THE FOUNDATIONS OF JUDAISM:
Method, Teleology, Doctrine
PART ONE: *Method*

MIDRASH

IN CONTEXT

Exegesis in Formative Judaism

JACOB NEUSNER

FORTRESS PRESS   PHILADELPHIA

————————————

Library of Congress Cataloging in Publication Data

Neusner, Jacob, 1932–
    Midrash in context.

    (The Foundations of Judaism : method, teleology,
doctrine ; pt. 1, method)
    Bibliography: p.
    Includes indexes.
    1. Midrash—History and criticism. 2. Bible. O.T.—
Criticism, interpretation, etc., Jewish. 3. Rabbinical
literature—History and criticism. I. Title.
II. Series: Neusner, Jacob, 1932–   . Foundations
of Judaism ; pt. 1.
    BM601.N48 1983 pt. 1 [BM514] 296s [296.1'406] 83–5705
    ISBN 0–8006–0708–2

————————————

131B83   Printed in the United States of America   1–708

Acknowledgments

The Dead Sea Scrolls in English, 2d ed., edited and translated by Géza Vermès (London: Pelican Books, 1975), copyright © 1962, 1965, 1968, 1975 by G. Vermès. Reprinted by permission of Penguin Books, London.

Mishnah's Theology of Tithing, translated by Martin Jaffee (Chico, Calif.: Scholars Press, 1981). Reprinted by permission.

Midrash Rabbah, edited by H. Freedman and M. Simon (London: Soncino Press, 1939). Reprinted by permission.

Contents

Preface

Like Saul, I went in search of asses. I found a kingdom. I wanted to know about the historical setting of the making of a particular kind of Jewish book by a distinctive political and religious group. I discovered I had therefore to confront a perpetual perplexity facing any religious tradition based on revelation preserved in a book. Let me explain.

The original problem before me was to make some sense, in the framework of the history of Judaism, of the earliest work of collecting biblical exegeses, called *midrashim*, produced by the Talmudic rabbis. The first of these books of exegeses were brought to closure, it is universally agreed, in the fifth and sixth centuries of the Common Era ("C.E.") in the Land of Israel ("Palestine," "The Holy Land"). They consisted of exegeses, amplifications, and discursive essays on the Pentateuch and Lamentations, Esther, the Song of Songs, and Ruth. Some of these compositions serve as word-for-word or verse-for-verse commentaries. Others present filigrees of scriptural verses so arranged as to make a point through dazzling bursts of proof-texts. What they have in common is the simple fact that they represent a totally new kind of book in their sort of Judaism. The Judaism called Talmudic, rabbinic, normative, or classical, which has predominated from the earliest centuries of the Common Era to the present day, had never before known such collections. Other kinds of Judaism had made them for close to a thousand years.

Let me emphasize that fact. Beforehand, no one in Rabbinic Judaism, then nearly five hundred years in the making, had ever, so far as we know, conceived of writing that kind of book of biblical exegeses. But afterward, the composition of such collections, using the names of Talmudic heroes and pseudepigraphically assigning to them a wide variety of opinions, rapidly became a literary and theological convention in Judaism. Even the thirteenth-century Zohar, a mystical speculation, was given the literary framework of biblical exegeses written in the names of Talmudic sages. What was done in Rabbinic Judaism for the first time in the fifth and sixth centuries thus would set the model for well over a thousand years, down to the eighteenth century: systematic collection, arrangement, and composition of biblical exegeses into authoritative books. So one acceptable mode of creative expression in the profoundly traditional world of Judaism turned out to have come to full exposure at just this time, in just this place, and I wanted to know why.

Let me be crystal clear about the problem by restating it. Why, in particular within the circles of Talmudic rabbis in the fifth and sixth centuries C.E., did people begin to compile exegeses of Scripture and make books of them? That is a very limited, narrowly historical problem in the history of the religion and literature of Rabbinic Judaism. But, as you will soon see, it becomes a theological problem and turns out to encompass a comprehensive theory of the character and formation of Rabbinic Judaism, its structure, and its entire literature. I stress, then, that the problem is *not* why Jews in general began to undertake exegesis of the Hebrew Scriptures. Many other kinds of Jews had done so, as we all know, certainly throughout the preceding thousand years, back to the sixth century B.C.E. Since the Hebrew Bible itself is rich in exegetical materials, with the books of Chronicles constituting a systematic commentary and revision of the books of Kings, for example, we cannot ask why at just this time people read and interpreted Scriptures. Judaism in all forms had always done that.

Nor was there anything new even in collecting exegeses and framing them for a particular polemical purpose, that is, creating a book out of comments on the Scripture and in the form of a commentary. The Essene library at Qumran presents us with compositions of biblical commentary and exegesis, on the one side. The school of Matthew provides an ample picture of another sort of exercise in systematic composition based on the amplification and application of Israel's ancient Scriptures, on the other. We recognize, moreover, that both Israelite communities—the Essenes, the Christian Jews around Matthew—produced their collections not merely to preserve opinions, but to make important statements in a stunning way. We also know, surely in the instance of Matthew, that the power of a brilliantly composed exegetical collection and arrangement can make its impact even after two thousand years. That is why, to begin with, people made and preserved such collections and arrangements—to say what they believed God had told them.

But within the formation of the holy literature—the canon—of Rabbinic Judaism in particular, so far as we know, no one before the fifth century had produced a composition of biblical exegeses formed into collections—holy books. The rabbinic movement thus had flourished for nearly half a millennium without making this type of book. By the fifth century in this kind of Judaism there were at least two other ways in which to compose books, represented, as I shall explain at length, first by the Mishnah and secondly by the Talmud of the Land of Israel ("Palestinian Talmud," "Yerushalmi" or Jerusalem Talmud). More important, the exegesis of Scripture itself had within rabbinical circles long constituted a well-established mode of thought and expression. The Talmud, for its part, is full of exegeses. But it is not organized as a book of exegeses of Scripture. So the question is now fully exposed. We ask about making systematic collections—books—of biblical exegeses among people who formerly had never made books of that type. Why then? Why do it at all?

My answer—the substance of my account of *midrash* in context—is that making such collections defined the natural next step in the process precipitated by the Mishnah and the exegesis of the Mishnah. The Talmud, the great work of exegesis of the Mishnah, set the pattern and shaped the mold. The compilers of the exegetical collections then followed the Talmud's pattern and conformed to the mold of exegesis of the Mishnah by the Talmud. They composed discourses for Scripture within precisely the same taxonomical framework as the Talmud's discourses for the Mishnah. So the context of the composition of *midrash* collections and the Talmud alike was defined by the Mishnah.

I started out with a question of literary history, with implications for the history of a religion. Success then would mean I might say something about the relationship of literature and society—the making of a particular kind of book, the social setting in which that kind of book came into being and won acceptance. But almost at the very beginning I found something quite different.

First, I had to ask about the canon of Judaism into which the collections under discussion rapidly found acceptance (so far as we know). Indeed, the ongoing work of compiling books of exegeses in Judaism turned out to form a principal convention of the religious literature of Judaism for so long, and under so wide a variety of conditions, that I began to wonder what meaning, if any, the category "canon" might enjoy within Judaism. Is the basket ever filled to overflowing? Can we speak of a canon at all?

Second, faced with the issue of canon and the place of the exegetical compositions in the canon, I had to turn to the more profound problem both concealed and revealed within that same category. For canon rests upon authority. In Judaism, authority always appeals in the end to the will and word of God contained within the Torah. Accordingly, as soon as I stumbled over the issue of whether there is a canon of Judaism, I found I had fallen into the depths of reflection on the nature and meaning of "Torah" as revelation. What are the limits of canon, and what are the possibilities of continuing to receive God's will and word, so long after Sinai? Exegesis is not Torah. But books of exegeses became part of Torah. How come? Is the category "canon" ever relevant to Judaism?

So here are the asses, and here is the kingdom. The asses bear books. The kingdom is God's will and word for Israel, the Jewish people. I claim here to outline the parameters of the problem of revelation, canon, and authority in the literature and history of Judaism. I thought to describe the life-situation—Sitz im Leben—of a particular kind of book. I end up perplexed by the relationship of established Scripture—literature, its content and form alike—to the enduring encounter with God. That is, I wondered how ongoing revelation, as the encounter with God, in all forms of Judaism, takes its form. How to contain and express the interplay of a new generation's encounter with an age-old matrix of religious experience turns out to be the implicit issue of the kind of book under discussion.

The kingdom is humanity's. The issue belongs to everyone. For, as I shall explain, the materials assembled in the exegetical compilations produced by the fifth- and sixth-century rabbis served a particular purpose. They claimed a distinctive status of authority. They stood in relationship to the authority of revelation. These compositions constituted not mere literature, reference books, encyclopedias of this and that about various biblical books or verses in them.

The contrast to the standing for Jerome's biblical commentaries therefore is striking. The earliest compilations of biblical exegesis stood in clear and close relationship to the Torah, that is, the canon, of Israel; they were not merely collections of explanations, provided by a great exegete. Jerome treated books of the canon; his commentaries were not canonical. The earliest *midrash* compilations spoke not for an individual but for the collectivity of sages; they demanded and gained a place within the canon of rabbinical writings, thus entering the Torah. The difference is fundamental. The compositions themselves claimed authority. So they took their place as statements of Judaism in the literature of Judaism. They were holy. And, being holy, they had to be brought into relationship with other, earlier holy books.

So, as I said, at the foundations are the issues of canon, scriptural authority, revelation. The definition of the canon of Judaism demands attention. The issue of the composition of these particular books has to come under analysis in the context of the place, in the canon of Judaism, of all books composed beyond the writings of the Hebrew Scriptures known in Judaism as the written Torah or as Tanakh (explained below), and in Christianity as the Old Testament. Beyond canon, then, looms the issue of scriptural authority and the place of exegesis in the processes of revelation—weighty questions.

The twin issues of revelation and canon frame the question in theological language. But the facts upon which theology meditates and to which theology assigns meaning derive, to begin with, from the history of literature: the story of the formation of particular holy books and their reception and sanctification within the believing community. The definition of the canon, after all, hardly demands attention, except for books people want to put there. When does the dilemma of ongoing revelation in a historical community, a community already defined by the increment and authority of revelation received in times past, become acute? It is only when new claims to say the word of God insistently press from latter-day saints. Then the entire foundations of the authority of Scripture come under close scrutiny within the community of the faithful because of, not doubt about old, but vivid faith in new, writings.

Accordingly, here I tell the story of when and why and how, in the formative centuries of Judaism, from the first through the sixth centuries, people composed a particular kind of book. Others may draw out of the tale strands of meaning for the twin issues of biblical authority in Judaism: the definition of canon, the nature and limits of revelation.

Even at this early stage in the argument, you must have wondered at my effort to use as little as possible a word commonly used in discourse on biblical exegesis, the word *midrash*. Let me define the word and explain why I shall use it only seldom. To avoid that word, I pay the price of using somewhat awkward circumlocutions, in particular, "collections of exegeses of Scripture," and the like. "*Midrash*" stands for at least three specific things, as well as a great many things in general.

It refers, first, to a particular kind of *book*, a compilation of biblical exegeses, amplifications, and compositions, as in *Midrash Rabbah*—a vast collection of compilations of biblical exegesis, covering the Pentateuch, the five scrolls. *Genesis Rabbah* is a *midrash*.

It speaks, second, to an *activity* of explaining or applying the meaning of a biblical verse (or group of verses), as in "the *midrash* of this verse is. . . ." In this sense, the Gospel of Matthew is not a *midrash*, but it contains much *midrash*. A word so rich in ambiguities is best avoided; other words, each of them standing for some one thing, will prove more useful.

That is still clearer when we realize that the word *midrash* may stand for yet a third thing: *hermeneutics* of a particular kind. As a mode of interpretation, people use the word *midrash* to mean the reading of one thing in terms of some other. This usage is so general as to defy concrete application, as in the statement, "Life itself is a *midrash* on the Torah." That is to say, things that happen constitute amplifications and applications of statements made in Scripture.

The range of definitions of the word *midrash*, of the modes of exegesis encompassed within that word (as well as those excluded by it, if there are any), of the sorts of books that constitute *midrash* (and those that do not)—these are so vast as to make the word, by itself, more of a hindrance than a help in saying what we mean.

In this connection I call attention to Gary G. Porton, "Defining Midrash," in *The Study of Ancient Judaism*, ed. J. Neusner (New York: KTAV Publishing House, 1981) 1:55–92. Ranging over the boundless plains of meanings imputed to the word *midrash*, from "*anything but* the plain meaning of Scripture," to "*everything said* about Scripture" or particular verses of Scripture, Porton comes to a simple definition (p. 62):

> Midrash [is] a type of literature, oral or written, which stands in direct relationship to a fixed, canonical text, considered to be the authoritative and the revealed word of God by the midrashist [the one who makes the midrash] and his audience, and in which this canonical text is explicitly cited or clearly alluded to.

That definition encompasses a vast range of Judaic and early Christian literature—as Porton says, "A broad area of activity . . ." The definition is, in his words, "broad enough to include a large variety of treatments of the canonical texts and traditions, and yet narrow enough to distinguish this activity from other literary activities."

Since I find these statements accurate, I cannot here use the word *midrash* at all. For we address the genre of writing and thinking known as *midrash* in only one context, namely, that of Rabbinic Judaism. We take up only one question, one aspect of the activity of *midrash*, namely, why people compiled (1) *midrashim* = exegeses of various verses of Scripture into (2) *midrashim* = systematic units of discourse made up mainly of exegeses of various verses of Scripture into (3) *midrashim* = whole books, that is, compilations of compositions (discourses) constituted by exegeses of verses of Scripture. Since we are able to use the same word for three things, and since, moreover, that same word is made to serve by others for many more things, I shall generally avoid use of the word *midrash*. But I shall always mean it.

So, to sum up the purpose of this book and its genesis, I wanted to know why people collected biblical exegeses into compositions. I found I had ultimately to ask about three things. First, what did they understand as the canon of Judaism? Second, how did they believe God revealed *torah*, that is, revelation, to Israel? Third, what importance did they assign to the written Torah they already had, that is, scriptural authority in Judaism? These three theological issues emerge from the rather simple, but never-asked, historical question that had demanded my attention at the outset.

All that has been said speaks about action upon a black and empty stage, lacking lights, scenery, furniture, even live actors. Up to now we have spoken about a literary problem—why people made such-and-such a type of book—and its theological ramifications. So we hear voices—ideas, opinions. But we see no bodies, no faces, no real people facing a concrete problem. I am a historian of a religion, interested in the history of religion. Accordingly, I am constrained to raise another range of external questions, about concrete social and political matters, in addition to internal ones of literature out of context and theology as the ahistorical logic of faith. These questions of mine concern when and where people did their work, and what else was happening at the same time. When, in chapter 5, I approach this final set of questions, I make the effort to show that the formation of both the Talmud of the Land of Israel and also the earliest collections of scriptural exegeses bear profound and important implications for the encounter—in my judgment, the first serious and important one—between Judaism and Christianity in its new, dominant position. It may then appear that one reason why people long after the fifth and sixth centuries would continue to nurture the work of making biblical exegeses and collecting them in books derives from the context and reason for their doing so to begin with—that and the persistence of that same context and condition for so long thereafter. But in so stating, I have signaled matters which, in the end, must come only as the last step in what will be a simple, but protracted and sustained, argument.

To summarize the entire book in five (somewhat long) sentences.

In chapter 1 we take up the traits of the Mishnah, the first document of the Judaism of which the Talmuds and the compilations of exegeses of Scripture form the principal early expression, asking how these traits defined the work of the heirs and continuators of the Mishnah.

In chapter 2 we consider the relationship of the Mishnah to Scripture and the exegetical challenge posed by the Mishnah to the rabbinical sages of the next two hundred years, from ca. 200 to ca. 400 C.E., the time of the closure of the Talmud of the Land of Israel.

In chapter 3 we form a typology of units of discourse of the Talmud of the Land of Israel, showing the exegetical choices before the authorities of that document responsible for the interpretation of the Mishnah.

In chapter 4 we then undertake the taxonomy (in fact, two taxonomies) of units of discourse of Genesis Rabbah, the first exegetical composition prepared in the period beyond the closure of the Talmud of the Land of Israel, comparing the types of units of discourse in that document with those of which the Talmud is constructed, and showing that, taxonomically, the two compositions are identical.

In chapter 5 we consider the interpretation, from both political and theological perspectives, of the results of the facts adduced in the preceding chapters.

That is the entire argument of the book—simple, sustained (I hope), cogent from beginning to end.

Since I am a teacher, with the problem of conveying a simple argument about remote documents and unfamiliar facts, I try to write as I try to teach. I proceed very slowly, with ample illustrations, and I repeat the main point at all crucial turnings in the argument. I offer summaries at the end of each chapter and a reprise of the argument where I think it is needed. Accordingly, the book is designed so that anyone interested in its topic should be readily able to follow the argument, fully informed as to the texts at hand and what is alleged about them. Everything needed to understand this book is found within its covers. That is why the reader will find extensive abstracts of sources, on the one side, and a deliberate pattern of repeating the main point where I think it bears restatement, on the other. I want the book to be clear and totally lucid. If, in the trade-off, the reader finds a few passages tedious or repetitious, it is a price willingly paid. You can always skip a paragraph or a page.

Up to now I have presented the problem and thesis of this book as a historian and a historian of a religion. But at the end of chapter 5 I offer a theological judgment. It is best at the outset to state what I believe to be the theological meaning of the historical and literary facts adduced in this book. The theological implication of this book is that, from its beginnings in late antiquity, Judaism as we know it means to provide for the faithful an enduring and ever-present encounter with the living God. The meeting is through the medium of revelation contained in the Torah learned through rabbinical modes of exegesis. It follows that Judaism is, further, the faith of the eternally-open canon—which is no canon at all. Revelation continues in time, so new *torah* becomes part of the Torah, as God speaks to generations without end. The particular form of religious encounter afforded by Judaism in its classical and enduring form, in both the Talmud to the Mishnah and the compilations of *midrash* to Scripture, is a meeting with God in the here and now. We Jews encounter God through the power of the human intellect to enter into intelligible and reliable dialogue with God, to learn the rules of life. In particular, when we use our minds to learn in the Torah what God has to say to us, what God wants us to be, we receive *torah*, that is, revelation. That is how we know God and try—always failing—to become what God wants us to be: like God.

JACOB NEUSNER

Program in Judaic Studies
Brown University
Providence, Rhode Island

28, July 1982
My fiftieth birthday

Abbreviations

A.Z.	Abodah Zarah	M.	Mishnah
b.	ben, "son of"	Mal.	Malachi
B.M.	Baba Mesia	Meg.	Megillah
ca.	circa	Mic.	Micah
Chron.	Chronicles	Mt.	Matthew
Dan.	Daniel	Neh.	Negaim
Deut.	Deuteronomy	Nid.	Niddah
Eccl.	Ecclesiastes	Num.	Numbers
Est.	Esther	Obad.	Obadiah
Ex.	Exodus	Prov.	Proverbs
Ezek.	Ezekiel	Ps.	Psalms
Gen.	Genesis	R.	Rabbi
Hos.	Hosea	Sam.	Samuel
Isa.	Isaiah	San.	Sanhedrin
Jer.	Jeremiah	Song	Song of Songs
Josh.	Joshua	T.	Tosefta
Judg.	Judges	Y.	Yerushalmi, the Talmud of
Ket.	Ketubot		the Land of Israel
Lam.	Lamentations	Zek.	Zekariah
Lev.	Leviticus		

1

The Enduring Dilemma

REVELATION AND CANON

When revelation stops, what then? The issue confronts Judaism and Christianity, in particular, because both religious communities receive and live by the statement of God's will to Moses and the prophets. Standing in direct succession to Sinai, Judaism speaks about a holy life framed in accord with God's will revealed in the Torah. Affirming and claiming to appropriate the entire heritage of ancient Israel and Judaism to its time, Christianity in nearly all its forms speaks of fulfilling the law and the prophets in the person of Jesus and the salvation of Christ. Accordingly, for Judaism and Christianity, the statement of God to Moses and the prophets stands for a single word, but with a double meaning: both then and now. That is to say, both religious traditions speak about God's will now, not merely revelation then. Both affirm an ongoing relationship between God and Israel—after the flesh, after the spirit—in which revelation of God's will and word endures as a fact of life.

But then revelation does *not* stop. For Judaism God's will is ever present. God now speaks, in the Torah today, as always in the past. For Christianity in its diverse traditions God endures in the Church, in tradition, in the preaching of the Word. And therein, for both faiths, we uncover the enduring dilemma. If God speaks through Torah, then, for Judaism, the issue turns upon what we receive or define as Torah. What finds room in the canon? And just how and to whom does God speak? The issue of ongoing encounter with the living God and of life in accord with the word of God joins to the definition of the canon of Torah. That is, what do we admit and what exclude?

For Judaism and Christianity the presence of the Hebrew Scriptures, which Jews know as Tanakh (for the biblical writings of the Pentateuch, Torah, hence T; prophets, Nebiim, hence N; and writings, Ketubim, hence K), and Christians as the Old Testament,

1

presents no answer to the question of canon. Rather Israel's Scriptures press the deeper question and frame the dilemma. For once people recognize that there is a Tanakh or an Old Testament, that is, a finished scripture, the issue of the place and relationship of all subsequent revelation, both written and not written, comes to acute formulation. If *torah*, in the sense of revelation, becomes *The Torah*, a particular set of compositions, then one must wonder whether revelation has come to an end. Can there be more Torahs, more Sinais? If there is a completed Testament, then the place and role we might define for a further testament demand attention. So the existence of a completed document of revelation presents, in chronic form, the dilemma about the authority and standing of further revelations later on.

The dilemma reaches an acute stage when new holy books, records of revelation, take shape and demand admission to the canon. The demand turns out to be irresistible when the consensus of believers bestows upon the new books the status of revelation, the standing of sanctification. Now it is one thing to interpret and apply the existing revelation to a new situation. Exegesis and amplification present no break with existing Scripture but confirm it. It is quite another to reckon with writings outside of the established canon, yet widely understood to contain not merely more words of faith and truth, but God's word too. Accordingly, the life of faith, assuredly rich in encounter with the living God, has perpetually to present new fruits for that compendious basket we know as the canon: the authoritative documents of the faith. So far as Judaism and Christianity abide, the issue of the interplay between old and new, canon and ongoing writing down of revelation, lives and vivifies. That is the issue before us.

THE CRISIS PRECIPITATED BY
THE MISHNAH

The advent of the Mishnah in ca. 200 C.E. demanded that people explain the status and authority of the new document. In consequence, in the Judaism of rabbis the canon of the religion of Israel had reopened. It would remain eternally open, for *torah* would encompass rabbis' teachings for all time to come. Accordingly, the conception of the form and possibilities of revelation reached wholly fresh definition. As we shall see, moreover, the lines of structure emanating from the Mishnah led to the formation of a vast and unprecedented literature of Judaism. The explosive force of the return to Zion, in the time of Ezra, had produced the formation of the Torah-book and much else. The extraordinary impact of the person and message of Jesus (among other things) had led to the creation of an unprecedented kind of writing in a sector of Israel's life. So too would be the case with the Mishnah.

Before spelling out what happened when the Mishnah came into being, I have in a preliminary way to define the document and explain its importance. The Mishnah is a vast set of statements about what Israel, the Jewish people, is supposed to do on its farms and in its homes, in the Temple in Jerusalem and in the courts of its villages, on ordinary days and on the Sabbath and festival days. It is a kind of law code, in that it contains statements that say what one does. It is a kind of schoolbook, in that it presents many opinions about what in theory we are supposed to do. If you study the deeper issues underlying many statements in the Mishnah, furthermore, you find that the sages confront perennial issues of philosophy, expressed in concrete and humble details. It is as if they prefer to talk about the acorn and the oak than potentiality and actuality. So the Mishnah in all is a philosophical essay, rich in theoretical initiatives, which also serves as a law code.

The reason the document proved decisive in the history of Judaism, from its time to ours, is that, to begin with, it enjoyed the sponsorship of the autonomous ruler of the Jewish nation in the Land of Israel, namely, Judah the patriarch, with the result that the Mishnah served for purposes other than simply learning and speculative thought. At its very beginnings the Mishnah was turned into an authoritative law code, the constitution, along with Scripture, of Israel in its Land. Accordingly, when completed, the Mishnah emerged from the schoolhouse and forthwith made its move into the politics, courts, and bureaus of the Jewish government of the Land of Israel. Men who mastered the Mishnah thereby qualified themselves as judges and administrators in the government of Judah the patriarch, as well as in the government of the Jewish community of Babylonia. Over the next three hundred years, the Mishnah served as the foundation for the formation of the system of law and theology we now know as Judaism.

The vast collection constituted by the Mishnah therefore demanded explanation: What is this book? How does it relate to the (written) Torah revealed to Moses at Mount Sinai? Under whose auspices, and by what authority, does the law of the Mishnah govern the life of Israel? These questions, we realize, bear both political and theological implications. But, to begin with, the answers emerge out of an enterprise of exegesis, of literature. The reception of the Mishnah followed several distinct lines, each of them symbolized by a particular sort of book. Each book, in turn, offered its theory of the origin, character, and authority of the Mishnah. For the next three centuries these theories would occupy the attention of the best minds of Israel, the authorities of the two Talmuds and the numerous other works of the age of the seed-time of Judaism.

One line from the Mishnah stretched through the Tosefta, a supplement to the Mishnah, and the two Talmuds, one formed in the Land of Israel, the other in Babylonia, both serving as exegesis and amplification of the Mishnah.

The second line stretched from the Mishnah to compilations of biblical exegesis of three different sorts. First, there were exegetical collections framed in relationship to the Mishnah, in particular Sifra, on Leviticus, Sifre on Numbers, and Sifre on Deuteronomy. Second, exegetical collections were organized in relationship to Scripture, with special reference to Genesis and Leviticus. Third, exegetical collections focused on constructing abstract discourse out of diverse verses of Scripture but on a single theme or problem, represented by Pesikta de Rab Kahana.

This simple catalogue of the types, range, and volume of creative writing over the three hundred years from the closure of the Mishnah indicates an obvious fact. The Mishnah stands at the beginning of a new and stunningly original epoch in the formation of Judaism. Like the return to Zion and the advent of Jesus in Israel, the Mishnah ignited a great burst of energy. The extraordinary power of the Mishnah, moreover, is seen in its very lonely position in Israelite holy literature. The entire subsequent literature refers back to the Mishnah or stands in some clearcut hermeneutical relationship to it. But for its part, the Mishnah refers to nothing prior to itself—except (and then, mostly implicitly and by indirection) to Scripture. So from the Mishnah back to the revelation of God to Moses at Sinai—in the view of the Mishnah—lies a vast desert. But from the Mishnah forward stretches a fertile plain.

The crisis precipitated by the Mishnah therefore stimulated wide-ranging speculation, inventive experiments of a literary and (in the

4

nature of things) therefore also political, theological, and religious character. I shall argue in chapters 2, 3, and 4 that the Talmuds' work of defining and explaining the Mishnah in relationship to the (written) Torah, interpreting the meaning of the Mishnah, expanding upon and applying its laws, ultimately yielded the making, also, of compilations of the exegeses of Scripture. The formation of the Talmuds and exegetical collections thus made necessary—indeed, urgent—extraordinary and original reflection on the definition of canon, the nature of scriptural authority, and the range and possibilities of revelation. The results of that work all together would then define Judaism from that time to this. So the crisis presented an opportunity. And Israel's sages took full advantage of the occasion. That, in a word, is the story before us. What then was this crisis?

Let me begin the tale by returning to the Mishnah itself. I have first of all to explain why and how the Mishnah presented such an unprecedented problem to the patriarch's sages who received the Mishnah. It is easy to do so in a way accessible to people to whom all of these events and writings have been, up to now, entirely unknown or, if known, alien and incomprehensible. To phrase the theological question so that anyone in the West may grasp it, I need simply point out one fact. So far as Judaism was concerned, revelation had been contained in the Tanakh, the written Torah. True, God may have spoken in diverse ways. But revelation had come down in only one form, in writing. The last of the biblical books had been completed—so far as Jews then knew—many centuries before. How then could a new book now claim standing as holy and revealed by God? What validated the authority of the people who knew and applied that holy book to Israel's life? These questions, as we shall see, would define the critical issue of formative Judaism, from 200 to 600 C.E. The resolution of the problem defines Judaism today. Accordingly, the crisis precipitated by the Mishnah came about because of the urgent requirement of explaining, first, just what the Mishnah was in relationship to the Torah of Moses; second, why the sages who claimed to interpret and apply the law of the Mishnah to the life of Israel had the authority to do so; and, third, how Israel, in adhering to the rules of the Mishnah, kept the will of God and lived the holy life God wanted them to live.

But why should the Mishnah in particular have presented these critical problems of a social and theological order? After all, it was hardly the first piece of new writing to confront Israel from the clo-

5

sure of Scripture to the end of the second century. Other books had found a capacious place in the canon of the groups of Israelites that received them and deemed them holy. The canon of some groups, after all, had made room for those writings of apocryphal and pseudepigraphic provenance so framed as to be deemed holy. The Essene library at Qumran encompassed a diverse group of writings, surely received as authoritative and holy, that other Jews did not know within their canon. So we have to stand back and ask why, to the sages who received and realized the Mishnah, that book should have presented special, particularly stimulating, problems. Why should the issue of the relationship of the Mishnah to Scripture have proved so pressing in the third, fourth, and fifth centuries' circles of Talmudic rabbis? After all, we have no evidence that the relationship to the canon of Scripture of the Manual of Discipline, the Hymns, the War Scroll, or the Damascus Covenant perplexed the teacher of righteousness and the other holy priests of the Essene community. To the contrary, those documents at Qumran appear side by side with the ones we now know as canonical Scripture. The high probability is that, to the Essenes, the sectarian books were no less holy and authoritative than Leviticus, Deuteronomy, Nahum, Habakkuk, Isaiah, and the other books of the biblical canon they, among all Israelites, revered.

The issue, as we shall shortly see, had to be raised because of the peculiar traits of the Mishnah itself. But the dilemma proved acute, not merely chronic, because of the particular purpose the Mishnah was meant to serve, and because of the political sponsorship behind the document. As I said above, it was to provide Israel's constitution. It was promulgated by the patriarch—the ethnic ruler—of the Jewish nation in the Land of Israel, Judah the Patriarch, who ruled with Roman support as the fully recognized Jewish authority in the Holy Land. So the Mishnah was public, not sectarian, nor merely idle speculation of a handful of Galilean rabbinical philosophers, though, in structure and content, that is precisely what it was. It was a political document. It demanded assent and conformity to its rules, where they were relevant to the government and court system of the Jewish people in its land. So the Mishnah could not be ignored and therefore had to be explained in universally accessible terms. Furthermore, the Mishnah demanded explanation not merely in relationship to the established canon of Scripture and apology as the constitution of the Jew's government, the patriarchate of second-century Land of Israel. The nature of Israelite life, lacking all capacity to distinguish as secular any detail of the common culture, made it natural to wonder about a deeper issue. Israel understood its collective life and the fate of each individual under the aspect of God's loving concern, as expressed in the Torah. Accordingly, laws issued to define what people were supposed to do could not stand by themselves; they had to receive the imprimatur of Heaven, that is, they had to be given the status of revelation. Accordingly, to make its way in Israelite life, the Mishnah as a constitution and code demanded for itself a theory of beginnings at (or relationship to) Sinai, with Moses, from God. As was pointed out above, other new writings for a long time had proved able to win credence as part of the Torah, hence as revealed by God and so enjoying legitimacy. But they did so in ways not taken by the Mishnah's framers. How did the Mishnah differ?

It was in the medium of writing that, in the view of all of Israel until about 200 C.E., God had been understood to reveal the divine word and will. The Torah was a written book. People who claimed to receive further messages from God usually wrote them down. They had three choices in securing acceptance of their account. All three involved linking the new to the old. In claiming to hand on revelation, they could, first, sign their books with the names of biblical heroes. Second, they would imitate the style of biblical Hebrew. Third, they could present an exegesis of existing written verses, validating their ideas by supplying proof-texts for them.

From the closure of the Torah literature in the time of Ezra, ca. 450 B.C.E., to the time of the Mishnah, nearly seven hundred years later, we do not have a single book alleged to be holy and at the same time standing wholly out of relationship to the Holy Scriptures of ancient Israel. The pseudepigraphic writings fall into the first category, the Essene writings at Qumran into the second and third. We may point to the Gospels, which take as a principal problem demonstrating how Jesus had fulfilled the prophetic promises of the Old Testament and in other ways carried forward and even embodied Israel's Scripture.

Insofar as a piece of Jewish writing did not find a place in relationship to Scripture, its author laid no claim to present a holy book. The contrast between Jubilees and the Testaments of the Patriarchs, with their constant and close harping on biblical matters, and the several books of Maccabees, shows the difference. The former claim

7

to present revealed truth, the latter, history. So a book was holy because in style, in authorship, or in (alleged) origin, it continued Scripture, finding a place therefore (at least in the author's mind) within the canon, or because it provided an exposition of Scripture's meaning.

But the Mishnah made no such claim. It entirely ignored the style of biblical Hebrew, speaking in a quite different kind of Hebrew altogether. It is silent on its authorship through sixty-two of the sixty-three tractates (the claims of Abot pose a special problem). In any event, nowhere does the Mishnah contain the claim that God had inspired the authors of the document. These are not given biblical names and certainly are not alleged to have been biblical saints. Most of the book's named authorities flourished within the same century as its anonymous arrangers and redactors, not in remote antiquity. Above all, the Mishnah contains scarcely a handful of exegeses of Scripture. These, where they occur, play a trivial and tangential role. So here is the problem of the Mishnah: different from Scripture in language and style, indifferent to the claim of authorship by a biblical hero or divine inspiration, stunningly aloof from allusion to verses of Scripture for nearly the whole of its discourse—yet authoritative for Israel. How come?

Still more vividly to grasp the dilemma presented by the Mishnah, we move far from the time and place of ancient Israel in 200 C.E. We take up the problem of revelation as received by a culture in the South Seas in nearly our own time.

Just how does God speak to us? When a shift takes place in the medium of revelation, it is a symptom that a far more profound turning in the formation of culture has been reached. Sam D. Gill, in *Beyond "the Primitive": The Religions of Non-Literate Peoples* (Englewood Cliffs, N.J.: Prentice-Hall, 1982), 102, points out that, in the precolonial way of life, peoples of Oceania and Melanesia referred to stories of origins to reveal the patterns of their culture, and relied "upon the spiritual communication with ancestors and deities to maintain a fertile and creative life in the physical world. Spiritual communication was essential to life." This took place through dreams and visions. Then, Gill says, the advent of the Europeans, with a quite different form of communication, changed everything. He notes, "Missionaries dwelt heavily upon the written word as the means of the revelation of God, and the colonial administration used writing to maintain contact with its home country, the source of its supplies. . . . [Literacy] was accepted as a spiritual mode of communication." Accordingly, the move from one medium of heavenly communication to another both precipitated a crisis and served as one of the symptoms of that crisis.

That fact is important to us, for, as we shall see in a little while, one of the principal theories of the origins of the Mishnah and vindications of its authority lay in the allegation that it constituted revelation, but in a different mode of communication from writing. Namely, it was revelation preserved in oral formulation and oral transmission, through memorization and repetition. For the moment, it suffices to prepare the way to a full appreciation of the problem posed by the Mishnah by noting that, until then, whatever other groups of Israelites laid claim to revelation took for granted that, like the revelation contained in the Hebrew Scriptures, a fair part of any further revelation would be written down.

Thus far we have noted that, in time to come, the Mishnah would find one principal justification and apology in the claim that it constituted oral tradition, going back to Moses at Sinai. To that remarkable claim we have now to join yet a second unusual trait of the Mishnah. The Mishnah is something like a law code. Accordingly, when we turn to the law codes of ancient Israel, we notice traits we have every reason to find, also, in the Mishnah. The first and most important of these is the telling of a tale to explain the authority and standing of the code and its laws. The Covenant Code (Ex. 20:22—23:33), for instance, starts with God's telling Moses to tell Israel, "You have seen for yourselves that I have talked with you from heaven." So all the laws that follow come from God in heaven. The Priestly Code iterates and reiterates the formula, "The Lord called Moses and spoke to him. . . ." The vast law collection in Deuteronomy begins only after a great address on the giving of the law has explained the origin and sanction of the law. Accordingly, Israel had every reason to expect that a law code would carry along its own myth of origin and authority. Later lawyers were quick to supply such myths. The framers of the so-called Damascus rule of the Essene Community at Qumran begin with a long exhortation, introducing the authority of the code, the teacher of righteousness, retelling the sacred history of Israel, and only then presenting the detailed laws. The Community Rule or Manual of Discipline starts with the statement that if people live in accord with the Book of the Community Rule, then they "may seek God with a whole heart and soul and do what is good and right before Him as He commanded by the hand of Moses and all his servants the prophets, that they may love all he has chosen and hate all that he has rejected" (G. Vermes, *The Dead Sea Scrolls in English* [Gloucester, Mass.: Peter Smith, 1975], 72). When, in a different setting altogether, people proposed to tell the story of Jesus, the Christ, they began by explaining who they were and how they knew what they knew, or who Jesus was and where he came from, or both. So, in a word, it was normal in Israelite culture to write books and to expect God to write books or dictate them. It was routine to provide an account of the origin of a book, to supply a myth of heavenly authority for a law code in particular. The Mishnah does not bother.

Precisely how the Mishnah inaugurates an unprecedented age in the literature of Judaism should be obvious to the reader from these points of emphasis in the preceding paragraphs. Let us now review where we stand in the unfolding argument of this book.

First, once closed and promulgated, the Mishnah would gain from its earliest apologists a myth of oral formulation and oral transmission through processes of memorization, a claim unusual in Israel, to which, for millennia, God had been conceived as communicating in writing.

Second, the Mishnah itself contains no myth of its origin in heaven, no account of its purpose, no claim or promise of the redemption of Israel through keeping its laws. (Abot 1:1–18 hardly presents a counterpart to Deut. 1:1ff.!)

Third, it already is clear that, in style, the Mishnah simply bypasses all of the aesthetic conventions of religious conviction commonplace among earlier Israelite writers, not bearing the name of a known, ancient authority, not imitating the style of biblical law codes or even their language, and not even providing its laws with an exegetical basis in relationship to biblical texts.

Fourth, had the Mishnah emerged from a circle of sectarians off in some wilderness plain, the Jewish nation at large need not have paid much attention to it. But the Mishnah comes down to us not through the medium of archaeology but through the living world of Judaism. So it clearly overcame the limits of sectarianism. Indeed, from the moment of closure and promulgation, the Mishnah enjoyed remarkable status. The Mishnah constituted the authoritative law code of Israel, the Jewish nation, living in its own land, the Land of Israel, and governed by its own authorities, the sages, or rabbis, of Israel, through the sponsorship of its own, internationally recognized ruler, the patriarch (*nasi*) of Israel. That, at least, is what the exegeses attached to the Mishnah, called the Talmuds, tell us. It is what every book of history about the world of Jewry and Judaism, from 200 C.E. onward, records.

So the Mishnah was not a statement of theory alone, telling us only how things will be in the eschaton. Nor was it a wholly sectarian document, reporting the view of a group without standing or influence in the larger life of Israel. True, in some measure it bears both of these traits. But the Mishnah was and is law for Israel. It entered the government and courts of the Jewish people, both in the motherland and also overseas, as the authoritative constitution of the courts of Judaism. The advent of the Mishnah therefore marked a turning in the life of the nation-religion. The document demanded explanation and apology.

The one thing you could not do, as a Jew in third-century Tiberias, Sepphoris, Caesarea, or Beth Shearim, in Galilee, was ignore the thing. True, you might refer solely to ancient Scripture and tradition and live out your life within the inherited patterns of the familiar Israelite religion-culture. But as soon as you dealt with the Jewish government in charge of your everyday life—went to court over the damages done to your crop by your neighbor's ox, for instance—you came up against a law in addition to the law of Scripture, a document the principles of which governed and settled all matters. So the Mishnah rapidly came to confront the life of Israel. The people who knew the Mishnah, the rabbis or sages, came to dominate that life. And their claim, in accord with the Mishnah, to exercise authority and the right to impose heavenly sanction came to perplex. Now the crisis should be fully exposed.

The sages in charge of Israel's courts and bureaucracy would spend three hundred years resolving that crisis, figuring out how to receive this new thing, this Mishnah. Receiving the Mishnah meant setting it into relationship with the ancient Scriptures. Let me now, in a single sentence, report what they did. The sages totally reformed the meaning of the word *Torah*, thereby, in the literary framework, reopening the canon of Judaism, and, in the theological setting, redefining the meaning and limits of revelation. The literary result would be the whole of Talmudic literature, on the one side,

11

and, later on, the formation of the earliest compilations of exegeses (the *midrashim*). The theological result would be Judaism as we know it: a living and enduring faith of everyday encounter with God through Torah and its holy way of life. Rabbis thus reshaped the meaning of the word *Torah* by exegetical processes which, to begin with, linked the statements of the Mishnah to verses of Scripture. The exegetical work, in consequence, overspread its original boundaries—the Mishnah—and encompassed Scripture within modes of exegesis and discourse of exactly the same taxonomic character.

So the Mishnah made necessary the formation of the Talmuds, its exegetical companions. Within the processes of exegesis of the Mishnah came the labor of collecting and arranging these exegeses, in correlation with the Mishnah, read line by line and paragraph by paragraph. The sorts of things the sages who framed the Talmud did to the Mishnah, they then went and did to Scripture. Within the work of exegesis of Scripture was the correlative labor of organizing what had been said verse by verse, following the structure of a book of the Hebrew Bible. The type of discourse and the mode of organizing the literary result of discourse which were suitable for the one document served the other too. The same people did both for the same reasons.

THE CHARACTER OF THE MISHNAH

Before proceeding to the next phase in the argument, the reader will want to know in greater detail just what the Mishnah is. The bare-bones statements presented before will take on flesh when we consider, first, two passages of the text in relationship to verses of Scripture on the same topics; and, second, a very brief account of the contents of the document as a whole. We begin with the aesthetic character of the Mishnah and then generalize from its literary theory to its theological convictions in the setting of Israel's revealed Torah.

We start with the interplay of Scripture and the Mishnah, attending to specific verses of Scripture and their counterparts in sentences or paragraphs of the Mishnah. But comparing the ways in which Scripture and the Mishnah, respectively, treat a given topic is easier said than done. The framers of the Mishnah devote entire tractates, running on for eight or ten chapters, each made up of seven or more paragraphs, to subjects dealt with in Scripture's law codes in a sentence or two. For example, Deut. 25:5–10 states that if a brother dies childless, his surviving brother marries his widow and produces a child to bear his name; if he refuses, a rite of removing the shoe is prescribed. These five verses find, in tractate Yebamot on the levirate connection and its dissolution, a counterpart of sixteen chapters, thus approximately one hundred fifty paragraphs. Deut. 24:1–4 delivers Scripture's entire message on the matter of divorce. The point of interest is that a divorcee, once remarried, may not then return to the husband who had earlier divorced her. Mishnah-tractate Gittin, on writs of divorce, requires no fewer than nine chapters to cover the same topic. Still, the aesthetic differences between the two documents—Scripture, Mishnah—and part of the meaning of these differences do emerge even from a brief comparison of how each document treats the same topic. While the approaches to the same topic—the issues raised in its regard—do not prove to be symmetrical to one another, still, the contrasts remain suggestive.

The first topic in common is tithing, on which Deut. 14:22 states, "You shall tithe all the yield of your seed, which comes forth from the field year by year." Lev. 27:30 says, "All the tithe of the land, whether of the seed of the land or of the fruit of the trees, is the Lord's; it is holy to the Lord." Let us now consider the opening paragraph of Mishnah-tractate Maaserot, tithes (trans. Martin Jaffee, in his *Mishnah's Theology of Tithing: A Study of Tractate Maaserot* [Chico, Calif.: Scholars Press for Brown Judaic Studies, 1981], 28):

[I.A] *A general principle they stated concerning tithes: Anything that is food, cultivated, and grows from the earth, is subject to the law of tithes.*
[II.A] *And yet another general principle they stated: Anything which at its first stage of development is food and which at its ultimate stage of development is food, even though the farmer maintains its growth in order to increase the food it will yield, is subject to the law of tithes, whether it is small or large.*
[B] *But anything which at its first stage of development is not food, yet which at its ultimate stage of development is food, is not subject to the laws of tithes until it becomes edible (M. Maaserot 1:1).*

Stylistically, the biblical verses and the Mishnaic paragraph have nothing at all in common. The framers of the Mishnah did not think it important that they should; they refrained from imitating biblical style in any detail. Where Scripture is specific, the Mishnah seeks to generalize. Where the Mishnaic language is closely balanced in run-on, carefully matched sentences as at II.A, B, Scripture exhibits no counterpart whatsoever. The point of interest in the Mishnah, by contrast, will not have surprised the biblical legislator. Scripture declares that one has to "tithe food." The Mishnah defines the sort of food that must be tithed. Scripture declares that the tithe of the land belongs to God. The Mishnah takes up the (mildly interesting) detail of the point at which God's claim takes effect, which is when the crop reaches the status of edibility. Accordingly, in the passage before us, the Mishnah looks to be the writing of rather philosophical minds, intent upon raising questions of secondary exposition of, and generalization about, facts of Scripture.

The important point must register once more: whatever the Mishnah was supposed to be, no one pretended it was an extension of Scripture. From the viewpoint of its literary traits, the Mishnah yields not a hint at that systematic archaizing and anachronizing at which the former Israelite writers had worked so hard for so many centuries in producing their holy books. Whether or not the authors of the Mishnah had in mind to write a holy book we do not know. If they did, they took a peculiar route. If they did not, they presented their successors and heirs with a remarkable set of problems in theological apologetics.

A second example of how the authors of the Mishnah both provide masses of new information (we do not know the source) and also systematize and reframe facts concerns the matter of the skin ailment described at Lev. 13:2–8. The priestly legislator speaks of the skin tone as a sign of whether or not the disease is present:

"When a man has on the skin of his body a swelling or an eruption or a spot, and it turns into a leprous disease on the skin of his body, then he shall be brought to Aaron the priest . . . and the priest shall examine the diseased spot on the skin of his body; and if the hair in the diseased spot has turned white and the disease appears to be deeper than the skin of his body, it is a leprous disease. . . . But if the spot is white in the skin of his body, and appears no deeper than the skin, and the hair in it has not turned white, the priest shall shut up the diseased person for seven days. . . ."

(Lev. 13:2–4)

Regarding this same matter, the Mishnah provides the following, using the word *nega*, translated by me as "plague," instead of Scripture's word choice, *Saraat*, "leprous disease":

[A] *The appearances of plagues are two, which are four:*
[B] *A bright spot is as bright-white as snow. And secondary to it is [a shade as white] as the lime of the Temple.*
[C] *"And the swelling is [as white] as the skin of an egg. And secondary to it is [a shade as white] as white wool," the words of R. Meir.*
[D] *And sages say, "The swelling is [as white] as white wool. Secondary to it is [a shade as white] as the skin of an egg" (M. Negaim 1:1).*

[A] *"The [reddish] mixture which is in the snow-white is like wine mixed in snow. The [reddish] mixture in the lime is like the blood which is mixed in milk," the words of R. Ishmael.*
[B] *R. Aqiba says, "The reddishness which is in this and in this is like wine mixed in water. But that which is in snow-white is strong, and that which is in lime is duller than it" (M. Negaim 1:2).*

[A] *R. Hananiah Prefect of the Priests says, "The appearances [colors] of plagues are sixteen."*
[B] *R. Dosa ben Harkinas says, "The appearances of plagues are thirty-six."*
[C] *Aqabya b. Mehallel says, "Seventy-two."*
[D] *R. Hananiah Prefect of the Priests says, "They do not examine the plagues in the first instance after the Sabbath [Sunday], for the end of that week will fall on the Sabbath; and not on the second day [Monday], for the end of its second week falls on the Sabbath; and not on the third day for houses, for the end of its third week falls on the Sabbath."*
[E] *R. Aqiba says, "At any time do they examine. [If] it [the next inspection] turns out to coincide with the Sabbath, they move [it] to after the Sabbath."*
[F] *And there is in this matter [ground] to rule leniently and to rule strictly (M. Negaim 1:4).*

Compared to Scripture, the traits of this passage are still more egregious than those of the first. We notice, to begin with, the appearance of proper names—Meir, Aqiba, Ishmael, Hananiah, and others. These are not biblical saints. Their standing and authority demand definition, even if they do not have to be identified. Second, where Scripture is rather vague and general about color, the

Mishnah's lawyers are very specific. Third, secondary disputes about the law governing unclean and clean skin tones raise the question of which opinion is to be followed and who decides. They hardly suggest that in hand is a law code deriving from Heaven, providing certainty as to God's will. The one thing Scripture always omits is disputes in the names of diverse authorities; it is the one ubiquitous trait of the Mishnah's discourse. Fourth, the further effort, at M. Negaim 1:4A–C, to systematize information for memorization through the provision of numeral mnemonics is to be noted. The closing dispute, M. 1:4D–E, ends with an important generalization demanding specific instances and exposition, which the continuation of the passage provides. What we see, in all, is a rather complex construction, following its own rules of discourse, its own *logoi* of organization and exposition, to make its own points. Once more, we note, these points take up rather loosely-framed statements of the biblical law and provide precise definition for interpreting and applying them. Finally, we observe, the two instances we have examined show us that the Mishnah will take an interest in matters of law important, in particular, to priests. So interests in the Temple and its sanctified work force, maintaining their rations ("tithes") and preserving the antisepsis, in a cultic sense, of their work area, played a role. The Mishnah could hardly claim to discuss only practical matters, things pressing at the moment (ca. 200 C.E.), if it devoted any part of its space to these issues. For, we recall, the Temple had by then lain in ruins for well over a century, and, after the calamity brought on by the rebellion led by Bar Kokhba, 132–135, everyone knew that the Temple would not rise in the near future. Accordingly, the Mishnah's traits, even in the snippets we have looked at, raise considerable puzzlement.

Before proceeding, let us once more review the catalogue of the issues confronting the Mishnah's apologists and heirs.

First, just what is the relationship of the Mishnah to the Torah of Moses? The passages we examined maintain perfect silence on that issue. They make no explicit reference to Scripture. They do not pretend to amplify or otherwise explain the meaning of a verse of Scripture. For our part, we know that they do. But the framers of the Mishnah in no way spelled out that fact.

Second, what is the standing, the authority, of the sages of the document? We now realize that the issue confronts not merely the heirs of the Mishnah, applying a law code. Named men figure within the document itself. Who are they? In disputes, how a decision is reached is not made explicit.

Third, the way in which, through keeping the rules of the Mishnah, Israel carries out God's will does not emerge from the discourse at hand. The name and will of God do not figure. The focus remains on close, niggling detail. The Mishnah organizes information. A reference book such as this may serve some useful purpose. Who can read it for inspiration? How anyone can have imagined that before us is another kind of Torah is hardly self-evident.

Phrasing the question in this way, we remind ourselves once again how other innovators in Israel's life had confronted the same problems and solved them. They signed the names of well-known saints of biblical times. They imitated biblical Hebrew. They attached their new ideas to ancient verses of Scripture, in a process of exegetical exposition. The reader hardly needs to be told that none of these traits emerge in the two passages just now reviewed. Accordingly, let us move outward from the specific passages at hand to a more general description of the Mishnah as a whole.

We are turning now from aesthetics to contents and context. The Mishnah is a six-part code of descriptive rules. The six divisions are: (1) agricultural rules; (2) laws governing appointed seasons, e.g., Sabbaths and festivals; (3) laws on the transfer of women, and property along with women, from one man (father) to another (husband); (4) the system of civil and criminal law (corresponding to what we today should regard as "the legal system"); (5) laws for the conduct of the cult and the Temple; and (6) laws on the preservation of cultic purity both in the Temple and under certain domestic circumstances, with special reference to the table and bed. These divisions define the range and realm of reality.

Since, as we know, in the aftermath of the war against Rome in 132–135, the Temple was declared permanently prohibited to Jews, and Jerusalem was closed off to them as well, in context the Mishnah's laws in part speak of nowhere and not now. There was no cult, no Temple, no holy city to which, at this time, ca. 200 C.E., the description of the Mishnaic laws applied. We again observe that a sizable proportion of the Mishnah deals with matters to which the sages had no material access or practical knowledge at the time of their work. They themselves were not members of the priestly caste. Yet we have seen that the Mishnah contains a division—the fifth—on the conduct of the cult, as well as one on the preservation of the cultic purity of the sacrificial system along the lines laid out in the book of Leviticus—the sixth division. Many of the tractates of the first division, on agriculture, deal with the rations provided for the priests by the Israelite farmers out of the produce of the Holy Land. The interests of the division overall flow from the Levitical taboos on land use and disposition of crops; the whole is an exercise of most acute interest to the priests. A fair part of the second division, on appointed times, takes up the conduct of the cult on special days, e.g., the sacrifices offered on the Day of Atonement, Passover, and the like. Indeed, what the Mishnah wants to know about appointed seasons concerns the cult far more than it does the synagogue, which plays a subordinate role.

The fourth division, on civil law, for its part, presents an elaborate account of a political structure and system of Israelite self-government based on Temple, priesthood, and monarchy, in tractates Sanhedrin and Makkot, not to mention Shebuot and Horayot. This system speaks of king, priest, Temple, and court. It was not the Jews, their kings, priests, and judges, but the Romans who conducted the government of Israel in the Land of Israel in the time in which the second-century authorities did their work. So it would appear that well over half of the document before us—the first, the second, part of the fourth, the fifth and sixth divisions—speaks of cult, Temple, government, priesthood. The Mishnah takes up a profoundly priestly and Levitical conception of sanctification as the principal statement on Israel's condition. When we consider that, in the very time in which the authorities before us did their work, the Temple lay in ruins, the city of Jerusalem was prohibited to all Israelites, and the Jewish government and administration which had centered on the Temple and based its authority on the holy life lived there were in ruins, the fantastic character of the Mishnah's address to its own catastrophic day becomes clear.

THE ENIGMA OF THE MISHNAH

The Mishnah does not identify its authors. In its authorities' patterns of language and speech, it permits only slight variations, so there is no place for individual characteristics of expression. It nowhere tells us when it speaks. It does not address a particular place or time. It rarely speaks of events in its own day. It never identifies its prospective audience. There is, in the entire mass of sayings and rules, scarcely a "you" of direct address to the reader and the world beyond. The Mishnah begins nowhere: "When do we do so and so?" It ends abruptly. There is no predicting where it will commence, no explaining why it is done. Where, when, why the document is laid out and set forth are questions not deemed urgent.

Indeed, as I noted above, the Mishnah contains not a hint about what its authors conceive their work to be. We asked before: Is it a law code? Is it a schoolbook? Since it makes statements describing what people should and should not do, or rather, do do and do not do, we might suppose it is a law code. Since it covers topics of both practical and theoretical interest, we might suppose it is a schoolbook, a work of philosophy. But the Mishnah never expresses a hint about its authors' intent. The reason is that the authors do what they must to efface all traces not only of individuality but even of their own participation in the formation of the document.

So it is not only a letter from utopia to whom it may concern. It also is a letter written by no one person—but not by a committee we can identify, either. When we turned to the contents of the document, we were helped not at all in determining the place of the Mishnah's origination, the purpose of making it, the reasons for its anonymous and collective plane of discourse and monotonous tone of voice. For the Mishnah covers a carefully defined program of topics. But the Mishnah never tells us why one topic is introduced and another is omitted, or what the agglutination of these particular topics is meant to accomplish in the formation of a system or of an imaginative construction. Nor is there any predicting how a given topic will be treated, why a given set of issues will be explored in close detail, and another set of possible issues ignored. Discourse on a theme begins and ends as if all things are self-evident—including, as I said, the reason for beginning at one point and ending at some other.

To conclude: Judaism in the first two centuries C.E. came into being on the other side of two wars, and produced, as its first and enduring testimony, a book of law and religion, a book to express a system of philosophy and a theory of society. Since the Mishnah emerges after a time of wars, the one thing we should anticipate is a message about the meaning of history, an account of events and their meaning. Central to the Mishnah's system should be a picture of the course of Israel's destiny, in the tradition of the biblical histories—Samuel, Kings, Chronicles, for instance—and in the tradition of the prophets of ancient Israel, the several Isaiahs, Jeremiah, and the rest. A theory of the Messiah should play a prominent role in this explanation of events.

The Mishnah's principal insistence is the opposite. It speaks of what is permanent and enduring: the flow of time through the seasons, marked by festivals and Sabbaths; the procedures of the cult through the regular and enduring sacrifices; the conduct of the civil society through norms of fairness to prevent unjust change; the pursuit of agricultural work in accord with the rules of holiness; the enduring, unchanging, invisible phobias of cultic uncleanness and cleanness. In the Mishnah there is no division devoted to the interpretation of history. There is no pretense even at telling what had just happened. There is scarcely a line to address the issue of the meaning of the disasters of the day. Others proclaimed Messiahs. The Mishnah knows none.

The Mishnah does not address singular men or one-time events of history. Its laws express recurrent patterns, eternal patterns of society as enduring as the movement of the moon and sun around the earth (as they would have understood it) and as regular as the lapping of the waves on the beach. These are laws on ploughing, planting, harvesting; birth, marriage, procreation, death; home, family, household; work, rest; sunrise, sunset—not the stuff of history. The laws speak of the here and now, not of state and tradition, past or future. Since, in the time in which the ideas of the Mishnah took shape, most other Jews expressed a keen interest in history, the contrast cannot be missed. The Mishnah imagines a world of regularity and order in the aftermath of the end of ancient certainties and patterns. It designs laws after the old rules all had been broken or fallen into desuetude. It speaks of an eternal present—generally using the continuous present tense and describing how things are—to people beyond all touch with their own past, their life and institutions.

2

Scripture and the Mishnah

THE MISHNAH AND SCRIPTURE

Before we consider how the Mishnah's heirs and continuators solved the problem of finding a place for the Mishnah in the Torah, that is, in the canon of Judaism, we briefly take up the facts of the matter. The place of Scripture in the Mishnah itself and the impact of the ideas of Scripture on the theories of the Mishnah's philosophers require some attention. Otherwise we shall not fully perceive the framework and context in which, from ca. 200 to 600 C.E., the founders of Judaism worked out the crisis precipitated by the role and character of the Mishnah.

I stress that the problem posed by the Mishnah was not formal but substantive. We are concerned not merely with the absence of proof-texts. These commonly appear in our eyes as mere pretexts. Indeed, the bulk of ancient exegesis in contemporary perspective is little more than crude, self-serving eisegesis. We want to know how the sixty-two tractates of the Mishnah (excluding Abot), all of them organized around specific topics and systematically investigating particular problems in connection with those topics, relate to Scripture. To this question, citation of proof-texts is not pertinent; the substance of the matter is what counts.

Still, at the outset, let us examine a specimen of how the writers of the Mishnah overall might have presented their ideas. For from antecedent Israelite literature, if they knew it, the exegetical form was available to them. Had they concurred with the school of Matthew that whatever they wished to say had to be framed in explicit response to what Scripture, clearly cited, had said, how would they have done their work? To answer that question, we look at a piece of the Mishnah purporting to amplify the meaning of Scripture. The biblical passage at hand is Deut. 20:2–6, rules governing exemptions from the Israelite army. The framer of the passage, at M. Sot. 8:1–2, systematically cited the verse and then added a few words to explain its meaning or to amplify and apply its law. The opening passage, M. Sot. 8:1, follows a style we shall see many times over in compilations of exegeses, that is, word-for-word commentary. The passage concludes with a small homily. What is striking is that the form of the exposition of the scriptural passage at M. Sot. 8:2 then takes up a decidedly "Mishnaic" character. That is, instead of word-for-word response to the statement of the Scripture, we find an autonomous construction of information, along highly formalized lines, in which there are six carefully matched and balanced sentences—a characteristically Mishnaic mode of expressing ideas. This kind of formulation of ideas, of course, is familiar to the reader, since in the opening chapter we encountered it in the Mishnaic extracts we considered. It is standard for the Mishnah as a whole. My guess is that approximately ninety-seven percent of the entire Mishnah is framed in this sort of generalizing, highly formalized style. But here the information, formulated in its own, Mishnaic way, is tacked on to verses of Scripture. That hardly constitutes a close exegetical reading of the Scripture's words. I include M. Sot. 8:3, finally, to show what a more commonplace mode of expressing ideas would look like; the contrast to the foregoing then is still more striking.

[A] *The anointed for battle, when he speaks to the people, in the Holy Language did he speak,*

[B] *as it is said, "And it shall come to pass when you draw near to the battle, that the priest shall approach [this is the priest anointed for battle] and shall speak to the people [in the Holy Language] and shall say to them, 'Hear, O Israel, you draw near to battle this day'" (Deut. 20:3)—*

[C] *"against your enemies" (Deut. 20:3)—and not against your brothers,*

[D] *not Judah against Simeon, nor Simeon against Benjamin.*

[E] *For if you fall into their [Israelites'] hand, they will have mercy for you,*

[F] *as it is said, "And the men which have been called by name rose up and took the captives and with the spoil clothed all that were naked among them and arrayed them and put shoes on their feet and gave them food to eat and something to drink and carried all the feeble of them upon asses and brought them to Jericho, the city of palm trees, unto their brethren. Then they returned to Samaria" (2 Chron. 28:15).*

[G] *"Against your enemies" do you go forth.*

[H] *For if you fall into their hand, they will not have mercy upon you.*

[I] *"Let not your heart be faint, fear not, nor tremble, neither be afraid" (Deut. 20:3).*

[J] *"Let not your heart be faint"—on account of the neighing of the horses and the flashing of the swords.*

[K] *"Fear not"—at the clashing of shields and the rushing of the tramping shoes.*

[L] *"Nor tremble"—at the sound of the trumpets.*

[M] *"Neither be afraid"—at the sound of the shouting.*

[N] *"For the Lord your God is with you" (Deut. 20:4)—*

[O] *they come with the power of mortal man, but you come with the power of the Omnipresent.*

[P] *The Philistines came with the power of Goliath. What was his end? In the end he fell by the sword, and they fell with him.*

[Q] *The Ammonites came with the power of Shobach (2 Sam. 10:16). What was his end? In the end he fell by the sword, and they fell with him.*

[R] *But you are not thus: "For the Lord your God is he who goes with you to fight for you"*

[S] *(—this is the camp of the ark) (M. Sot. 8:1).*

[A] *"And the officers shall speak to the people, saying, What man is there who has built a new house and has not dedicated it? Let him go and return to his house" (Deut. 20:5).*

[I.B] *All the same are the ones who build a house for straw, a house for cattle, a house for wood, and a house for storage.*

[II.C] *All the same are the ones who build it, who purchase it, who inherit it, and to whom it is given as a gift.*

[D] *"And who is the man who has planted a vineyard and has not used the fruit thereof?" (Deut. 20:6)—*

[III.E] *All the same are the ones who plant a vineyard and who plant five fruit-trees,*

[F] *and even if they are of five different kinds.*

[IV.G] *And all the same are the ones who plant such a tree, who sink them into the ground, and who graft them.*

[V.H] *And all the same are the ones who buy a vineyard, and who inherit it, and to whom it is given as a gift.*

[I] *"And who is the man who has betrothed a wife" (ibid)—*

[VI.J] *All the same are the ones who betrothe a virgin and who betrothe a widow—*

[K] *and even a deceased childless brother's widow who awaits the Levir.*

[L] *And even if one heard during the battle that his brother had died,*

[M] *he returns and comes along home.*

[N] *All these listen to the words of the priest concerning the arrangements of battle and go home.*

[O] *And they provide water and food and keep the roads in good repair (M. Sot. 8:2).*

[A] *And these are the ones who do not return home:*

[B] *He who builds a gate-house, a portico, or a porch;*

[C] *he who plants only four fruit-trees or five barren trees;*

[D] *he who remarries a woman whom he has divorced,*

[E] *or [he who marries] a widow in the case of a high priest, a divorcee or a woman who has undergone the rite of* halisah *in the case of an ordinary priest, or a* mamzeret *or a Netinah in the case of an Israelite, or an Israelite-girl in the case of a* mamzer *or a Netin—*

[F] *such a one did not go home.*

[G] *R. Judah says, "Also: He who builds his house on its original foundation did not go home."*

[H] *R. Eleazar says, "Also: He who builds a house of bricks in the Sharon does not go home" (M. Sot. 8:3).*

With M. Sot. 8:3 in hand, we are able in microcosm to see the character of the issue at hand. We realize that the Mishnah's statement at M. Sot. 8:3 addresses a theme of a passage of Scripture. We know that, ordinarily, Israelite writers for nearly seven hundred years had preferred to formulate their ideas through constant recourse to biblical verses, as at M. Sot. 8:1–2, or, at the very least, through imitating biblical language and style. These writers normally do not. In consequence, the heirs of their document had to analyze their writing, sentence by sentence, to show precisely what the writers of the Mishnah hid: how *what* they said stood in close and subordinate relationship to sentences of Scripture.

Let us now turn to the actual relationships, as distinct from those to be alleged in time to come by the critics and commentators of the Mishnah: how do tractates relate to their thematic counterparts among the legal codes and ideas of Scripture? Let me begin by reminding the reader of facts already adduced in the first chapter.

Formally, redactionally, and linguistically the Mishnah stands in splendid isolation from Scripture. It is not possible to point in prior Israelite religious writing to many parallels, that is, cases of anonymous books, received as holy, in which the forms and formulations (specific verses) of Scripture play so slight a role. People who wrote holy books commonly imitated the Scripture's language. They cited concrete verses. They claimed at the very least that direct revelation had come to them, as in the angelic discourses of IV Ezra and Baruch, so that what they say stands on an equal plane with Scripture. The internal evidence of the Mishnah's sixty-two usable tractates (excluding Abot), by contrast, in no way suggests that anyone pretended to talk like Moses and write like Moses, claimed to cite and correctly interpret things that Moses had said, or even alleged to have had a revelation like that of Moses and so to stand on the mountain with Moses. There is none of this. So the claim of scriptural authority for the Mishnah's doctrines and institutions is difficult to locate within the internal evidence of the Mishnah itself.

Let us now rapidly survey the conceptual relationships between various Mishnah tractates, on the one side, and laws of Scripture, on the other.

First, there are tractates which simply repeat in their own words precisely what Scripture has to say, and at best serve to amplify and complete the basic ideas of Scripture. For example, all of the cultic tractates of the second division, on Appointed Times, which tell what one is supposed to do in the Temple on the various special days of the year, and the bulk of the cultic tractates of the fifth division, which deals with Holy Things, simply restate facts of Scripture. For another example, all of those tractates of the sixth division, on Purities, which specify sources of uncleanness, completely depend on information supplied by Scripture. Every important statement, for example, in Niddah, on menstrual uncleanness, the most fundamental notions of Zabim, on the uncleanness of the person with flux referred to in Leviticus 15, as well as every detail in Negaim, on the uncleanness of the person or house suffering the uncleanness described at Leviticus 13 and 14—all of these tractates serve only to reiterate the basic facts of Scripture and to complement those facts with other derivative ones.

There are, second, tractates which take up facts of Scripture but work them out in a way that those scriptural facts could not have led us to predict. A supposition concerning what is important about the facts, utterly remote from the supposition of Scripture, will explain why the Mishnah tractates under discussion say the original things they say in confronting those scripturally-provided facts. For one example, Scripture (Num. 19:1ff.) takes for granted that the red cow will be burned in a state of uncleanness, because it is burned outside the camp (Temple). The priestly writers cannot have imagined that a state of cultic cleanness was to be attained outside of the cult. The absolute datum of Mishnah-tractate Parah, on burning the red cow, by contrast, is that cultic cleanness not only can be attained outside of the "tent of meeting"; the red cow was to be burned in a state of cleanness even exceeding the cultic cleanness required in the Temple itself. The problematic which generates the intellectual agendum of Parah, therefore, is how to work out the conduct of the rite of burning the cow in relationship to the Temple: Is it to be done in exactly the same way, or in exactly the opposite way? This mode of contrastive and analogical thinking helps us to understand the generative problematic of such tractates as Erubin and Besah, to mention only two.

Third, there are, predictably, many tractates which either take up problems in no way suggested by Scripture, or begin from facts at best merely relevant to facts of Scripture. In the former category are Tohorot, on the cleanness of foods, with its companion, Uqsin; Demai, on doubtfully tithed produce; Tamid, on the conduct of the daily whole-offering; Baba Batra, on rules of real estate transactions and certain other commercial and property relationships, and so on. Representative of the latter category is Ohalot, which spins out its strange problems within the theory that a tent and a utensil are to be compared to one another (!). Other instances are these: Kelim, on the susceptibility to uncleanness of various sorts of utensils; Miqvaot, on the sorts of water which effect purification from uncleanness; Ketubot and Gittin, on the documents of marriage and divorce; and many others. These tractates here and there draw facts of Scripture. But the problem confronted in these tractates—the generative problematic—in no way responds to issues or even facts important to Scripture. What we have here is a prior program of inquiry, which will make ample provision for facts of Scripture in an inquiry generated, to begin with, essentially outside of the framework of Scripture. First comes the problem or topic, then, if possible, attention to Scripture.

So there we have it: some tractates merely repeat what we find in Scripture. Some are totally independent of Scripture. And some fall in-between. We find everything and its opposite. But to offer a final answer to the question of Scripture-Mishnah relationships, we have to take that fact seriously. The Mishnah in no way is so remote from Scripture as its formal omission of citations of verses of Scripture suggests. It also cannot be described as contingent upon, and secondary to Scripture, as many of its third-century apologists claimed. But the right answer is not that it is somewhere in-between. Scripture confronts the framers of the Mishnah as revelation, not merely as a source of facts. But the framers of the Mishnah had their own world with which to deal. They made statements in the framework and fellowship of their own age and generation. They were bound, therefore, to come to Scripture with a set of questions generated elsewhere than in Scripture. They brought their own ideas about what was going to be important in Scripture. This is perfectly natural.

The philosophers of the Mishnah conceded to Scripture the highest authority. At the same time what they chose to hear, within the authoritative statements of Scripture, would in the end form a statement of its own. To state matters simply: all of Scripture was authoritative. But only some of Scripture was found to be relevant. And what happened is that the framers and philosophers of the tradition of the Mishnah came to Scripture when they had reason to. That is to say, they brought to Scripture a program of questions and inquiries framed essentially among themselves. So they were highly selective. That is why their program itself constituted a statement *upon* the meaning of Scripture. They and their apologists of one sort hastened to add that their program consisted of a statement *of*, and not only upon, the meaning of Scripture.

The way in which the sages of the Mishnah utilized the inherited and authoritative tradition of Scripture therefore is clear. On the one hand, wherever they could, they repeated what Scripture says. This they did, however, in their own words. So they established a claim of relevance and also authority. They spoke to their own day in their own idiom. On the other hand, they selected with care and precision what they wanted in Scripture, ignoring what they did not want. They took up laws, not prophecies, descriptions of how things are supposed to be, not accounts of what is going to happen.

So much for the role of Scripture in the Mishnah. We turn now to ask how the heirs and continuators of the Mishnah, the rabbinical sages who inherited the document after ca. 200 C.E., sorted out the diverse questions before them, the questions of (1) canon, (2) scrip-

27

tural authority, and (3) revelation. Specifically, they had to make a judgment on the place and authority of the Mishnah within the total corpus of revelation called, in Judaism, "the Torah." Second, in order to reach such an assessment, they further had to impose their own view, through exegesis of the Mishnah, about the place and authority of Scripture within the Mishnah, forming a concomitant position on the relationship of the Mishnah to Scripture. We now take up the principal documents produced in the rabbinical estate after the closure of the Mishnah.

As I indicated earlier, three different kinds of literature flow from the Mishnah and refer to it. One, Tosefta, supplements to the Mishnah, is a wholly dependent, secondary, and exegetical form, in which the Mishnah provides the whole frame of organization and redaction for all materials, and in which citation and secondary expansion of the statements of the Mishnah define the bulk, though not the whole, of the work. The next, Sifra, exegeses of Leviticus, focuses not upon the Mishnah but upon Scripture and proposes to provide a bridge between the two. Sifra, and to a lesser degree, Sifre to Numbers and Sifre to Deuteronomy, fall into this second category. The last is in the middle, both dependent upon, and autonomous of, the Mishnah, taking up its individual statements and amplifying them, but also expanding and developing autonomous discussions. The two Talmuds, one produced in the Land of Israel, the other in Babylonia, constitute this kind of writing. Our task is now to outline the ways in which each of these kinds of literature defines the role of Scripture in the Mishnah.

The order in which we take up these three types of rabbinical writing produced in the aftermath of the Mishnah bears no implications whatever about the historical sequence in which they were written. That historical issue, while interesting, in no way relates to the problem at hand. My order of presentation simply presents, among the three possible approaches to the question, a thesis, an antithesis, and a synthesis. As we shall now see, the Tosefta makes no systematic effort to adduce scriptural proof-texts for Mishnaic statements. The Sifra commonly attempts to show the Mishnah's links to the Scripture, so that whatever is right in the Mishnah derives from, is secondary to, statements of Scripture. The Talmud takes up a far more complex position, in rough balance between these two extreme views. That fact accounts for the order of topics in the remainder of this chapter.

SCRIPTURE AND THE MISHNAH
IN THE TOSEFTA

The Tosefta presents no general theory of the Mishnah. The Mishnah is read in parts, but not viewed as a whole. The Mishnah is the lattice for the Tosefta's vine. That accounts for the simple fact that the Tosefta proposes to take up and explain fragments of the Mishnah's sentences, but never systematically to provide an overview. Indeed, the absence of system is a symptom of the exegetes' failure to form an overall picture. And, as we shall see, that accounts for the place of Scripture in the Tosefta's reading of the Mishnah. We find no evidence of a systematic effort to give the Mishnah what it lacks, proof-texts for its assertions. Further, we shall observe nothing distinctive in the way in which the Tosefta's authors turn to Scripture in relationship to their exegesis of the Mishnah. Just as they looked into Scripture for proof-texts for opinions found in the Mishnah, so they did the same, without formal or substantive variation, in seeking for proof-texts for opinions not located in the Mishnah. The point of it all is not to buttress with scriptural proof-texts the Mishnah's statements in particular. The Mishnah does not define the issue. The routine and entirely natural recourse to Scripture does. This point will prove central to the argument of chapter 5.

Let me step back and explain the document at hand. The Tosefta, or collections of supplements, is a corpus of materials correlative to the Mishnah. Standing apart from the Mishnah, the greater part of Tosefta's materials is incomprehensible gibberish, bearing no autonomous meaning to be discovered wholly within the limits of a discrete passage. The Tosefta's units relate to corresponding ones in the Mishnah in one of three ways: (1) The Tosefta cites the Mishnah verbatim and then supplies glosses or further discussions of the Mishnah's rules; (2) the Tosefta complements the Mishnah without directly citing the corresponding passage; (3) the Tosefta supplements the Mishnah with information relevant to, but in theme and meaning independent of, the principal document.

29

The first sort of relationship characterizes about half of the units of the book, the second about another third, and the last, about a sixth. This is a very rough approximation. The Tosefta's aggregations of materials normally are grouped in accord with their respective relationships to the Mishnah. A sequence serving a given chapter of the Mishnah, for example, may begin with pericopae in which the Mishnah is cited, then proceed to another set in which the Mishnah is complemented, and finally present materials in which the Mishnah is given supplementary but essentially separate materials. The formulary traits of the Tosefta run parallel to those of the Mishnah in the first, and, to a lesser extent, in the second sort of materials. But in the main the Tosefta's language is far less formalized than the Mishnah's. The Mishnah's redaction tends to produce aggregates of materials characterized by a common formulary pattern and a common theme. So far as the Tosefta may be divided into sizable groups of materials, by contrast, it is redacted primarily in accord with the single relationship to the Mishnah exhibited by a sequence of otherwise formally and thematically discrete units. In size, the Tosefta is approximately four times larger than the Mishnah.

What interests us in the Tosefta now comes to the fore. We begin with what we do not need to examine. Where the Tosefta speaks autonomously about issues in general shared with the Mishnah, we are not going to learn about its view of how the Mishnah's statements in particular are to be unpacked and explained. Where it contains its own traditions on these same matters, it goes without saying, we are not apt to learn how the Tosefta regards the role of Scripture in the Mishnah. When the Tosefta cites verbatim and then explicitly comments upon a passage of the Mishnah, however, we find out how the Tosefta wants to introduce scriptural proof-texts into the exegesis of the Mishnah. Introducing proof-texts where the Mishnah's authors supplied none, the Tosefta's authorities then indicate what they think the Mishnah lacks. That fact then tells us their judgment both upon the Mishnah and upon the Mishnah's relationship to Scripture. It is this: the Mishnah requires proof-texts, because, by itself, the Mishnah has no autonomous standing or authority. It is to be presented only as a secondary expansion of the Torah of Moses. If, on the other hand, the Tosefta's writers do not systematically and regularly add proof-texts, or if they use proof-texts for purposes other than to indicate their critique of the Mishnah's failure to use them, we draw other conclusions of their theory of the matter.

Let us start with examples of how the Tosefta will cite and amplify or otherwise make its comment upon a passage of the Mishnah. In the first instance, the Tosefta simply adds to the Mishnah a sizable exemplification of the opinion of sages. What follows is typical of how the Tosefta's writers cite, and then make their own comment upon, a passage of the Mishnah. The words in italics are verbatim in the Mishnah's corresponding passage. The rest, in boldface, is what Tosefta adds.

[A] *"***The sanctification of the new month** and the intercalation of the year are to be done by three [judges],"* **the words of R. Meir.**
[B] **And sages say,** *"Before three do they begin, and before five they debate the matter, and they reach a final decision with seven [judges] [M. San. 1:2D–E].*
[C] **"How so?**
[D] **"[If] one says to go into session, and two say not to go into session, the opinion of the individual is null as a minority.**
[E] **"[If] two say to go into session, and one says not to go into session—they add two more to their number and debate the matter with five.**
[F] **"[If] two say that it requires intercalation, and three say that it does not require intercalation—the opinion of the two is null because it is a minority.**
[G] **"[If] three say it requires, and two say it does not require [intercalation], then they add two more to their number.**
[H] **"Then they reach a final decision with seven.**
[I] **"For a quorum may not be less than seven"** [T. San. 2:1].

What we do not find is important. No verse of Scripture is adduced in behalf of the position of either party. What is important to the framer of the Tosefta's comment is to explain the case of the Mishnah, and not the source of the Mishnah's law.

An instance in which the Tosefta does exactly that is in the following. I cite a sizable extract, so that the interplay of the Mishnah and the Tosefta is clear, and the exact place of Scripture citations and proof-texts becomes apparent. In this extract, watch for the way in which Tosefta carries on its work of supplement. First, we see that the Mishnah paragraph is cited quite systematically, in sequence, at T. 4:1J, then T. 4:2G–I, K. So there can be no doubt of the intent of the framer of the passage. Second, we want to see whether or not the Tosefta's authorities thought it important, point by point, to cite a passage of the Scripture to sustain or prove the validity of the assertions of the Mishnah. Third, we have to ask ourselves for what purposes a verse of Scripture is cited.

[J] *[People may] not watch him while he is getting a haircut, [or while he is nude] or in the bathhouse [M. San. 2:5B]*,

[K] since it is said, "And he who is high priest among his brothers" (Lev. 21:10)—that his brethren should treat him with grandeur.

[L] But if he wanted to permit others to wash with him, the right is his.

[M] R. Judah says, "[If] he wanted to disgrace himself, they do not pay attention to him.

[N] "as it is said, "And you will keep him holy" (Lev. 21:8)—even against his will."

[O] They said to R. Judah, "To be sure [Scripture] says, "From the Temple he shall not go forth" (Lev. 21:12), [but this is referring] only to the time of the Temple service" [M. San. 2:1/IJ].

[P] He goes out to provide a funeral meal for others, and others come to provide a funeral meal for him.

[4:2.A] *An Israelite king does not stand in line to receive comfort [in the time of bereavement]*,

[B] *nor does he stand in line to give comfort to others*.

[C] *And he does not go to provide a funeral meal for others*.

[D] *But others come to him to give him a funeral meal [M. San. 2:3F]*,

[E] as it is said, "And the people went to provide a funeral meal for David" (2 Sam. 3:35).

[F] And if he transgressed a positive or a negative commandment or indeed any of the commandments, lo, he is treated like an ordinary person in every respect.

[G] *He does not perform the rite of removing the shoe, and others do not perform the rite of removing the shoe with his wife;*

[H] *he does not enter into levirate marriage, nor [do his brothers] enter into levirate marriage with his wife [M. San. 2:2C–D]*.

[I] *R. Judah says, "If he wanted to perform the rite of removing the shoe [M. San. 2:2E]*, he has the right to do so."

[J] They said to him, "You turn out to do damage to the glory owing to a king."

[K] *And [others] do not marry his widow [M. San. 2:3G]*, as it is said,

"So they were shut up to the day of their death, living in widowhood" (2 Sam. 20:3).

[L] And he has the right to choose wives for himself from any source he wants, whether daughters of priests, Levites, or Israelites.

[M] *And they do not ride on his horse, sit on his throne, handle his crown or sceptre [M. San. 2:5]* or any of his regalia.

[N] [When] he dies, all of them are burned along with him, as it is said, "You shall die in peace and with the burnings of your fathers, the former kings" (Jer. 34:5) [T. San. 4:1J–P, 4:2].

The facts are clear. What is important is the absence of a *systematic* effort to prove from Scripture what the Mishnah has said, or, at least to relate to Scripture. We note that at M. 4:1J, a passage of the Mishnah is cited, then given a proof-text, while an opinion *not* cited from the Mishnah, M–O, is treated in exactly the same way. This means that, in providing proof-texts, no distinction was made between the points of origin of statements. Some appearing in the Mishnah were given proof-texts, some not; and so too is the pattern with some not appearing in the Mishnah. As to the Mishnah paragraph as a whole, it is cited again at T. 4:2G–H–I, continuous then with T. 4:1J, and then forward to T. 4:2K. Some clauses bear proof-texts, some do not.

That brings us to the main point. In the Tosefta, verses of Scripture serve a variety of purposes. But the Tosefta's framers in no way make the effort point by point to validate a passage of the Mishnah through adducing proof-texts of Scripture in its behalf. So while to those philosophers of the law Scripture constituted a paramount source of facts, even served as the place of ultimate appeal, the issue of the Mishnah's relationship to Scripture proved entirely secondary. It was part of the larger issue of validating whatever seemed to someone to demand and sustain proof in Scripture. The Mishnah therefore formed a small part of the larger problem. It did not define the problematic. To state matters in a more relevant way, the issue of the place of Scripture in the Mishnah in particular hardly proved paramount in anyone's mind.

Let us proceed to the final phenomenon, Tosefta's citation of Scripture in contexts quite independent of the exegesis of the Mishnah. The fact that this occurs proves the validity of what has just been stated. The focus lay upon Scripture, not upon the Mishnah. Interest in the Scripture as a pool of proof-texts proved generalized and unexceptional, not particular and polemical. The reason for my stressing that distinction will become clear in the next section.

Here is an instance in which the Tosefta's authors resort to Scripture as a mere source of well-established facts.

[A] *Cities surrounded by a wall from the time of Joshua ben Nun read [the Scroll of Esther] on the fifteenth [M. Meg. 1:1C].*

[B] R. Joshua b. Qorha says, "[If they were surrounded by a wall] from the time of Ahasueros [they read the Scroll of Esther on the fifteenth of Adar]."

[C] Said R. Yose b. Judah, "Where do we find evidence concerning Shushan, the capital, that it was surrounded by a wall from the time of Joshua b. Nun?

[D] "But: '[. . . that these days should be remembered and kept throughout every generation,] in every family, province, and city' (Est. 9:28)" [T. Meg. 1:1].

The characteristic traits of the Tosefta's use of Scripture emerge in this brief passage. The formulation of C–D tells the entire story. We ask for a source of evidence, and we turn naturally to Scripture. No other proof is required—or even thought possible. We must not miss the remarkable fact that, to the mentality before us, "proof" and "proof-texts" are redundant words.

The conclusions of this brief review require little amplification. The framers of the Tosefta turned to Scripture for diverse purposes. They proposed, first, to prove points important to themselves; second, to provide proof-texts for statements of the Mishnah; third, to find proofs for facts already in hand. We cannot then maintain that the principal interest of the Tosefta was systematically and routinely to prove that what the Mishnah's framers stated must derive from Scripture and therefore requires such proof. We may observe only a sporadic and unsystematic effort in that regard. Where, by contrast, the Tosefta's framers did read the Mishnah with order and consistency, it was simply to expand and explain what the Mishnah had to say. They introduced secondary refinements and considerations to the Mishnah's basic law and otherwise focused upon the Mishnah as an autonomous and important body of law. Scripture then was pertinent but incidental. Why that fact is striking becomes clear when we consider the opposite extreme, a fairly systematic effort to link Scripture to the Mishnah, such as Sifra provides.

SCRIPTURE AND THE MISHNAH
IN THE SIFRA

The Sifra, a systematic exegesis of Leviticus, applies rigorous logic to the exegesis of Scripture. But its interest is not in Leviticus alone. The framers undertake to show again and again that principal assertions of the Mishnah are either to be linked with Scripture (a common exercise) or derive not from logic but, in particular, from scriptural exegesis. Revelation, and not logic alone, is necessary for the discovery of the law. Sifra frequently asks about the scriptural foundations of laws, including laws it shares with the Mishnah, in the effort to prove that Mishnaic and other laws are based not upon logic but upon revelation and that alone. That obvious and pointed polemic against the non-exegetical character of the Mishnah also is directed against the non-exegetical character of laws distinctive to Sifra. It would appear to be a critique of reason in the name of revelation. The Mishnah presents a target of opportunity, not the cause of inquiry.

The Sifra derives from the period after the Mishnah. That fact is shown in the numerous verbatim citations of passages of the Mishnah by the authors of the Sifra. The book is made up of two types of materials. The first is simple. A verse (or a few words of a verse) will be cited, followed by a few words stating the meaning of the cited passage. This type rarely contains the name of an authority. The second type is complex; in it the simple exercise just described is augmented in an important way. There will be a sequence of questions and answers raising and rejecting diverse legal theories. (This rhetoric, based on the dialectic, or moving, argument, is entirely familiar in both Talmuds.) The construction is important in that it exhibits substantial development. This second type often will bear the names of authorities behind its opinions. The primary stratum of the Sifra consists of the former type. But many of the more complex paragraphs of the Sifra begin in this same simple type. Other undeveloped items can have been served by the secondary expansion of questions, theses and counter-theses.

The Sifra is predominantly exegetical. The paragraphs which are not exegetical normally appear also in the Mishnah or Tosefta and accord with the formal and syntactic traits of those documents, traits otherwise unknown in the Sifra. Where the Sifra does not draw

35

upon materials common to those collections, it is wholly exegetical in character. So the Sifra as a whole is a composite document, with an early stratum of simple exegeses and a later, larger stratum of dialectical ones. The purpose of the bulk of these later entries, as we noted just now, is to apply rigorous logic to the exegesis of Scripture and to demonstrate that revelation, not logic alone, is necessary for the discovery of the law. In doing so, therefore, the authors of the Sifra used the inherited, simple form. They spun out their theses by presenting ideas in that uncomplicated form and then challenging their ideas in various ways. They used an equally simple disciplined form.

When the framers of the Sifra drew, in addition, upon materials from completed paragraphs appearing in the Mishnah or the Tosefta, were they citing completed documents? Since these paragraphs exhibit the definitive editorial and stylistic traits of the Mishnah or the Tosefta and not those otherwise paramount in the Sifra, I am inclined to conclude that materials occurring in both the Sifra and in the Mishnah or the Tosefta originally were formulated for use in the latter documents. Hence they emerged from the period after the Mishnah, possibly also the Tosefta, had reached closure.

So the framers of the Sifra maintained that statements of the Mishnah should be closely tied to verses of Scripture. That position is worked out in a line-by-line reading of Leviticus, with frequent reference to pertinent passages of the Mishnah (in italics) or the Tosefta (again given in boldface type). The authors, second, took the more extreme position that *only* in Scripture, and not in reason uncorrected by Scripture, may we gain certainty about the true foundations of the law. The former position appears in the simple, the latter in the complex and dialectical, sorts of discussions of the Sifra. Let us begin with the simple procedure, linking a passage of the Mishnah or the Tosefta to a statement in Leviticus (other such instances occur in the appendix). We take up the simplest instance, in which the Sifra's citation of the Mishnah on the surface is lacking in all polemic.

[A] "[But if the scall, spreading, will spread] after he is purified" (Lev. 13:35)—

[B] I know only that this is after the clearance. And how do I know that this applies even at the end of the first week and at the end of the second week?

[C] Scripture says, "It will spread, and if spreading, it will spread" (Lev. 13:35).

[D] One certified him unclean because of golden hair, and the golden hair went away, and returned, and so with spreading, in the first instance, at the end of the first week, at the end of the second week, after the clearance, after he has certified him unclean—lo, he is as he was.

[E] On this account it is said "It will spread, and if spreading, it will spread" (Lev. 13:35).

[F] One certified him unclean through spreading, the spreading went away, and the spreading returned, and so with golden hair, at the end of the first week, at the end of the second week, and after the clearance, lo, he is as he was [M. Negaim 10:5].

[G] Scripture says, "It will spread, and if spreading it will spread" (Lev. 13:35).

Sifra Negaim 9:10

What we see is that, in the exegesis of Lev. 13:35, a passage of the Mishnah is entered verbatim, with no further comment. The focus of interest simply is in collecting materials pertinent to the exegesis of Leviticus. Whether or not one must cite a verse of Scripture to prove the point of M. Negaim 10:5 we do not know.

In the next two instances, we have a clearer polemic. Following a sequence of simple statements about the reasons and possibilities for Scripture's laws, we proceed to a simple statement cited from the Mishnah. The question then is the basis on which one proves that Mishnaic rule. The answer is a citation of a verse of Leviticus. So the polemic is now implicit.

[A] Another matter:

[B] "In all the sight of the eyes of the priest" (Lev. 13:12)

[C] This excludes a priest the light of whose eyes has dimmed.

[D] On this basis have they said:

[E] A priest the light of whose eyes has darkened and one who is blind in one of his eyes or the light of whose eyes has dimmed should not examine the plagues [= M. Negaim 2:3A].

Sifra Negaim 4:4

[A] "And the priest shall look, and behold, the leprosy has covered [all his body; he shall pronounce him clean]" (Lev. 13:13).

[B] Why does Scripture say this?

37

[C] Because one might [argue]: I know only that breaking forth renders him clean only from the [white shade of the] eruption alone.

[D] How do we know that we should include all other colors?

[E] Scripture says, "The leprosy" (Lev. 13:13)—

[F] "All his flesh" (Lev. 13:13)—

[G] to include the space between the fingers of the hands and the toes of the feet.

[H] *Another matter:*

[I] Why does Scripture say, "All his flesh" (Lev. 13:13)?

[J] On what basis do you rule:

[K] *[If] it broke forth throughout his body but not over about a half-lentil [of flesh] near the head or the beard or the boil and the burning and the blister—*

it returned to the midst of his head and beard but they became bald—

the boil, the burning, and the blister and they formed a scab
[= M. Negaim 8:5]—

[L] Might one say he is clean?

[M] Scripture says, "All his flesh" (Lev. 13:13)—until it will break forth over his entire body.

Sifra Negaim 4:5

This brings us to the more complex case in which the Sifra's authors cite Scripture specifically to prove one of two propositions. First, the Mishnah's proposition derives *not* from reason but only from Scripture. Second, reason unaided by the corrective of Scripture leads to false conclusions. In the context of the Mishnah's neglect of proof-texts, the two propositions are not much different from one another. Let us first take up an example of the Sifra framers' attack on logic unaided by Scripture. In the following passage, the Mishnah does not appear. In the exegesis of the cited verse, we ask why the proposition opposite the one attached to the verse of Scripture is not logical. The result is to prove that logic alone is misleading.

[A] "A reddish white plague" (Lev. 13:42: "diseased spot")—this phrase teaches that it [the bald spot] is rendered unclean with a variegation.

[B] "A leprosy" (Lev. 13:42)—this phrase teaches that it is rendered unclean with quick flesh.

[C] And is [the opposite proposition] not logical?

[D] If the boil and the burning, which are unclean because of white hair, are not unclean because of quick flesh, a bald spot on the forehead and a bald spot on the scalp, which are not made unclean with white hair, logically should not be made unclean with quick flesh.

[E] Scripture says, "Leprosy" (Lev. 13:42)—

[F] teaching that it is made unclean with quick flesh.

[G] "Breaking forth" (Lev. 13:42)—this phrase teaches that it is made unclean through spreading.

[H] "It" [Lev. 13:42: "It is leprosy breaking forth on his bald head or on his bald forehead"]—it is not made unclean through white hair.

[I] Is [the opposite proposition] not logical:

[J] If the boil and the burning, which are not made unclean because of quick flesh, are made unclean through white hair, a bald spot on the forehead and a bald spot on the scalp, which are made unclean through quick flesh, logically should be made unclean through white hair.

[K] Scripture says, "It" (Lev. 13:42).

[L] It is not made unclean through white hair.

Sifra Negaim 11:1–2

The point of C is that the *opposite* of the scriptural law would seem to be required by logic. Scripture therefore has to specify the rule. The same issue is raised at I–J. Bald spots are unclean if they spread or if they contain the specified spots, just as Scripture says. There is no reference to white hair, but obviously the exegetes could have shown through Scripture that white hair would be a sign of uncleanness, if they themselves thought so. G–L depend upon the result of A–F, that is, we cannot analyze G–L's problem without knowing that quick flesh is a token of uncleanness.

In the final extract from Sifra, we confront an explicit attack on the use of logic, unaided by exegetical support, by the Mishnah in particular. A logical argument is overturned, and the Mishnaic authority, Simeon, is turned into a critic of the absence of biblical proof-texts from the Mishnah.

[A] "And when the priest will examine the plague [diseased place] of the scall" (Lev. 13:30).

[B] Said R. Simeon, "Why does Scripture say, 'A plague, a scall' (Lev. 13:30)?

[C] "Scripture intends to link the diseased spot to the scall, to teach that just as in the plague the white hair renders unclean only when it has been turned white [after the appearance of, and by, the bright spot], so in the case of the scall the golden hair which is in it is not a sign of uncleanness unless it is turned golden after the appearance of the scall—

[D] "'And in it is [already located] thin golden hair' (Lev. 13:30).

[E] *It is an argument a fortiori:*

[F] *"If white hair, from the power of which other hair does not afford protection, renders unclean only when it has been turned [white after the appearance of the bright spot], thin golden hair, from the power of which other hair [namely black] does afford protection, is it not logical that it should render unclean only when it has been turned [golden after the appearance of the scall [M. Negaim 10:2]?*

[G] "No. If you have said so concerning white hair, the power of which is not sufficient to render unclean in any color [but only the specified four shades of white], will you say so concerning thin golden hair, the power of which is sufficient to render unclean in any shade [of gold]?

[H] "Since its power is sufficient to render unclean in any shade, it should render unclean both when turned [gold before the appearance of the scall] and when not turned [gold before the appearance of the scall].

[I] "Scripture says, "A plague, a scall" (Lev. 13:30), thus linking a plague to a scall. Just as in the plague the white hair which is in a diseased spot renders unclean only when turned [white after the appearance of the diseased spot], so the golden hair in the scall renders unclean only when it has been turned [golden after the appearance of the scall]."

Sifra Negaim 8:1–2

The Sifra's version of the issue debated by Judah and Simeon in M. Negaim 10:2 gives Simeon a scriptural foundation for his opinion that only if the scall is present before the golden hair grows up is the golden hair a token of uncleanness for the scall. The Sifra has a two-fold purpose. First, it provides Simeon with the stated proof on the basis of exegesis of Scripture. Second, it also makes him admit that the logical argument, stated at E–F and in M. 10:2D, is insufficient. Scripture also will prove his point.

Simeon's proof is at C. Scripture speaks of a *plague, a scall*. Yet what trait of a plague pertains to the scall? Even though there is no plague mark in the scall, but we have only the scall itself (that is, the place from which hair has fallen out), it is still unclean. The reference to *plague, scall* therefore means to link the one to the other. Just as, Simeon holds (M. Negaim 4:6), white hair in the plague spot must be turned white after, and by the disease of, the plague spot itself, for it to serve as a token of uncleanness, so the golden hair must appear after, and be turned golden, by the scall. But G–I refute this logic. The Sifra gives the refutation to Simeon, so as to represent him as a critic of logic, as I said. Then I repeats C.

The Sifra therefore proposes a systematic critique of the Mishnah. As we observed in the Tosefta, however, so too here the interest in Scripture is not limited to the search for proof-texts for the Mishnah. But, unlike the Tosefta, the Sifra approaches the Mishnah in a fairly systematic way. For the authors take up one paragraph after another of the Mishnah to indicate how Scripture alone validates what the Mishnah's rule maintains. So, in all, the Sifra undertakes to provide in an orderly and fairly complete way precisely what the Mishnah does not regard as called for at all. We note, finally, that while, in the Tosefta, we do not discover a context for the making and systematic collection of exegeses of Scripture, in the Sifra, we do. That is the single most important outcome of this protracted study of how the Sifra approaches the exegesis of Scripture and why the framers of the document thought it important to form and collect such exegeses. The argument of the exegeses constituted a polemic; composing them into a document made an important, and unmistakable, statement on theology and canon alike.

SCRIPTURE AND THE MISHNAH IN THE TALMUD OF THE LAND OF ISRAEL

The Talmud of the Land of Israel takes up an intermediate position between the ones imputed just now to the Tosefta and the Sifra. Like the Sifra, the Talmud of the Land of Israel investigates the relationship between the laws of the Mishnah and various biblical verses. Implicitly, the Talmud takes the view that the Mishnah requires support of scriptural authority, therefore is secondary and subordinated to the (written) Torah of Moses. Further, when the Talmud asks about the source of a law stated by the Mishnah, it invariably cites a verse of Scripture and no other source of certainty and truth. But the polemic of the Sifra against reason uncorrected by scriptural revelation finds slight place in the Talmud. In this regard the Talmud stands closer to the Tosefta's view that Scripture is a source of facts, thus serviceable for many purposes, including, among other things, validation of the Mishnah's laws. The pointed character of the Sifra's use of Scripture finds no counterpart in the Talmud. That is why I see the Talmud as holding an intermediate position between the two extremes before us.

If, then, we ask how the Talmud defines the place of Scripture in the Mishnah, the answer is readily at hand. The Mishnah rarely cites verses of Scripture in support of its propositions. The Talmud routinely adduces scriptural bases for the Mishnah's laws. The Mishnah seldom undertakes the exegesis of verses of Scripture for any purpose. The Talmud consistently investigates the meaning of verses of Scripture and does so for a variety of purposes. Accordingly, the Talmud, subordinate as it is to the Mishnah, regards the Mishnah as subordinate to, and contingent upon, Scripture. That is why, in the Talmud's view, the Mishnah requires the support of proof-texts of Scripture.

By itself, in the view of the framers of the Talmud, the Mishnah exercises no autonomous authority and enjoys no independent standing or norm-setting status. The task of the framers of the Talmud is not only to explain Mishnah law but to prove *from Scripture* the facticity of rules of the Mishnah. Accordingly, so far as the Talmud has a theory about the Mishnah as such, as distinct from a theory about the work to be done in the exposition and amplification and application to the Israelite court system of various laws in the Mishnah, it is quite clear. To state matters negatively, the Mishnah does not enjoy autonomous and uncontingent authority. That conclusion is made ineluctable by the simple fact that one principal task facing sages, as I just said, is to adduce proof-texts for the Mishnah's laws. It follows that, without such texts, those laws stand on infirm foundations.

Let us now proceed to review the types of ways in which the Talmud presents proof-texts for allegations of passages of the Mishnah, a sizable repertoire. We begin with three of the simplest examples, in which a passage of the Mishnah is cited, then linked directly to a verse of Scripture, deemed to constitute self-evident proof for what has been said. The Mishnah's rule is given in italics.

1. Y. *Abodah Zarah 4:4*. [III.A] [Citing M. A.Z. 4:4:] *An idol belonging to a gentile is prohibited forthwith*, in line with the following verse of Scripture: "You shall surely destroy [all places where the nations whom you shall dispossess served their gods]" (Deut. 12:2)—forthwith.

[B] *And one belonging to an Israelite is prohibited only after it will have been worshipped*, in line with the following verse of Scripture: "Cursed be the man who makes a graven or molten image, an abomination to the Lord, a thing made by the hands of a craftsman, and set it up in secret" (Deut. 27:15)—when he will set it up.

[C] There are those who reverse the matter:

[D] An idol belonging to an Israelite is prohibited forthwith, as it is written, "Cursed be the man who makes a graven or molten image."

[E] And one belonging to a gentile is prohibited only after it will have been worshipped, as it is written, "You shall surely destroy all the places where the nations whom you shall dispossess served their gods."

[F] R. Isaac bar Nahman in the name of Samuel derived that same view [that an idol belonging to a gentile is prohibited only after it will have been worshipped] from the following: If one has inherited [the idol] when it [already] is deemed a god, "in fire will you burn it," and if not: "whom the nations whom you shall dispossess . . . their gods. [You shall tear down their altars and dash in pieces their pillars and burn their Asherim with fire . . .]" (Deut. 12:2–3).

2. Y. *Abodah Zarah 4:4*. [IV.A] [With reference to the following passage of the Mishnah: *A gentile has the power to nullify an idol belonging either to himself or his fellow, but an Israelite has not got the power to nullify an idol belonging to a gentile (M. A.Z. 4:4),*] R. Yohanan in the name of R. Yannai derived that view from the following verse of Scripture: "You shall not covet the silver or the gold that is on them or take it for yourselves" (Deut. 7:25). "You may not covet and take [that gold], but others may covet [the gold], and then you may take it."

3. Y. *Niddah 2:6*. [A] *Five [colors of] blood are unclean in a woman [M. Nid. 2:6]*.

[II.A] Whence do we derive evidence that there are five varieties of unclean blood specified by the Torah? [Not all vaginal discharges are regarded as unclean menstrual blood.]

[B] Said R. Joshua b. Levi: "'And she has uncovered the fountain of her bloods' (Lev. 20:18) [= two], 'And she will be clean from the

source of her bloods' [= two], a discharge of blood from her body
(Lev. 15:19) [= one, thus five]."
[C] And lo: "And if a woman has a discharge of blood" (Lev.
15:25)—this blood [too] should be part of that number.
[III.A] And how do we know that there is unclean blood, and there
is clean [blood], [so not all blood is unclean, but only the five which
are listed]?
[B] R. Hama bar Joseph in the name of R. Hoshaiah: "It is written,
'If any case arises requiring a decision . . .' (Deut. 17:8). Now 'between blood and (W) blood' is not written, but 'of one kind of blood
from (L) another.'
[C] "On this basis there is proof that there is blood that is unclean,
and blood that is clean."

The preceding instances follow a single pattern. A statement of the
Mishnah is given, followed by a verse of Scripture regarded as proof
of the antecedent conception. The first instance, Y. A.Z. 4:4, is the
obvious one, since all we have are sentences from the one document, the Mishnah, juxtaposed to sentences from the other, the
Scripture. In the next, out of the same passage, Yohanan-Yannai first
cite, then restate the meaning of, a verse. In the third, at Y. Niddah
2:6, the words of a verse of Scripture are treated one by one, each
yielding a number of types of blood. So the sense of the verse is less
important than its formal character.

Along the lines of the foregoing, but somewhat more complex, are
examples in which the language of the Mishnah rule is not cited verbatim, but its underlying proposition is stated, then provided with a
proof-text. Here is an instance of this phenomenon. Again the passage of the Mishnah is in italics,

Yerushalmi Baba Mesia 2:1. [A] *What lost items are [the finder's], and
which ones is he liable to proclaim [in the lost-and-found]?*
[B] *These lost items are his [the finder's]:*
[C] "*[if] he found pieces of fruit scattered about, coins scattered
about, small sheaves in the public domain, cakes of figs, baker's
loaves, strings of fish, pieces of meat, wool-shearings [as they come]
from the country [of origin], stalks of flax, or tongues of purple—lo,
these are his,*" *[the words of R. Meir].*
[I.A] [Since the operative criterion in M. B.M. 2:1 is that, with
undistinguished items such as these, the owner takes for granted he
will not recover them and so despairs of them, thus giving up his

rights of ownership to them, we now ask:] Whence do we know from the Torah the law of the owner's despair [of recovering his property constitutes relinquishing rights of ownership and declaring the property to be ownerless, hence available to whoever finds it]?

[B] R. Yohanan in the name of R. Simeon b. Yehosedeq: "'And so you shall do with his ass; so you shall do with his garment; so you shall do with any lost thing of your brother's, which he loses and you find; you may not withhold your help' (Deut. 22:3)—

[C] "That which is [perceived as] lost by him and found by you, you are liable to proclaim [as having been found], and that which is not [perceived as] lost by him [because he has given up hope of recovering it anyhow] and found by you, you are not liable to proclaim.

[D] "This then excludes that for which the owner has despaired, which is lost to him and to any one."

What is striking in the preceding instance is the presence of a secondary layer of reasoning about the allegations of a verse of Scripture. The process of reasoning then derives from the verse a principle not made explicit therein, and that principle turns out to be precisely what the Mishnah's rule maintains. Accordingly, the Mishnah's law is shown to be merely a reversal of the Scripture's, that is, the obverse side of the coin. Or Scripture's rule is shown to deal only with the case pertinent to the Mishnah's law, rather than to what, on the surface, that biblical law seems to contain.

We proceed to an instance in which a disputed point of the Mishnah is linked to a dispute on the interpretation of Scripture. What is important is that the dispute in the Mishnah is made to depend upon, not principles of law, but readings of the pertinent verse of Scripture. Once again the net effect is to turn the Mishnah into a set of generalizations of what already is explicit in Scripture, a kind of restating in other language of what is quite familiar—therefore well-founded.

Y. Makkot 2:2. [A] [If] the iron flew from the heft and killed someone,
[B] Rabbi says, "He does not go into exile."
[C] And sages say, "He goes into exile."
[D] [If] it flew from the wood which is being split,
[E] Rabbi says, "He goes into exile."
[F] And sages say, "He does not go into exile."
[I.A] What is the Scriptural basis for the position of Rabbi [at M. 2:2D–E]?

45

[B] Here it is stated, ". . . [and the head] slips [from the handle and strikes his neighbor so that he dies . . .]" (Deut. 19:5).

[C] And later on, the same verb-root is used: "[. . . for your olives] shall drop off . . ." (Deut. 28:40).

[D] Just as the verb-root used later means, "dropping off" so here it means, "dropping off."

[E] What is the Scriptural basis for the position of the rabbis [at M. 2:2F]?

[F] Here the verb-root "slipping" is used.

[G] And later on we have the following: ". . . and clears away many nations before you . . ." (Deut. 7:1).

[H] Just as the verb-root, clearing away, refers to an [active] blow there, so here too it speaks of an [active] blow [by an object which strikes something, e.g., the ax, not chips of wood].

We see that both parties to the Mishnah's dispute read the same verse. The difference then depends upon their prior disagreement about the meaning of the verse. The underlying supposition is that the Mishnah simply restates in general language the results of the exegesis of biblical law.

We consider, finally, an instance in which the discussion of the Talmud consists wholly in the analysis of the verses of Scripture deemed to prove the point of the Mishnah. The upshot is that we deal not with a mere formality but a protracted, sustained inquiry. That is to say, the discussion of the Talmud transcends the limits of the Mishnah and becomes a well-developed discourse upon *not* the Mishnah's rule but Scripture's sense. What is important is the fact that the search for proof-texts in Scripture sustains not only propositions of the Mishnah, but also those of the Tosefta as well as those of the Talmud's own sages. This again indicates that the search of Scriptures is primary, the source of propositions or texts to be supported by those Scriptures secondary. There is no limit, indeed, to the purposes for which scriptural texts will be found relevant.

Y. Sanhedrin 3:8. [II. A] **How do they carry out a judgment?**

[B] **The judges seat themselves, and the litigants remain standing before them.**

[C] **Whoever brings claim against his fellow is the one who opens the proceedings [T. San. 6:3],**

[D] as it says, ". . . Whoever has a complaint, let him go to them [Aaron and Hur, as judges]" (Ex. 24:14).

[E] And how do we know that the one who lays claim against his fellow bears the burden of proof?

[F] R. Qerispa in the name of R. Hananiah b. Gamaliel: "'. . . let him go to them. . . .,' [meaning,] Let him bring his evidence to them."

[G] R. Yohanan raised the question, "In the case of a childless sister-in-law, who brings claim against whom?"

[H] R. Eleazar replied, "And is it not written, '. . . then the brother's wife shall go up to the gate to the elders' (Deut. 25:7)?"

[I] R. Yohanan said, "Well did R. Eleazar teach me."

At Y. San. 3:8, we see, the search for proof-texts is provoked equally by citation of a passage of the Tosefta and by an opinion of a rabbi. D, E–F, give an instance of the former, and G–I, the latter. There is no differentiation between the two processes. The main point is that, in the mind of the framers of the Talmud, Scripture is the main thing, its authority paramount. They in no way differentiated among the diverse sources of propositions requiring scriptural support. Whether a statement occurred in the Mishnah, the Tosefta, or in the name of an authority of their own day made no difference. All stood on the same plane, subordinated to Scripture. But that fact, as I shall emphasize in the final chapter, is critical. The living sage of the fourth century presented in his own name, not only in the name of authorities of ancient times represented in the Mishnah and the Tosefta, a judgment to be validated by Scripture and therefore to be related to God's will and word and to be given a location within the canon of the Torah. The authority of Scripture leveled all differences. Appropriate appeal to Scripture made possible the accommodation of even the last and the latest in the succession of Sinai. Revelation at Sinai extended even to the here and now.

In the end we see that the issue of the status and authority of the Mishnah, as part of the Torah, turns out to be secondary. It is derivative of the overriding issue of the status and authority of Scripture itself—that, and who has the right to explain and interpret Scripture. The appeal is ever to the authority of Scripture, in theological terms meaning to God's will and word to Moses. In linking to the Pentateuchal law the document entrusted to them for interpretation and application, the sages who interpreted the Mishnah and applied its law more really tied themselves to Moses, their rulings to God's law, their authority to Heaven. So, if we list the issues in ascending order of priority, they end up the opposite of what they seem: (3)

the standing of the Mishnah in relationship to (2) the Scripture as interpreted by (1) the sages who received and claimed to declare the meaning of both documents. This observation will take on more weight when we observe, as we shall in the next two chapters, that the modes of thought that generated discourse on the Mishnah in the Talmud fall into the same taxonomical categories as encompass discussions on the meaning of verses of Scripture in the compilations of scriptural exegeses called *midrashim*.

REPRISE

Sufficient numbers of extracts of rabbinic texts have now passed the reader's eyes that it is easy to forget why, to begin with, I thought we had to examine them. Furthermore, we have made ourselves acquainted with so considerable a collection of rabbinic compilations—Tosefta, Sifra, Talmud—that the thread of argument may well have fallen from view. At the end, therefore, let us review why we have done the exercises of this chapter and what we have now to accomplish, in order to attain the point of the labor. I here propose a context, so as to account for the work of compiling exegeses of Scripture undertaken in the fifth and sixth centuries. I further ask about the broader implications of that editorial work for Judaism's theory (or theology) of the canon, of the authority of Scripture, and of the character and nature of revelation. Since yet another chapter of defining and illustrating the context for the making of exegetical collections lies ahead, a rapid reprise of the fundamental argument will prove timely.

Let me begin by restating the thesis of the book as a whole. The original work of collecting and arranging the compilations of exegeses of Scripture followed the patterns set in collecting and arranging exegeses of the Mishnah. Just as the Talmud, which is Mishnah exegesis, treats the Mishnah, so the earliest collections of scriptural exegesis treat Scripture. To unpack the components of that thesis, I have had to begin the tale in 200 C.E., several hundred years before the formation of the earliest exegetical compilations, in the fifth and sixth centuries. We started our venture with the issue of the Mishnah itself. I presented an account of why and how the Mishnah's advent precipitated an acute crisis in politics and theology.

The character of the Mishnah itself and the context of its reception defined the crisis and made it acute. The book was the first in Judaism to ignore the character of antecedent holy literature, specifically the marks of consecration used by all former writers to gain for their writing the status of holiness. Had the Mishnah remained an idle fantasy, a mere philosophical vision of utopia, it would have presented no critical theological problem. It also would never have come down to us—at least not under the auspices of what became normative Judaism. But the Mishnah rapidly found the chief place in the Jewish government of the Land of Israel as the constitution and bylaws of the Jewish nation in its land. Accordingly, the heirs of the Mishnah demanded for themselves a theory of its origin, standing, claim to authority, and grounds for compelling obedience, whether in sanctions or in a myth of supernatural origin in revelation.

In the nature of Israelite national life from the beginnings to the time at hand (and long afterward), the established mode of theorizing about such matters in regard to equivalent writings required a myth of supernatural origin. The Mishnah therefore gradually made its way into the framework of revealed law. It found for itself ample place within the category of *torah*, that is, revelation, and, ultimately, within the Torah itself, that is, the canon of Judaism. The route took the exegetes of the Mishnah squarely into the heart of the matter, the already-available written Torah of Moses. Now, as we observed at some length, the path from the Mishnah to the Torah hardly runs straight and true. For the Mishnah frames its ideas in modes different from those of the written Torah's law codes. And many of its ideas and points of emphasis indeed proved alien to those of Scripture. Always in style and often in substance, the Mishnah appears to be anything but an appendage to the Mosaic law codes.

How to pave the road from the Mishnah to Scripture? The answer lay in one age-old and commonplace mode of dealing with precisely the same problem. A conventional way of reading Scripture commonly called *midrash* and here called simply *exegesis*, had long proved acceptable. Why change now? As we know full well, Israelite thinkers—whether lawyers and philosophers, like the heirs of the Mishnah in the Talmuds, or visionaries and prophets, like the Essenes at Qumran, or messianists and evangelists, like the members of the school of Matthew—routinely read one thing in relationship to something else, old Scripture in the setting of fresh concerns and sure knowledge of new truth. So there is nothing remarkable in what the heirs of the Mishnah did. To seek, through biblical exegesis, to link the Mishnah to Scripture, detail by detail, represented a well-trodden and firmly-packed path.

What captures our attention is not the techniques of exegesis but, in particular, the place and purpose assigned to the larger labor of exegesis. Why was it important to accomplish exegesis of Scripture in the light of the Mishnah, and of the Mishnah in the light of Scripture? And how important? In the chapter now completed, we have repeatedly asked about the place assigned to Scripture in the exegesis of the Mishnah by one document after another. Precisely what significance was attached to that exercise of reading the one document in the light of the other defined our work. The result, now fully spelled out, hardly requires much repetition. Work on Scripture, merely routinely encompassing the scriptural basis for the Mishnah's statements, represents one extreme. The Mishnah, by itself, required no systematic linkage to Scripture. Or work on Scripture repeatedly demanded attention to laws in the Mishnah, with the polemical implication that the latter without the former stood naked. This stands at the opposite extreme. Work on Scripture, in the assumption that, wherever possible, support for the Mishnah, to be sure, should derive from Scripture, represented the third and mediating position. It is not a polemic but an assertion of veneration.

So to the Tosefta, Sifra, and Talmud of the Land of Israel alike, the paramount issue was Scripture, not merely its authority, but especially, its sheer mass of information. The decisive importance of the advent of the Mishnah in precipitating the vast exegetical enterprise represented by the books at hand emerges from a simple fact. The three documents before us all focus attention on the Mishnah in particular. Two of them, the Tosefta and the Talmud of the Land of Israel (not to mention the other, larger Talmud, made in Babylonia) organize everything at hand around the redactional structure supplied by the Mishnah itself. The third's—Sifra's—obsession with the Mishnah is still more blatant.

For it is all the more striking what the redactional choice of the Sifra's framers called to the fore: the selection of a book of Scripture, rather than of the Mishnah, as the focus for exegesis. That choice conforms entirely to the polemic of the writers and compilers of the Sifra: Scripture is important, the Mishnah subordinate. How better say so than organize things not around the Mishnah, but around a book of the law of Moses itself? So the Mishnah now is cited in a work about Scripture. Let me unpack this point. Down to the editing of the Sifra, Scripture had been cited in works on the Mishnah. Since the Sifra draws upon materials of the Mishnah and the Tosefta, we have every reason to suppose the redactors of the Sifra knew full well the ways taken by others. They rejected those ways, reversing the redactional convention based on the Mishnah's structure and choosing what was, in context, a fresh and different route. To be sure, that way, in the setting of antecedent Judaism, had been entirely familiar. Earlier writers had laid out their exegesis of Scripture side by side with a text of Scripture. So doing things the way the Sifra's composers did the work was nothing new. Earlier writers also had expressed their own ideas through their arrangement of verses of Scripture.

But the Mishnah is the first document of its kind of Judaism. Afterwards, the Tosefta and the Talmud came along—probably at roughly the same time. Their materials derived both from the period in which the Mishnah was taking shape and also from the period after which the Mishnah had reached closure. And, it would seem, the Sifra comes later on, surely after both the Mishnah and the Tosefta. Its assertions are more extreme, its redactional definition more radical. We noticed a correspondence, therefore, between the kind of material that is collected and the way that material is arranged. It follows that the polemical purposes of the document are expressed not only in what is said, but in how what is said is collected and arranged. That fact will strike us, in chapter 4, as still more critical to the larger task of interpreting the context in which *midrash* collections come into being.

In making these observations about the Sifra, I have moved far ahead of my argument. Since I wish to place into the context established by the formation of the Talmud of the Land of Israel the labor of collecting and arranging the earliest compilations of scriptural

3

The Talmud Is
to the Mishnah . . .

COMPONENTS OF THE TALMUD

The Talmud of the Land of Israel was not written by a single person. Nor is it made up of sustained chapters, compositions running on along a simple path and pursuing a cogent issue or thesis. Still more important, the Talmud does not take up as a whole either the Mishnah, a tractate of the Mishnah, or even a chapter of a tractate of the Mishnah. The Talmud is made up only of brief discussions, which I call units of discourse, whole and complete in themselves, focused upon fairly brief snippets—at most a paragraph, but more commonly a sentence or even a phrase—of a chapter of a tractate of the Mishnah. The first point of comparison between the Talmud's treatment of a passage of the Mishnah and an exegetical compilation's approach to a passage of Scripture, therefore, is that both attend to bits and pieces, rarely transcending the narrow bounds of a sentence or two. The affect upon the documents—the Mishnah, Scripture—is to reduce them to their smallest intelligible components and deconstruct their systems into their (random) constituents. Then the exegetes can say pretty much whatever they like.

To compare the Talmud's treatment of the Mishnah to an exegetical composition's treatment of Scripture, the point that is subject to comparison has to undergo exceptionally precise definition. For the reason just now given—the shared approach of the framers of discourse in both the Talmud and the exegetical collections to atoms, but rarely to molecules—to begin with, we undertake the comparison of the components (units of discourse) of the two wholes. The suggestive facts come at the level of how these units of discourse relate to the respective documents served by them, the Mishnah and Scripture respectively. I shall establish one simple fact. The editors of the earliest compositions of exegeses of Scripture write books of

exegesis of Scripture in much the same way that the authors of the
Talmud of the Land of Israel put together exegesis of the Mishnah.
They build out of the same types of units of discourse. That observation marks a significant step forward in discovering the historical
context—the life situation—in which the earliest collections of
scriptural exegesis came into being. In chapter 5 we explore its
implications.

To begin with, therefore, we have to pursue the simple question
of how the framers of the Talmud chose to talk about the Mishnah.
By this, I mean, what *sorts* of discussion did they enter into? What
types of units of discourse make up the Talmud of the Land of Israel? Once these have been defined and their mode of analyzing
passages of the Mishnah (paragraphs, sentences, words) exposed,
then we shall turn directly to the kinds of materials of which the earliest collection of biblical exegeses is made up. At that point we shall
be able to compare the traits of the units of discourse we find in the
Talmud of the Land of Israel with the characteristics of the units of
discourse we find in the exegetical compilations brought to closure
in the period following the conclusion of the Talmud.

TALMUDIC EXEGESIS OF THE MISHNAH

A taxonomy of the diverse units of discourse of the Talmud of the
Land of Israel finds its organizing categories in the relationships of
these units to the Mishnah itself. For the Mishnah defines the constant among the variables of types of units of Talmudic discourse
about the Mishnah. The first and single most important category is
the type of unit of discourse devoted to the close reading and exegesis of sentences, phrases, and even words of a passage of the Mishnah. These exegetical units of discourse themselves are somewhat
varied, but for the present purpose a single taxon suffices.

Before proceeding, let me give one example of what I mean by a
simple exegesis of a passage of the Mishnah. In the next sections we
shall consider examples of other sorts of Talmudic units of discourse
constructed in relationship to passages of the Mishnah. Here is a
passage of the Mishnah, given in italics, followed by a unit of discourse I call the exegetical type. In the later sections we shall refer
to this same passage of the Mishnah, so here we consider it
completely.

M. Niddah 1:1

[A] *Shammai says, "[For] all women it is sufficient [to reckon menstrual uncleanness from] their time [of discovering a flow]."*

[B] *Hillel says, "[They are deemed unclean retroactively] from [the time of] an examination [at which the flow of menstrual blood was discovered] to the [last] examination [made beforehand, at which no flow of menstrual blood was discovered],*

[C] *"even for many days."*

[D] *And sages rule not in accord with the opinion of this one nor in accord with the opinion of that one but:*

[E] *[the woman is held to have been unclean only] during [the preceding] twenty-four hours [when] this lessens the period [of uncleanness demarcated by the span] from examination to examination.*

[F] *[And she is held to have been unclean only] during the period from [one] examination to [the preceding] examination [when] this lessens the period of twenty-four hours [of retroactive uncleanness].*

[G] *Any woman who has a fixed period—sufficient for her is her fixed period [in which case there is no retroactive uncleanness at all].*

[H] *And she who makes use of test-rags—lo, this [form of examination] is equivalent to an examination [and so marks the point before which the woman is assumed to have been clean],*

[I] *which lessens either the period of twenty-four hours [of retroactive contamination] or the period from examination to examination.*

Meaning of Phrases

Y. *Nid. 1:1.* [I.A] What is the meaning of the phrase, "*It is sufficient [to reckon menstrual uncleanness from] their time [of discovering a flow]*"?

[B] [Such women] do not retroactively impart uncleanness to food subject to the laws of cleanness.

Amplification of Phrases

Y. *Nid. 1:1.* [II.A] *And sages rule not in accord with the opinion of this one nor in accord with the opinion of that one.*

[B] Not in accord with the opinion of Shammai, who placed no limit to his view of the matter [in entirely dismissing the possibility of retroactive uncleanness].

[C] Nor in accord with the opinion of Hillel, who took an extreme position.

Of the same type is the exegesis of a passage through its scriptural roots, but I see no need at this point to give yet another example of how the Talmud's unit of discourse will provide a scriptural proof-text for a statement in the Mishnah. The unit of discourse at hand is a brief account of the meaning of a phrase. How it does the work is self-evident.

Let us now ask, in general, what are the sorts of things a Talmudic rabbi would wish to accomplish in taking up a passage of the Mishnah?

First, the Talmud of the Land of Israel will aim at establishing the correct text of various passages of the Mishnah. This text criticism nearly always is in the context of deciding the law. It is not a random search for a "perfect" text. It rather represents a deliberate and principled inquiry into the law as revealed by the phrasing of a passage. That is why, in the bulk of such passages, the legal consequences of one reading as opposed to those of the other are carefully articulated, sometimes even tied to a range of other points subject to conflict.

Before proceeding, let me clarify something that the careful reader will have noticed. In chapter 1 I laid great stress on the fact that the Mishnah was "published" by being composed to facilitate memorization, so that it was an oral, not a written, statement. What this means is that the Mishnah was issued by having professional memorizers learn the authorized version. No single, original, written version, then, was deposited in an archive, against which other versions might be checked. Saul Lieberman, in "The Publication of the Mishnah," (*Hellenism in Jewish Palestine* [New York: Jewish Theological Seminary of America, 1950], 83–99) has spelled out the basis for this view.

Now, you have observed, I speak of a "correct text," just as, later on, you will hear about "text criticism," "commentary," and other processes and categories pertinent to a written, but not to an oral, document. By "text criticism" I mean, more precisely, "establishing the correct version of a formula subject to memorization and transmission." By "commentary" I mean the addition to a lemma of explanatory matter of some sort, perhaps notes or a kind of *obiter dicta* attached to the official formula of a saying. At this time we have no established theory about how the two Talmuds took shape, the way in which ideas made the movement to a medium of preservation and transmission, how, in all, people formulated and handed on the official writings of the rabbinical estate. That the Mishnah's statements were formulated and transmitted orally seems to me the sole demonstrated fact. Accordingly, the reader will have to muster a measure of patience as the metaphor of literature shifts back and forth across the frontier between orality and writing.

Let us now return to the problem at hand. The connection, in context, to this digression seems to me clear. We have to deal with the governing trait of the exegesis of the Mishnah by the Talmud: the decision to explain only one small thing at a time, the incapacity to grasp the totality of an issue or an argument all at once. The Talmud's capacity to deal with words, phrases, or sentences, but rarely with paragraphs and never with whole chapters, let alone tractates, of the Mishnah, may well derive from the character of the material at hand. If you face a memorized sentence, you can readily parse it and analyze its traits. But how do you hold within your mind and systematically deal as a whole with fifty, two hundred, or a thousand memorized sentences? The limits of the exegetical task, to begin with, may well receive definition from the formal traits of the document subject to exegesis.

Second, one principal interest among the framers of the Talmud's materials was simply to understand, essentially within its own terms and implicit meanings, the Mishnah's discrete passage at hand. What that means is that when people read a passage of the Mishnah, they wanted to know mainly what it meant in its own terms and setting. They had only limited interest in how one passage related to some other.

Third, as I indicated above, the Talmud's exegetical procedures commonly include attention to locating a scriptural proof-text for what the Mishnah's law requires. That fact brings us no surprises. But it is important to restate it in the present context. The Mishnah, as is well known, rarely finds it necessary to cite a scriptural proof-text for its propositions. Just as the Mishnah ignores the scriptural ways of stating propositions in general, and laws in particular, favoring instead its own highly distinctive and disciplined syntax and morphology and word choices, so the Mishnah rephrases whatever it borrows from Scripture into its own terms. Accordingly, only rarely does the Mishnah invoke in behalf of its own ideas the authority of Scripture, and that is more commonly in discussions of theological than of narrowly legal matters. The Talmud, by contrast, finds it appropriate whenever possible to cite scriptural proof-texts for the propositions of the Mishnah.

What is still more striking is that this inquiry appears to be systematic and not random. We find long sequences of pericopes in which proof-texts are adduced one after another. It is tempting to suggest that, whenever people could, they would supply scriptural citations for the Mishnah. But that cannot be demonstrated. The best we can say is that the Talmud's approach to a given passage of the Mishnah (shown in my *Talmud of the Land of Israel* [Chicago: University of Chicago Press, 1983] 35, introduction), two out of three times is to provide some sort of gloss or exegesis, and in half of these instances, one out of three times, a proof-text as well.

The principal taxa for units of discourse devoted to the close reading and exegesis of a passage of the Mishnah are these:

1. *Citation and gloss of the language of the Mishnah (meaning of a phrase or concrete illustration of a rule):* A unit of discourse of this type will contain a direct citation of a sentence of the Mishnah. The word choices or phrasing of the Mishnah will be paraphrased or otherwise explained through what is essentially a gloss. Or the rule of the Mishnah will be explained through an example or a restatement of some kind. (It should be noted that a great many passages of the Tosefta constitute citations and glosses, or paraphrases, of the Mishnah passage they cite.)

2. *Specification of the meaning of the law of the Mishnah or the reason for it:* Items in this taxon stand very close to those in the former. What differentiates the one from the other is the absence, in the present set of units of discourse, of direct citation of the Mishnah or close and explicit reading of its language. The discussion then tends to allude to the Mishnah or to generalize, while remaining wholly within its framework. Units of discourse in which scriptural proof-texts are adduced in evidence of a passage fall into this category. These frequently spill over into discussion of the reason for a rule.

3. *Secondary implication or application of the law of the Mishnah:* Units of discourse may generalize beyond the specific rule of the Mishnah. The discussion will commonly restate the principle of the rule at hand or raise a question invited by it. Hence if the Mishnah's law settles one question, participants in this type of discourse

will use that as the foundation for raising a second and consequent question. Two or more rules of the Mishnah (or of the Mishnah and Tosefta) may be contrasted with one another and then harmonized. Alternatively, two or more rulings of a specific authority will be alleged to conflict, then shown not to stand at variance with one another.

4. *The matter of authorities and their views. Decided law:* This taxon contains that handful of items in which concrete decisions are attached to specific laws of the Mishnah, or in which the harmonization or identification of the opinions of the Mishnah's authorities form the center of interest. What makes these items worth noting is that the statements stand in close relationship to the Mishnah's rule itself. Hence they do not necessarily tell us how things were laid out in the rough-and-tumble of the rabbinic courts of the third and fourth centuries. They reveal rather the state of legal theory spun out of the Mishnah's conflicts themselves. Not uncommonly, this type of unit of discourse trails off into an exercise in harmonization.

The upshot is that there was a severely circumscribed repertoire of intellectual initiatives available to the authorities of the Talmud of the Land of Israel. Approaching a given rule of the Mishnah, a sage would do one of two things: (1) explain the meaning of the passage, or (2) extend and expand the meaning of the passage. Within these two categories, we may find a place for all units of discourse in which the focus of the Talmud's discussion is a passage of the Mishnah, ninety percent of the entire Talmud of the Land of Israel's units of discourse. Of the two sorts, the work of straightforward explanation of the plain meaning of a law of the Mishnah by far predominates. If we may state the outcome very simply: what the framers of the Talmud want to say is what they think the Mishnah means in any given passage.

TALMUDIC AMPLIFICATION OF
THE MISHNAH

Let us first consider how units of discourse of the Talmud amplify the meaning of a passage of the Mishnah. For this purpose, I present two instances of expansion or amplification: first, clarification of a passage in the Mishnah through reference to the expansion of that passage in the Tosefta; second, provision of cases meant to illustrate the law of the Mishnah. The two passages are associated with Mishnah Niddah 1:1, presented above.

Clarification of the Law of
the Mishnah Through Citation of
a Passage of the Tosefta

Y. Nid. 1:1. [VII.A] [If] a woman examined herself and found blood the status of which is subject to doubt, it is self-evident that this [examination] does not function as does an examination to impose a limit on the retroactive uncleanness during the antecedent twenty-four hours.

[B] But as to the status of the blood itself, what is the rule as to its imparting uncleanness as matter of doubt?

[C] We may infer the rule from the following teaching:

[D] **One whose sex is unknown and an androgyne who produced a drop of blood—sufficient for them [to impart uncleanness to objects they have touched] is their time** [of actually having discovered the blood; we do not impose uncleanness, by reason of doubt as to their status as women, on objects they have touched from the last examination, or for the preceding twenty-four hours] [T. Nid. 1:3A].

[E] Now what do you wish to infer from this passage?

[F] Said R. Yose, "One whose sex is unknown and an androgyne are cases of doubt [as to whether they are women or men], and the matter of imputing retroactive contamination during the antecedent twenty-four hours is a case of [doing so by reason of] doubt. Now [we do not impute uncleanness by adding] one matter of doubt to yet another matter of doubt.

[G] "Here too producing a drop of blood is a case of doubt [as to the status of the blood], and imputing uncleanness for the antecedent twenty-four hours is by reason of doubt. Now [we do not impute uncleanness by adding] one matter of doubt to yet another matter of doubt."

Cases to Illustrate the Law
of the Mishnah

Y. Nid. 1:1. [XIII.A] And she who makes use of test-rags—lo, this [for examination] is equivalent to an examination [and so marks the point before which the woman is assumed to have been clean].

[B] What would be a concrete case?

[C] [If] a woman examined herself at dawn [finding no blood], and had sexual relations toward noon, making use of a test-rag, and then produced blood at dusk—unclean [are only those objects which she touched] retroactively to the time of her having had sexual relations [but not earlier].

[D] Levi said, "Concerning the test-rag used after having sexual relations [the Mishnah] speaks, but the test-rag used before having sexual relations is swept clean by her vagina, so it does not effect a good examination."

[E] R. Abun in the name of R. Zeira [said], "The Mishnah speaks of a test-rag used before sexual relations, but as to the test-rag used after sexual relations, it is discolored on account of semen."

What we have is a sort of exegesis, but not an effort to explain a passage word-for-word or phrase-for-phrase. The discussion is still quite close to the specific assertions of the passage of the Mishnah at hand, and what is clarified is that passage, not its implications or points of intersection with other passages. Accordingly, the character of the unit of discourse under discussion is clear from these passages. It falls within the range of taxa of Talmudic exegesis of the Mishnah.

TALMUDIC EXPANSION ON PROBLEMS OF THE MISHNAH

A Talmudic unit of discourse may present an analysis of a passage of the Mishnah in which the contents, rather than the language, of the Mishnah's paragraph will form the center of interest. This type of unit of discourse may deal with the passage at hand and present reflection primary to it. Or it may treat the paragraph under discussion as a pretext for a wide-ranging discussion of an underlying principle. Further, there may be speculation superficially independent of the Mishnah passage to which a given unit of discourse is attached, yet at some point that speculation will intersect with the sentences of the Mishnah cited at the outset. Let me first present two instances of some of them, then spell out the broader range of possibilities. Once more we make reference to M. Niddah 1:1, given in full above.

Secondary Expansion

Y. Nid. 1:1. [V.A] Up to now [we have assumed that we deal with a case] in which a woman examined herself and found herself wholly dry.

[B] [But what is the law] if a woman examined herself and found blood which [in fact] is clean [and not a source of uncleanness at all]?

[C] R. Ammi in the name of Rab, R. Ba in the name of R. Judah: "[If] a woman examined herself and found clean [blood], she is [in any case] prohibited to have sexual relations until the source [of her blood] has [entirely] dried up."

[D] R. Tobi said in the name of R. Abbahu, "She is prohibited to have sexual relations for twenty-four hours."

[E] Said R. Jacob bar Aha when he came up here [to the Land of Israel], "I heard from all the rabbis that she is permitted to have sexual relations forthwith [and need not await for twenty-four hours]."

Harmonization of Positions of Diverse Authorities

Y. Nid. 1:1. [IV.A] There have we learned the Tannaitic teaching: *A dead creeping thing which was found in an alleyway imparts uncleanness retroactively [M. Nid. 7:2].*

[B] R. Ammi asked [whether] the cited passage of the Mishnah might not be contrary to the position of Shammai.

[C] Said R. Yose, "If it is not in accord with the position of Shammi [who rejects the possibility of retroactive contamination entirely], then [the cited passage of the Mishnah also] is not even in accord with the position of Hillel.

[D] "For does Hillel not concur in the case of an alleyway which is [daily] swept out, and through which a water-course runs, that it is deemed clean [retroactively, in case a dead creeping thing is found therein]?"

[E] Shammai maintains this: In the case of a woman, because she customarily [examines herself when she] urinates, sages have treated her case as comparable to an alleyway which is swept out from day to day and through which a water-course runs, so that it is deemed clean [under normal conditions, until proven otherwise].

Let us now review the several possibilities for Talmudic expansion on problems of the Mishnah, that is, not merely exegetical but amplificatory units of discourse. These seem to me to fall into the following subdivisions.

1. *Legal Speculation and Reflection Primary to the Mishnah:* A unit of discourse may well carry forward a discussion superficially separate from the Mishnah. Upon routine inquiry, we notice that the discussion at hand speculates on principles introduced, to begin with, in the Mishnah's rule or in the Tosefta's complement to that rule.

2. *Harmonization of Distinct Laws of the Mishnah:* One of the most interesting kinds of Talmudic units of discourse is that in which principles are abstracted from utterly unrelated rules of the Mishnah (less commonly, of the Tosefta). These are then shown to intersect and to conflict; or opinions and principles of a given authority on one such matter will be shown to differ from those of that same authority on another, intersecting matter. These units tend to occur at several different tractates verbatim, since they serve equally well (or poorly) each Mishnah pericope cited therein. This type will vastly amplify the principles of the Mishnah. But it does not serve for a close exegesis of its wording or specific rule. These kinds of units always are substantial and difficult. The reason is that several different kinds of law have to be mastered, then the underlying principles made explicit and brought into juxtaposition with those of other laws on other topics.

3. *Legal Speculation and Reflection Independent of the Passage of the Mishnah at Hand:* There are units of discourse essentially independent of the Mishnah pericope with which they now are associated. These pursue questions not even indirectly generated by the law in hand. From time to time we may guess at why the redactor thought the discourse belonged where he placed it. While there are not a great many of these, as in the foregoing instance they are long and involved, always difficult and unusually interesting. They tend to occur not at the initial stages of a Talmudic passage attached to a pericope of the Mishnah, but rather late in the sequence of types of units of discourse.

TALMUDIC ANTHOLOGIES ON TOPICS
OF THE MISHNAH

There are sizable units of discourse joined together only by a common theme, and joined to the Mishnah pericope at which they occur only because, in some rather general way, someone supposed their themes and those of the Mishnah passage at hand intersected. Most such anthologies are rich in collections of citation of, and comment upon, verses of Scripture. But in the present category they are by no means the bulk of the Talmud's scriptural exegeses and comments.

To illustrate the anthological mode of constructing a unit of discourse, we review only part of a sizable extract on the theme of

Ahithophel, Y. Sanhedrin 10:2. What we now ask is whether we see some sort of unifying problem exhibited by the unit as a whole, a purpose or problematic that generates a drawing of the materials together. Alas, I do not perceive it, and I doubt the reader will. What we have is simply a collection of this-and-that about Ahithophel. The Talmud's units of discourse constituting little more than thematic anthologies are not limited to collections joined by a single biblical authority; there are anthologies on common themes of theology, scriptural exegesis, and law. They invariably form composites of evidently available material. We discern no effort to impose formal coherence, let alone stylistic unity. So the trait of the anthology is, by definition, the absence of definitive, unifying traits, either of a formal or of a substantive, intellectual character. The Talmud of the Land of Israel contains few such anthologies. (They are still less common in the earlier collections of exegeses.)

> *Y. Sanhedrin 10:2.* [X.A] Ahithophel was a man mighty in Torah learning.
> [B] It is written, "David again gathered all the chosen men of Israel, thirty thousand. [And David arose and went with all the people who were with him . . . to bring up from there the ark of the Lord']" (2 Sam. 6:1–2).
> [C] R. Berekiah in the name of R. Abba bar Kahana: "Ninety thousand elders did David appoint on a single day, but he did not appoint Ahithophel among them."
> [D] This is in line with that which is written in Scripture: "David again gathered all the chosen men of Israel, thirty thousand. . . ." That is, "And he added" means, "thirty." And "again" means "thirty." The Scripture explicitly speaks of thirty. Lo, there are then ninety in all.
> [E] You find that when David came to bear the ark of the covenant of the Lord, he did not bear it in accord with the Torah:
> [F] "And they carried the Ark of God on a new cart, [and brought it out of the house of Abinadab which was on the hill; and Uzzah and Ahio, the sons of Abinadab, were driving the new cart]" (2 Sam. 6:3). [That is, the Torah requires that the priests carry it, but they carried it in a cart instead.]
> [G] Now the ark carried the priests on high, but let them fall down; the ark carried the priests on high, but let them fall down to the ground.
> [H] David sent and brought Ahithophel. He said to him, "Will you not tell me what is with this ark, which raises the priests up high and casts

them down to the ground, raises the priests on high and casts them down to the ground?"

[I] He said to him, "Send and ask those wise men whom you appointed!"

[J] Said David, "One who knows how to make the ark stop and does not do so in the end is going to be put to death through strangulation."

[K] He said to him, "Make a sacrifice before [the ark], and it will stop."

[L] This is in line with the following verse which is written in Scripture: "And when those who bore the ark of the Lord had gone six paces, he sacrificed an ox and a fatling" (2 Sam. 6:13).

[M] R. Haninah and R. Mana—

[N] One of them said, "At every step an ox and a fatling, and at the end, seven oxen and seven rams."

[O] And the other said, "At every step seven oxen and seven rams, and at the end, an ox and a fatling."

[P] Said the Holy One, blessed be he, to Ahithophel, "A teaching which children say every day in the school you did not report to him!

[Q] "'But to the sons of Kohath he gave none, because they were charged with the care of the holy things *which had to be carried on the shoulder*' (Num. 7:9).

[R] "And this [to sacrifice] you never told him!"

The passage runs on for a considerable space, but nothing would be gained by reading the rest. The point is clear from what we have seen. The passage has no unifying idea or problem. It exhibits no aim. The composer does not even pretend to present a protracted argument. All the framers do is collect and arrange thematically congruent materials. Whether these materials are abundant or sparse has no bearing on the editorial principle at hand.

THE TALMUD IS TO THE MISHNAH . . .

Let us turn from the specific to the general. We now know how the Talmud will frame coherent discussions of passages of the Mishnah, the types of units of discourse presented by the Talmud as its exegesis of the Mishnah. These, as I said, constitute approximately ninety percent of the bulk of the Talmud. Let us now turn to list and interpret the more general approaches of the Talmud of the Land of Israel to the exegesis and amplification of the Mishnah.

First, and most important, the Mishnah was laid forth by Rabbi—

whole and complete, a profoundly unified, harmonious document. The Talmud, by contrast, insists upon obliterating the marks of cogency. It treats in bits and pieces what was originally meant to speak in a single way. That simple fact constitutes what is, by definition, Talmudic.

Second, the Mishnah, also by definition, delivered its message in the way chosen by Rabbi. The Talmud ignores that way. That is to say, by producing the document as he did, Rabbi left no space for the very enterprises of episodic exegesis undertaken so brilliantly by his immediate continuators and theirs. For the Mishnah not only came to closure. It also forms a closed system, that is, a whole, complete statement. It does not require facts outside of its language and formulation, so makes no provision for commentary and amplification of brief allusions, as (for its part) the Talmudic style assuredly does.

This characterization of the Mishnah as a closed system requires a measure of amplification. What I mean by a closed system is a statement that (evidently) covers all of the ground initially intended and provides all the information one (evidently) is supposed to require to understand and make sense of the whole. The Mishnah, with its highly systematic exposition of the principal components of Israel's natural and supernatural world—its economy, society, civil life, cult, seasons, realm of unclean and holy alike—presupposes only one thing. The framers of the Mishnah take for granted knowledge of Scripture, with special reference to the laws of the Pentateuch. No other information is required, so far as I can see, to make sense of what the Mishnah says and to grasp the design of the world the Mishnah proposes. At best, the Mishnah's authors presuppose a vast corpus of facts not in Scripture, and also not made articulate in the layers of dispute through which the Mishnah's framers express their own contribution. But this subterranean layer of fact is not part of the Mishnah's particular conception of the world, only its foundation, as much as Scripture, also not made articulate, forms the foundation.

To choose a convenient analogy, if the Constitution of the United States spelled out principles covering all of the law codes and civil institutions, instead of simply outlining the principal parts of the system, then we should call the Constitution a closed system. The opposite is the case. The writers of the Constitution take for granted not only a vast amount of information. They also address a future, the construction of a government and society, for the life of which they provide little or no legislation, or even guiding principles. They thus leave open doors of entry into the politics they create. The topical scheme of the Tosefta and the two Talmuds, closely adhering to the thematic and conceptual framework defined by the Mishnah, shows us the very opposite. That is why, if we call the one an open system, we must regard the other as a closed. So, while, I think, Rabbi may have been surprised had he known what the Talmud would do to his Mishnah, I do not think the framers of the Talmud would have been amazed by the development of a vast literature of commentary, responsa, and codification generated by *their* document. They expressed their ideas in such a way as to demand continuation and extension. Rabbi in the Mishnah did not.

Third, the Mishnah refers to nothing beyond itself. As I just now stressed, it promises no information other than what is provided within its limits. More strikingly, it raises no questions for ongoing discussion beyond its decisive, final, descriptive statements of enduring realities and fixed relationships. By contrast, the Talmud's single and irrevocable judgment is the opposite. The Talmud's very beginning initiative is to reopen the Mishnah's closed system, to treat as open questions closed or not even raised. That at the foundations is what is definitive about the Talmud of the Land of Israel: its daring assertion that the concluded and completed demanded clarification and continuation.

When we return to the taxa just now found encompassing, we discover a program of criticism of the Mishnah framed by independent and original minds. The meanings and amplification of phrases represent the judgment that Rabbi's formulation, while stimulating and perhaps provocative, left much to be desired. These indications of independence of judgment among people disposed not merely to memorize but to improve upon the text provided by Rabbi hardly represent judgments of substance. The most important point is the one that first won our attention. The propositions of the Mishnah cannot stand by themselves but must be located within the larger realm of scriptural authority. If Rabbi presented his Mishnah without proof-texts in the view that such texts either were self-evident or unnecessary, his continuators and successors rejected his judgment on both counts.

So far as the Mishnah was supposed to stand as a law code independent of the revelation of Torah to Moses at Mount Sinai, it was received by people to whom such a supposition was incredible. So far as Rabbi took for granted the scriptural facticity of the facts of his law code, that was regarded as insufficient. What was implicit had to be made explicit. So, in all, the creation of the Talmud of the Land of Israel (as well as the other one, produced in Babylonia) constituted a profound judgment upon the Mishnah: authoritative, yet insufficient; definitive, yet demanding the participation of successors and continuators, in partnership with the framers of the original document itself. The main point then is that the Mishnah, if once closed, was reopened. The authorities of the Talmud in no way claimed for themselves a position on the same plane as that of the framers of the Mishnah. But what they did, as distinct from what they said about themselves, implicitly declares they had the right to do things too. So if less than the founders, they stood in a direct line with the founders. They too could participate in the work of the Mishnah, carry it forward, reshape it in line with their own brilliant minds. What later rabbis' work of exegesis of Scripture implicitly states about their position in relationship to Moses, the prophets, the scribes and sages of the Torah, remains to be seen.

To conclude: The Talmud is a composite of three kinds of materials—exegeses of the Mishnah, exegeses of Scripture, and accounts of the men who provide both. Perhaps one might then wish to see the Talmud as a synthesis of its two antecedent documents: the Mishnah, lacking all reference to Scripture, and the Scripture itself. The Talmud brings the two together into a synthesis of its own making, both in reading Scripture into the Mishnah, and in reading Scripture alongside and separate from the Mishnah. Further, since, as I have stressed, the next major phase in the formation of the literature of Judaism, beyond the Talmud, will be the making of compilations of scriptural exegeses, we may say that the Talmud forms the bridge from the formation of the Mishnah to the making of the earliest midrashic compilations and collections.

Focused upon the Mishnah, the Talmud opens the way to the creation of compilations of midrashic passages. All authorities concur that that is the chronological fact of the matter. The Talmud came to closure at the end of the fourth and beginning of the fifth centuries. The earliest work of composing collections of exegeses of Scripture began with Genesis Rabbah in the fifth century and continued, in the first seven collections of exegeses, through the sixth. (Separate but parallel work on the compilation of exegeses of legal passages of Leviticus, Numbers, and Deuteronomy, using the names of Mishnaic authorities, went forward at this same time.) So if we seek a bridge from the Mishnah, at the end of the second century, to the collections of exegeses begun in the fifth century, we find that, in time, the Talmud of the Land of Israel fills the gap and therefore forms the bridge. We have now to ask whether or not that bridge is merely chronological. Whether it is a matter of sequence or of substance remains to be seen.

4

. . . As Compilations of Exegeses Are to Scripture

THE ARGUMENT FROM TAXONOMY

The vast and various writings of the Talmud of the Land of Israel turn out to fall into just a handful of categories or types. It follows that a taxonomy of the document yields an important fact. The Yerushalmi presents the result of a systematic and carefully thought-through program of (1) exegesis and (2) amplification of the Mishnah. While the Mishnah itself is an immense document, the Talmud's varieties of discourse and, consequently, the modes of thought generative of discourse, form an amazingly cogent and uniform body of hermeneutic inquiry. The Talmud's framers' questions addressed to the Mishnah's text, the exegetical possibilities inhering in the Mishnah and explored by the sages of the Talmud—these turn out to take up only a handful of very closely related positions upon the vast continuum of potential commentary. So among the many things they might have done with the text at hand, the framers of the Talmud chose to do only a few things, mainly verbatim exegesis and secondary amplification.

This fact brings us to the problem at hand after so long a preliminary bout. What we shall see is a simple and striking fact. It is that Genesis Rabbah, the document universally regarded as the first compilation of exegeses accomplished within the rabbinical circles in particular, is composed of units of discourse as cogent, in their way, as the ones in the Talmud of the Land of Israel.

More important, these units of discourse fall into precisely the same taxonomical categories as those of the Talmud of the Land of Israel. Accordingly, the way in which the rabbinical exegetes who selected passages of the Mishnah and so constructed the Talmud of the Land of Israel did their work turns out to be the same as the way in which rabbinical exegetes who selected passages of Scripture and so constructed Genesis Rabbah did their work. Self-evidently, what the one group had to say about the Mishnah bears no material relationship to what the other group had to say about Genesis. But the modes of thought, the ways of framing inquiries and constructing the results into formations of protracted and cogent discourse, serving quite specific and limited hermeneutical purposes—these, I shall show, are taxonomically uniform. Furthermore, as we shall see, even when we employ a taxonomical system defined not by the Mishnah's continuum but solely by formal traits of Genesis Rabbah's units of discourse, specifically the placement of a verse of Scripture and the mode of analysis of that verse within an exegetical construction, the result is the same. What the masters of biblical exegesis did in Genesis was what the masters of Mishnaic exegesis did in whatever Mishnah tractate they chose for study. It follows that the compiling of the first collection of biblical exegesis falls into the same intellectual framework as the Talmud of the Land of Israel, whether this was before, at the same time as, or in the aftermath of, the composition of Yerushalmi.

Once in this chapter I have made these claims stick, I shall be able, in the last chapter, to interpret the context of the making of compilations of biblical exegesis within the already-established historical, theological, and apologetic context of the making of compilations of Mishnaic exegesis—that is, within the setting of the formation of the Talmud of the Land of Israel. In consequence I hope to make sense of the entire literary corpus of maturing Rabbinic Judaism at the end of the late antiquity and on the threshhold of the Middle Ages. That brings us to the eve of the encounter with triumphant Christianity and militant Islam alike.

The things the exegetes of Scripture and compilers of exegeses might have done are many and diverse. The word *midrash* bears multiple and imprecise meanings. The activity of compiling such *midrash*, meaning exegesis of Scripture, turns out to express all of the differences among all of the diverse groups of ancient Israel that took up the work of framing their ideas in response to Scripture. That is to say, just as you could say anything you wanted about Scripture, so you could collect anything you wanted and call it *midrash* of anything—any text—you chose. *How* collections were made as much as *what* was compiled in them expressed the distinctive polemical purpose of the compilers. There is a natural and close correspondence between what one chose to say and the mode of organizing and expressing the message. What this means for our problem is simple. People did make choices and carry them out. From the things they did, we may therefore draw out a picture of what they chose to do and why they wished to do it. There is nothing accidental or self-evident in what is before us, even though familiarity suggests otherwise. Since that is the fact, we must find it noteworthy when we see the taxonomy of units of discourse characteristic of the first extant compilation of exegesis assigned to the ancient rabbis.

The procedure once more demands that the reader consider a sizable extract of a source. In this case, we take a chapter of Genesis Rabbah, chosen as randomly as possible. (A second chapter of Genesis Rabbah is given in the appendix, and I allude to both of them in my taxonomy.) Once we have read the entire chapter, I shall simply take up, taxon by taxon, exactly the same categories of units of discourse as I outlined in the preceding chapter. Then I shall attempt to assign to those categories all of the units of discourse of our chapter of Genesis Rabbah. If the thesis at hand is sound, we should find place among the taxa serviceable for the Talmud of the Land of Israel for all types of units of discourse produced in our chapters of Genesis Rabbah.

The reader need not remain in suspense for long. The fact is that all of the units of discourse (as designated by the framers of the text itself, not by me) in our chapters of Genesis Rabbah indeed may find a place among the taxa serviceable for all the units of discourse of the Talmud of the Land of Israel. All of the taxa yielded by the Talmud, moreover, prove serviceable in the present exercise, except for one. While I found in the Talmud of the Land of Israel a small number of units of discourse that did not seem united and cogent, presenting episodic sayings or observations rather than well-composed arguments and called, therefore, anthologies, Genesis Rabbah's chapters at hand provide no instances of anthologies. Whether or not that fact bears implications for our larger theory I cannot say. I perceive none pertinent to the circumstances of the formation of the units of discourse of Genesis Rabbah. What follows is Genesis Rabbah chapter 78, in the translation of H. Freedman.

[I.A] "And he said: 'Let me go, for the day is breaking'" (Gen. 32:26). It is written, "They are new every morning; great is Thy faithfulness" (Lam. 3:23). R. Simeon b. Abba interpreted this: Because Thou renew us every morning, we know that great is Thy faithfulness to redeem us. R. Alexandri interpreted it: From the fact that Thou renew us every morning, we know that great is Thy faithfulness to resurrect the dead.

[B] R. Samuel b. Nahman said in R. Jonathan's name: A celestial company never repeats [God's] praises. R. Helbo said: The Holy One, blessed be He, creates a new company of angels every day, and they utter song before Him and then depart [evermore]. R. Berekiah observed: I objected to R. Helbo: But it is written, "And he said, 'Let me go, for the day is breaking.'" But he retorted: Strangler! Think you to strangle me? It was Michael or Gabriel, who are celestial princes; all others are exchanged, but they are not exchanged.

[C] Hadrian—rot his bones!—asked R. Joshua b. Hananiah: "Do you maintain that the celestial company do not praise [God] and repeat [their praises], but that every day the Holy One, blessed be He, creates a company of new angels and they utter song before Him and then depart?" "Yes," he replied. "And whither do they go?" he pursued. "To the source whence they were created," was the answer. "And whence are they created?" he went on. "From Nehar Dinur," he replied. "And what is the nature of Nehar Dinur?" he enquired. "It is like the Jordan," said he, "which ceases not [to flow] by day or by night." "And whence is its source?" "The perspiration of the *Hayyoth*, caused by their bearing God's Throne." Said his adviser to him: "But the Jordan flows by day but not by night?" "Was I not watching at Beth Peor," he replied, "[and saw] that it flows by night just as it flows by day?"

[D] R. Meir, R. Judah, and R. Simeon each made an observation.

R. Meir said: Who is greater: the guardian or the guarded? Since it is written, "For He will give His angels charge over thee, to guard thee in all thy ways" (Ps. 91:11), it follows that the guarded is greater than the guardian.

R. Judah said: Who is greater, the bearer or the borne? Since it says, "They shall bear thee upon their hands" (Ps. 91:12), it follows that the borne is greater than the bearer.

R. Simeon said: Who is greater: the sender or the sent? From the verse, "And he said: Let me go" [lit. "send me away,"] it follows that the sender is greater than the sent.

[II.A] "And he said: 'Let me go, for the day is breaking'": For it is time to sing praises. "Let your colleagues sing praises," said he to him. "I cannot [arrange it so]," he replied, "for when I come to utter praise tomorrow, they will say to me: 'As you did not utter praise yesterday, so cannot you utter praise to-day.'" "Make an end [of pleading]; enough!" he [Jacob] answered him. "I will not let thee go, except thou bless me," adding: "The angels who visited Abraham did not depart without a blessing," "They had been sent for that purpose," he pleaded, "whereas I was not sent for that purpose." "Make an end! enough!" he retorted. "I will not let thee go, except thou bless me." R. Levi said in the name of R. Samuel b. Nahman: "Because the ministering angels revealed God's secrets," [pleaded the angel], "they were expelled from their precincts for a hundred and thirty-eight years; shall I then listen to thee and be banished from my precincts?" "Make an end, enough!" he answered, "I will not let thee go, except thou bless me." R. Huna said, Eventually he decided, I will reveal [the future] to him, and if the Holy One, blessed be He, upbraids me, saying, "Why did thou reveal it to him," I will answer Him: "Sovereign of the Universe! Thy children make decrees and Thou does not nullify them; could I then nullify their decrees?" Thereupon he told him: "He [God] will reveal Himself to you at Bethel and change your name, while I will be standing there." Hence it is written, "At Bethel He would find him, and there He would speak with us" (Hos. 12:5): it does not say, "with him," but "with us."

[III.A] "And he said unto him: 'What is thy name?' And he said: 'Jacob.' And he said: 'Your name shall be called no more Jacob'" (Gen. 32:28f.). (It is written, "That confirms the word of His servant, and performs the counsel of His messengers"—angels (Is. 44:26).) R. Berekiah said in R. Levi's name: Since He "confirms the word of His servant," do we not know that He "performs the counsel of His messengers," "and says of Jerusalem: she shall be inhabited; and of the cities of Judah: They shall be built" (Is. 44:26)? But "That confirms the word of His servant" refers to the one angel who appeared to our Patriarch Jacob and told him: "The Holy One, blessed be He, will reveal Himself to you at Bethel and change your name, while I too will be there," as it says, "At Bethel He would find him," etc. God did appear to him to fulfill the decree of that angel, who had said to him, "Your name shall be called no more Jacob," and God too spoke thus to him, as it says, "And God said unto him: Your name is Jacob; your name shall not be called any more Jacob" (Gen. 35:10). Then how much the more will God fulfill the words of His prophets concerning Jerusalem, for all the prophets prophesied about it!

[B] Bar Kappara said: Whoever calls Abraham 'Abram,' violates a positive command. R. Levi said: A positive and a negative command: "Neither shall your name any more be called Abram" (Gen. 17:5)—that is a negative command; "But your name shall be called Abraham" (Gen. 17:5)—that is a positive command. But surely the men of the Great Assembly called him Abram, for it is written, "Thou art the Lord God, who didst choose Abram" (Neh. 9:7)? There it is different, as it means that while he was yet Abram Thou didst choose him. Then, by analogy, does one who calls Sarah "Sarai" infringe a positive command? No, for only he [Abraham] was enjoined regarding her. Again, by analogy, if one calls Israel "Jacob," does one infringe a positive command? [No, for] it was taught: It was not intended that the name of Jacob should disappear, but that "Israel" should be his principal name and "Jacob" a secondary one. R. Zechariah interpreted it in R. Aha's name: At all events, "Your name is Jacob," save that, "But Israel [too] shall be your name" (Gen. 35:10): Jacob would be the principal name—"Israel" was added to it.

[C] "For you have striven with Elohim and with men, and have prevailed" (Gen. 32:29): you have striven with celestial beings and conquered them, and with mortals, and have conquered them. "With celestial beings" alludes to the angel. R. Hama b. Hanina said: It was Esau's guardian angel. That was what Jacob meant when he said to him: "Forasmuch as I have seen thy face, as one sees the face" of Elohim (Gen. 33:10): even as the face of God denotes judgment, so does your face denote judgment; even as with respect to the face of God [it is written], "And none shall appear before My face empty-handed" (Ex. 23:15), so art thou; none may appear before thy face empty-handed. "With mortals, and has conquered them"—by that, Esau and his chiefs are meant.

Another interpretation of "For thou has striven (saritha) with God": it is thou whose features are engraven on high.

[IV.A] "And Jacob asked him, and said: 'Tell me, I pray thee, thy name'" (Gen. 32:30). Rabbi said in the name of Abba Jose b. Dosay: One verse says, "He counts the number of the stars, He gives them as names" (Ps. 147:4); whereas another text states, "He who brings out their host by number, He calls them all by name" (Is. 40:26). This, however, teaches that there is no [permanent] name, but a [continuous] change, the present name [of an angel] not being the same as he may bear later on, for it says, "And the angel of the Lord said unto him: 'Wherefore do you ask after my name, seeing it is hidden?'" (Judg . 13:18)—I do not know to what my name will be changed.

[V.A] "And the sun rose for him," etc. (Gen. 32:32). R. Berekiah commented: The sun rose in order to heal him, but for others only to give light. R. Huna said in R. Aha's name: It was indeed thus: the sun healed Jacob and burned up Esau and his chiefs. Said the Holy One, blessed be He, to him: "Thou art an earnest for thy descendants: even as the sun heals thee while it burns up Esau and his chiefs, so will the sun heal thy descendants while it burns up the heathen." It will heal them: "But unto you that fear My name shall the sun of righteousness arise with healing in its wings" (Mal. 3:20); it burns up the idolaters: "For, behold, the day cometh, it burns as a furnace," etc. (Mal. 3:19).

[B] "And he limped upon his thigh." R. Joshua b. Levi went up to Rome; when he arrived at Acco [on his return], R. Hanina went out to greet him and found him limping upon his thigh, at which he remarked, You resemble your ancestor: "And he limped upon his thigh."

[VI.A] "Therefore the children of Israel eat not the sinew of the thigh-vein [gid ha-nasheh]" (Gen. 32:33). R. Hanina said: Why was it called Gid ha-nasheh? Because it slipped (nashah) from its place. R. Huna said: The ramifications of the thigh-vein are permitted, but Israel are holy [self-restrained] and treat it as forbidden. R. Judah said: He [the angel] touched only one of them, and only one was forbidden. R. Yose said: He touched only one of them, but both became forbidden. One tanna teaches: It is reasonable to suppose that it was the right one, which is R. Judah's view; while another tanna teaches: It is reasonable to suppose that it was the left one, which is R. Yose's view. The opinion that it was the right one [is based on the verse], "And he touched the hollow of his thigh" (Gen. 32:26), while the opinion that it was the left is based on the passage, "Because he touched the hollow of Jacob's thigh."

[VII.A] "And Jacob lifted up his eyes and looked, and behold, Esau came" (Gen. 33:1). R. Levi said: A lion was angry with the cattle and the beasts. Said they: "Who will go to appease him?" Said the fox: "I know three hundred fables and I will appease him." "Let it be so," they replied. He went a short distance and halted. "Why have you halted?" they asked. "I have forgotten a hundred," he answered. "In two hundred there are blessings," they replied. He went on a little and again halted. "What does this mean?" they demanded. "I have forgotten another hundred," he replied. "Even a hundred will do," they replied. When he arrived there he said: "I have forgotten them all, so every one must appease him for himself." So it was with Jacob. R. Judah b. Simon said: [Jacob declared]: "I have the strength to engage in prayer [against him]"; R. Levi said: [He declared]: "I have the strength to wage a battle." But when he arrived there, "Then he divided the children," etc. (Gen. 33:1) saying to them: "Let the merit of each one protect him."

[VIII.A] "And he put the handmaids and their children foremost, and Leah and her children after, and Rachel and Joseph hindermost" (Gen. 33:2): from this it follows that the further back one was the more beloved he was.

[B] "And he himself passed over before them" (Gen. 33:2): thus it is written, "Like as a father has compassion upon his children" (Ps. 103:13). R. Hiyya taught: It means, like the most compassionate of the Patriarchs. Who was that? R. Judah b. R. Simon said: Abraham, for Abraham said: "That be far from Thee to do after this manner" (Gen. 18:25). R. Levi said: It was Jacob: "And he himself passed over before them," saying, "Let him harm me rather than them."

[C] "And bowed himself to the ground seven times" (Gen. 33:3). Why seven? Symbolizing, "For a righteous man falls seven times, and rises up again" (Prov. 24:16). Another reason why seven: [In effect] he said to him: Regard thyself as though stationed behind seven gratings, sitting and giving judgment, while I am being judged by thee, and thou art filled with compassion for me. R. Hanian b. Isaac said: He did not cease from repeatedly prostrating himself until he converted judgment to mercy.

[IX.A] "And Esau ran to meet him . . . and kissed him" (Gen. 33:4). The word is dotted. R. Simeon b. Eleazar said: Wherever you find the plain writing exceeding the dotted letters, you must interpret the plain writing; if the dotted letters exceed the plain writing, you must interpret the dotted letters. Here the plain writing does not exceed the dotted letters, nor do the dotted letters exceed the plain writing: hence it teaches that he kissed him with all his heart. Said R. Yannai to him: If so, why is the word dotted? It teaches, however, that he wished to bite him (but that the Patriarch Jacob's neck was turned to marble and that wicked man's teeth were blunted and loosened). Hence, "And they wept" (Gen. 33:4): one wept because of his neck and the other wept because of his teeth. (R. Abbahu adduced it in R. Yohanan's name from the following verse: "Thy neck is as a tower of ivory" (Song 7:5).

[X.A] "And he lifted up his eyes . . . the children whom God has graciously given your servant" (Gen. 33:5). R. Benjamin b. Levi said: We thus hear of grace in connection with the eleven tribal ancestors, but not in connection with Benjamin. Where then do we hear it? Further on: "And he said: God be gracious to you, my son" (Gen. 43:29).

[B] "Then the handmaids came near" etc. (Gen. 33:6). In the case of all the others it states, "Then the handmaids came near, they and their children," etc., "And Leah also and her children came near," etc. (Gen. 33:7). But in the case of Joseph it is written, "And after came Joseph near and Rachel, and they bowed down" (Gen. 33:7). The fact is that Joseph said: "This wicked man has an aspiring eye: let him not look at my mother," whereupon he drew himself up to his full height and covered her. Hence it is written of him, "Joseph is a fruitful (*porath*) vine, a fruitful vine before the eye" (Gen. 49:22). "A fruitful vine" means: thou didst wax great, O Joseph; "A fruitful vine before the eye": because thou didst enlarge [thy stature] before [Esau's] eye; again, through the cows (*paroth*) didst thou wax great. "A fruitful vine before (*'ale*) the eye." R. Berekiah interpreted in R. Simon's name: It is for Me (*'alay*) to reward thee for that eye.

[XI.A] "And he said: What do you mean by all this camp which I met?" etc. (Gen. 33:8). The whole of that night the ministering angels formed into bands and companies and kept confronting Esau's troops. When they asked them to whom they belonged and were told, "To Esau," they exclaimed, "Give it to them!" "We belong to Isaac's son!" They still exclaimed, "Lay on!" "We belong to Abraham's grandson!" They still said, "Lay on!" But when they pleaded, "We belong to Jacob's brother," they said, "Let them go; they are of ours." In the morning he said to him: "What do you mean by all this camp which I met?" "Did they say anything to you?" he inquired. "I was crushed by them," he replied. "And he said: To find favour" (Gen. 33:8).

[B] "And Esau said: I have enough" (Gen. 33:9). R. Aibu said: His [Jacob's] hold on the blessings was in fact but weak. Where was it strengthened? Here: "My brother, let that which thou hast be thine." R. Eleazar said: The validity of a document is established by its signatories. Thus, lest you say, Had not Jacob deceived his father he would not have received the blessing, Scripture states, "My brother, let that which you have be for yourself."

[XII.A] "And Jacob said: 'No, I pray you, if now I have found favor in your sight, then receive my present from my hand; for as much as I have seen your face, it is as one seeing the face of God'" (Gen. 33:10). Even as the face of God denotes judgment, so does your face denote judgment; and even as with respect to the face of God [it is written], "And none shall appear before My face empty-handed" (Ex. 23:15), so are you: none may appear before your face empty-handed.

[B] "Take, I pray you, my gift that is brought to you" (Gen. 33:11): how much toil did I expend before it came to my hand, he exclaimed, yet to You it comes of itself. For it is not written, "That I brought," but "that is brought"—it came to you of itself.

[C] "And he urged him, and he took it" (Gen. 33:11): he pretended to draw back, but his hands were stretched out. R. Judah b. Rabbi said: "Every one submitting himself (*mithrappes*) with pieces of (*razze*) silver" (Ps. 68:31): that means, he opens his hand (*mattir pas*) and would be appeased (*mithrazzeh*) with silver.

[D] Resh Lakish went to pay his respects to our Teacher. "Pray for me," he [R. Judah] begged him, "for this Government [Rome] is very evil." "Take nothing from anyone," he [Resh Lakish] told him, "and then you will not have to give anything." While he was sitting there, there came a woman and brought him a salver with a knife on it, whereupon he took the knife and returned the salver. Subsequently a royal courier came and saw it, took a fancy to it, and carried it off. Toward evening Resh Lakish again went to pay his respects to our Teacher and he saw him sitting and laughing. "Why are you laughing?" he asked him. "That knife which you saw," replied he, "there came a royal courier and took it away." "Did I not tell you," he retorted, "that if you take nothing from anyone you will not have to give to anyone?"

[E] One of the common people said to R. Hoshaya: "If I tell you a good thing, will you repeat it in public in my name?" "What is it?" asked he. "All the gifts which the Patriarch Jacob made to Esau," replied he, "the heathens will return them to the Messiah in the Messianic era." "What is the proof?" " 'The kings of Tarshish and of the isles shall return tribute' (Ps. 72:10): it does not say, 'shall bring,' but '*shall return*.' " "By thy life!" he exclaimed, "you have said a good thing, and I will teach it in your name."

[XIII] "And he said unto him: My Lord knows that the children are tender" (Gen. 33:13). R. Berekiah said in R. Levi's name: "My Lord knows that the children are tender" alludes to Moses and Aaron; "And [that] the flocks and the herds" symbolizes Israel: "And ye My flock, the flock of My pasture, are men" (Ezek. 34:31). R. Huna said in R. Aha's name: But for the compassion of the Holy One, blessed be He, then, "They had overdriven them one day" and "All the flocks had died" already in the days of Hadrian. R. Berekiah said in R. Levi's name: "My God knows that the children are tender" alludes to David and Solomon; "And [that] the flocks and the herds" alludes to Israel: "And ye My flock," etc. R. Huna said in R. Aha's name: But for God's mercy, then "All the flock had died" already in the days of Haman.

[XIV.A] "Let my Lord, I pray you, pass over before his servant" (Gen. 33:14). He [Esau] proposed: "Are you willing that we should be partners in your world?" "Let my Lord, I pray you, pass over before his servant," he replied. "Do you not fear then my generals, lieutenants, and commanders?" he demanded. "And I will journey on gently— [*le'itti*]" (Gen. 33:14), he replied, i.e., meekly: I will walk meekly, [*le'itti*] having the same sense] as in the verse, "The waters of Shiloah that go softly [*le'at*]" (Isa. 8:6). I will walk with face wrapped [in humility], as in the verse, "Behold, it is here wrapped [*lutah*] in a cloth" (1 Sam. 21:10).

[B] "Until I come unto my Lord unto Seir" (Gen. 33:14). R. Abbahu said: We have searched the whole Scriptures and do not find that Jacob ever went to Esau to the mountain of Seir. Is it then possible that Jacob, the truthful, should deceive him? But when would he come to him? In the Messianic era: "And saviors shall come up on Mount Zion to judge the mount of Esau" etc. (Obad. 1:21).

[XV.A] "And Esau said: Let me now leave with you some of the folk," etc. (Gen. 33:15). He offered to accompany him, but he [Jacob] declined it. When our Teacher had to travel to the Government, he would look at this text and would not take Romans with him. On one occasion he did not look at it, and took Romans with him, and before he reached Acco he had already sold his coat.

[B] "So Esau returned that day," etc. (Gen. 33:16). Where were the four hundred men? They had slipped away one by one. Said they: "Let us not be scorched by Jacob's burning coal." When did the Holy One, blessed be He, reward them? Later on: "And there escaped not a man of them, save four hundred young men, who rode upon camels and fled" (1 Sam. 30:17).

[XVI.A] "And Jacob journeyed to Succoth," etc. (Gen. 33:17). How many years did the Patriarch spend in Bethel? R. Abba b. Kahana said: Eighteen months, [for he dwelt in] booths, in a house, and again in booths.

[B] R. Berekiah said in R. Levi's name: During all the months that our ancestor spent in Bethel, he kept on presenting Esau with that gift. R. Abin said in R. Aha's name: For nine years he presented Esau with that gift. R. Phinehas said in R. Abin's name: During all the years spent by the Patriarch in Bethel he did not refrain from offering libations. R. Hanan said: Whoever knows how many libations were offered by Jacob in Bethel would be able to calculate the quantity of the waters of Tiberias.

CATEGORIES OF UNITS OF DISCOURSE
OF EXEGETICAL COLLECTIONS

Let us begin with the definition of the primary category at hand, the notion of a "unit of discourse." By a unit of discourse, in the context of compilations of exegeses as in the Talmud, I mean a complete discussion of a particular problem, with a beginning, middle, and end. Such a unit of discourse constitutes a composition exhibiting traits of reflection and both careful organization and planning. A unit of discourse by definition consists of a set of sentences, formed into a well-framed paragraph. So a unit of discourse is a cogent statement of a complete thought, starting somewhere and proceeding purposefully to a foreordained and considered goal. The fact that the compilation under discussion is made up of these units of discourse is what makes possible the taxonomy of a text and then comparison between one rabbinic document and another. For, as we have already seen, the Talmud of the Land of Israel for its part also is composed of complete exhibitions of cogent thought, that is, units of discourse, formed into fairly sizable discussions—three or more coherent sentences—of carefully framed questions or problems.

The alternatives of discourse are many, for people may frame and express ideas in ways without number. In the penultimate section of this chapter, we shall review other ways of saying other things—that is, different approaches to making up and putting together exegeses of Scripture. These approaches expressed different purposes, formed by different groups of Jews, all of whom read the same holy book. Only when we contrast the ways taken by the framers of the earliest exegetical compositions in rabbinical circles with the paths explored by others shall we see the true state of affairs.

The upshot—I stress again—is that before us are the results of considered choice, yielding distinctive and readily distinguishable forms of composition. The choices were to say one thing, not some other, to say it in one way, not some other, and to draw together everything that had been said into one sort of composition or collection, not some other. Later on, the ways not taken will indicate alternatives. The way taken by the framers of the Talmud of the Land of Israel and of Genesis Rabbah alike is simple: to work out a complete thought, a proposition of some sort; in a cogent and intelligible way; in a discourse we may liken to a paragraph or a short essay, in its careful traits of providing a proposition and then expounding or exemplifying said proposition.

If the taxonomy workable for the Talmud is to prove truly suitable for the present passages of Genesis Rabbah, in our chapters we should come up with only two fundamental types: first, phrase-by-phrase exegesis of Scripture, second, amplification of the meaning of a verse of Scripture. These are the two ways in which a Talmudic sage might approach the problem of the Mishnah. He had the choice of explaining the meaning of a particular passage or of expanding upon the meaning, or the overall theme, of a particular passage—nothing else. True, in dealing with Scripture he might systematically interpret one thing in terms of something else, a verse of Scripture in light of an autonomous set of considerations not explicit in Scripture but (in his mind) absolutely critical to its full meaning. But that is still not much more than the exegesis of the passage at hand for a given purpose, established a priori. That is an exercise fully familiar to the framers of the units of discourse of the Talmud in their confrontation with the Mishnah.

Now to define our taxonomical categories: we shall take up four, of which the first two are closely related, and the fourth of slight consequence.

The first category encompasses close exegesis of Scripture, by which I mean, a word-for-word or phrase-by-phrase interpretation of a passage. In such an activity, the framer of a discrete composition will wish to read and explain a verse or a few words of a verse of the Scripture at hand, pure and simple.

The second category, no less exegetical than the first, is made up of units of discourse in which the components of the verse are treated as part of a larger statement of meaning, rather than as a set of individual phrases, stitches requiring attention one by one. Accordingly, in this taxon we deal with wide-ranging discourse about the meaning of a particular passage, hence an effort to amplify what is said in a verse. Here the amplification may take a number of different forms and directions. But the discipline imposed by the originally cited verse of Scripture will always impose boundaries on discourse.

The third taxon encompasses units of discourse in which the theme of a particular passage defines a very wide-ranging exercise. In this discussion the cited passage itself is unimportant. It is the theme that is definitive. Accordingly, in this third type we take up a unit of discourse in which the composer of the passage wishes to expand on a particular problem, (merely) illustrated in the cited passage. The problem, rather than the cited passage, defines the limits and direction of discourse. The passage at hand falls away, having provided a mere pretext for the real point of concern.

The fourth and final taxon deriving from the Yerushalmi takes in units of discourse shaped around a given topic, but not intended to constitute cogent and tightly-framed discourse on said topic. These units of discourse then constitute topical anthologies, rather than carefully composed essays. As I said, I find none in the two chapters at hand.

We now proceed to review the passage of Genesis Rabbah cited in the foregoing unit. The first and most important fact is simply that that passage *is* made up of what I have called "units of discourse." That is to say, we do not have a mere mass of discrete sayings, in which the number of sentences is the same as the number of completed thoughts or fully spelled out exercises of cognition. Rather, we can break up the entire chapter of Genesis Rabbah into a finite number of cogent discussions, paragraphs, each with its beginning, middle, and end. Upon that simple and self-evident fact everything else rests. For what it means is that the whole has been made up of parts. These parts, in turn, exhibit the abilities of not mere collectors, or collectors and arrangers, but masters of composition and cogent reflection.

So, like the Talmud of the Land of Israel, Genesis Rabbah's chapter at hand emerges in two stages: first, from people who worked out its components; second, from people who arranged them. These may well have been the same people, but the work was in separate and distinct stages. First came writing compositions expressive of complex ideas, framed in sophisticated ways. Second, there was the work of selecting and arranging these units of discourse into the composition now before us. This second process need not detain us; it has no bearing on the argument at hand. Our principal concern is now to find out whether or not, as I have alleged, the taxonomical framework suitable for all units of discourse of the Talmud of the Land of Israel may move, without significant variation or revision, to encompass and categorize the materials of the earliest composition of scriptural exegesis, Genesis Rabbah.

For that purpose, through the next four sections, I present a brief definition, then a list of the pertinent entries of the chapter cited at the outset. The reader may then refer back to the text to see why I

think a given unit of discourse falls into the category to which I assign it.

EXEGESIS OF SCRIPTURE

Exegesis of Scripture in the simplest and narrowest sense involves
reading a given verse and explaining in a systematic way words or
phrases of which the verse is made up. The substance of the exegesis may vary. We may have the explanation of a given passage
through the introduction of another passage of Scripture itself. The
notion is that the latter, the meaning of which is known, amplifies or
clarifies the unclear meaning of the former. We may, second, find
that a phrase is restated in other words, serving to add to the meaning of the passage at hand. The exegete, third, may simply take a
word and provide a synonym or otherwise clarify the meaning of the
phrase in a word-for-word way. Finally, a story may be cited to illustrate the meaning of a phrase. In the catalogue that follows, I signify
the type of exegesis I think is at hand through these indicators: first,
parallel passage; second, rephrasing; third, synonym; and fourth, il-
lustrative story, respectively.

The instances in Genesis Rabbah chapter 78 are as follows:

78:3A	: Parallel passage		78:11B	: Parallel passage
78:4	: " "		78:12A	: " "
78:5B	: Illustrative story		78:12B	: Illustrative dialogue
78:6	: Synonym			invented
78:7	: Illustrative story		78:12C	: Parallel passage
78:8B	: Parallel passage		78:13	: " "
78:8C	: " "		78:14A	: Rephrasing and
78:10A	: " "			synonym
78:10B	: " "		78:14B	: Parallel passage
78:11A	: Illustrative story		78:15A	: Illustrative story
			78:15B	: Parallel passage

In addition, the reader will find in Genesis Rabbah chapter 32,
given in the appendix, the following further examples of this type of
unit of discourse.

32:3B	: Parallel passage		32:8E	: Illustrative story
32:4A	: " "		32:10	: Illustrative story,

32:5B	: Parallel passage		Parallel passages
32:7A(2)	: " "	32:11A	: Rephrasing
32:8B	: Rephrasing	32:11B	: Synonym
32:8C	: "	32:11D	: Interpretation of a
32:8D	: Parallel passage		particle (AK)

AMPLIFICATION OF SCRIPTURE

In the collection of exegeses before us, we find a mode of inter-preting a verse of Scripture separate from the one in the preceding unit, though, as I said, closely related to it in purpose. In this other way, the exegete amplifies the meaning of a verse of Scripture, without a close account of the words of the passage and without trying to tie the amplification of the sense of meaning of the passage to a literal account of the verse's phrasing and word choices. What I mean by "amplification," therefore, is that the exegete greatly expands upon the meaning of the passage without attempting to link to the verse he has cited his sense of this broader and more encompassing meaning.

The instances in Genesis Rabbah chapter 78 are as follows:

78:2	: Why let him go? Why bless?
78:3B	: Change of Jacob's name.
78:3C	: Jacob's striving.
78:5A	: Sun rose.
78:8A	: Point of the deed is generalized.
78:9	: Why is the passage dotted?
78:16A	: How many years did Jacob spend in Bethel?
78:16B	: What Jacob did in Bethel.

In addition, the reader will find in Genesis Rabbah chapter 32, given in the appendix, the following further examples of this type of unit of discourse.

32:4B	: Why seven of each kind?
32:5A	: Why forty days?
32:5C	: Verse refers to . . .
32:6A	: Year of the flood.
32:6B	: Noah entered the ark only when he had to.

32:7A(1)	: Respite of seven days
32:7B	: Appropriateness of water as a means of punishment.
32:8A	: Why Noah entered the ark by day.
32:9A	: Ark sank.
32:9B	: Ark floated.
32:11C	: Fish not killed in flood.

EXPANSION ON PROBLEMS OF SCRIPTURE

Now, in this third taxon, the exegete leaves behind the verse at hand. He travels the route indicated solely by the theme or overall problem introduced by, or merely implicit in, the verse. Transcending the details of the verse, the exegete takes up the main point (I might say, the problematic) of the verse. He composes a sizable and impressive discourse upon that large-scale theme. This expansion so obscures the original bounds of the verse that they no longer serve to define discourse at all. Yet in the mind of the compiler of the chapter before us, the occasion for discourse remains the cited passage. That is why the rather abstract discussion is placed here. Of great importance, the unit of discourse of the present sort exhibits a profoundly unified and cogent character. It is never a mere anthology, framed around a common topic. It rather makes a pointed and purposeful argument. The exegete of a verse of Scripture aims to serve as a philosopher of the problem presented (also) by the verse at hand. As a good thinker, he presents his ideas in a carefully composed paragraph, conforming to distinctive conventions of cogent exposition.

The instances in Genesis Rabbah chapter 78 are as follows:

78:1A–D	: God's faithfulness is shown in renewal.
[78:6	: Thigh-vein.]
78:12D–E	: Theme of accepting gifts.

In addition, the reader will find in Genesis Rabbah chapter 32, given in the appendix, the following further examples of this type of unit of discourse.

| 32:1A | : Truth and falsehood. |
| 32:1B | : Punishment of the generation of the flood. |

32:2 : God loves his fellow-craftsmen
32:3A : Testing the righteous.

ANTHOLOGIES ON TOPICS OF SCRIPTURE

Proof that the entries listed in the foregoing catalogue constitute well-composed discussions of large-scale topics derives from this final taxon, the (mere) anthology. This taxon encompasses units of discourse that cannot fairly be called unified discussions at all. Rather, in this sort of unit, we have nothing more than collections of sayings on a common theme. No effort goes into linking these sayings to one another or to showing their points in common. No cogent statement emerges from the joining of the sentences on the stated topic. Instead we find that the composer of the unit regards his work as a task of collection, and that alone. The conceptual and aesthetic failures of the items of this type highlight the achievement of the framers of the ones in the earlier three categories. Their work, with its reflection, and its adherence to canons of rational discourse and conventions of intelligible expression, finds no counterpart in the anthology. There are no anthologies in the two chapters of Genesis Rabbah at hand. This type also is uncommon in the Talmud of the Land of Israel. That fact underlines the traits of care, reflection, and thoughtful expression characteristic of the rabbinical exegetes of both Scripture and the Mishnah, showing both the Talmud and the compilations of scriptural exegeses to be purposeful compositions.

AN ALTERNATIVE TAXONOMY

Up to now we have differentiated sages' units of discourse by reference to substantive matters involving a measure of subjective judgment, e.g., the way in which they relate to and take up the verse at hand. For example, we asked, do the framers propose to cite and explain the meaning of a verse word for word? Do they expand upon its meaning? Do they expatiate upon its theme? Or do they simply collect materials pertinent to its topic? We now differentiate a much larger number of units of discourse by asking solely about their formal construction. For the reader may well object that the taxonomy just now carried out depends upon use of differentiating categories lifted directly from the Talmud of the Land of Israel. A fairer picture of how the units of discourse of Genesis Rabbah may be classified should emerge from traits not borrowed from some other place but rather revealed by the document at hand, preferably gross literary ones. Accordingly, I now present a second taxonomy, this one encompassing chapters 1–30 and 85–90 of Genesis Rabbah.

This far larger sample is worked out on the basis of the citation and placement of the key verse of a given unit of discourse. We deal with the traits of the opening part of a unit of discourse (or clearly distinct segments of the unit of discourse thereafter). We now use as our taxonomic criterion the location of the key verse—that is, the verse of the chapter of Genesis that is subject to exegesis in some way or other. I cannot think of a more superficial and formal taxonomic criterion than that. In what follows, then, to begin with we distinguish units of discourse in which a key verse is cited and *then* explained, from units of discourse in which discussion proceeds along different lines, e.g., with the key verse cited at the end. What we see is that the taxa employed just now—based upon the function of a unit of discourse—turn out to serve equally well to differentiate and categorize units of discourse as the ones followed in this unit, framed in relationship to gross formal and external traits of the passage at hand.

The taxa employed here are explained and then instances in which units of discourse exhibit the definitive traits are listed. Once again, we discover the striking fact that all the conceptual components (paragraphs) of Genesis Rabbah exhibit remarkable conceptual cogency. All units of discourse turn out to conform to one or another of a severely limited repertoire of formal possibilities, just as, we saw earlier, they conform to an equally narrow range of logical-conceptual ones. I am inclined to think the possibilities for so economical a taxonomy constitute the single most important result of this inquiry. But, as we shall see at the end, we cannot lose sight of our main point, which is to compare the way in which framers of units of discourse in Genesis Rabbah did their work with the way in which framers of units of discourse in the Talmud of the Land of Israel carried out theirs.

1. *Citation of the key verse + materials amplifying or expanding that key verse.* These materials take up the word-for-word exe-

gesis of the key verse, cited at the outset of the discourse. Amplification may be through citation of other verses.

1:4D	9:10	17:2	22:11
2:3	9:11	17:3	22:12
2:4A	9:12	17:4	23:2
2:5	9:13	17:5	23:3
3:1	9:14	17:6	23:4
3:6	10:1	18:2	23:5B–C
3:6D	10:5B	18:4	25:1
3:7	11:1	18:5	25:2
4:1	12:1	18:6	26:4
4:2	12:3	19:2	26:5
4:3	12:4	19:5	27:4
4:6A	12:9	19:6	28:4
4:7	12:10	19:8	28:6
5:1A	13:1	19:9A	28:8C
5:6	13:2	20:4	29:1
5:8	13:7	20:5	29:3–4
5:9	13:8	20:6B	30:1
6:1B	14:2	20:7	30:5
6:2	14:3	20:8	30:7
6:3A	14:4	20:9	30:8
6:5A	14:5	20:10	30:9
6:6	14:6	20:11	———
6:9	14:7	20:12	85:4
7:1	14:9	21:5	85:7
7:2A	14:10	21:6	85:9
7:4	15:2	21:8	85:10
7:5A	15:3	21:9	85:11
8:12A, C, D	15:4	22:3	85:13
9:3	15:5	22:5	85:14
9:5A	16:2	22:6A–E, I	86:2
9:6	16:3	22:7	86:3
9:7	16:4	22:8	86:6:B–D
9:8	16:5	22:9	87:8
9:9	16:6	22:10	88:2

88:4	89:4	90:2	90:5A
88:5	89:5	90:3	90:6
88:6	89:9	90:4	

2. *Citation of the key verse + materials amplifying or expanding the theme or topic of the key verse.* These materials do not take up the word-for-word exegesis of the key verse, cited at the outset.

2:1	13:12	22:13	85:6
2:2	13:14	23:1	85:8
5:2	13:16	23:5A	85:12
7:5B	13:17	23:6	86:1
8:3	14:1	24:1	86:4
8:4	15:1	24:2	86:5
8:8	15:6	24:4	86:6A
8:9	15:7	24:5	87:1
8:11A	17:1	24:6	87:4
8:12B	18:1	24:7	87:5
8:13	18:3	25:2	87:6
10:3	19:1	26:1	87:7
10:4	19:3	26:2B	87:9
10:8	19:7	26:3	87:10
10:9	19:10	28:1	88:1
11:2	19:11	28:2	88:3
11:9	19:12	28:5	88:7
11:10	20:1	30:1	89:1
12:1	20:2B	30:4	89:6
12:5	20:3	30:6	89:7
12:6	20:6A	30:10	89:8
12:15	21:1	————	90:1
12:16	21:7	85:1	90:5B
13:3	22:1	85:2	
13:9	22:2	85:3	
13:10	22:4	85:5	

3. *Discourse leading up to the citation of the key verse, e.g., an invented speech, or a parable.* This type lacks other introductory matter. The key verse then comes at the end, as the climax rather than the precipitant of discourse.

1:3B	7:3	21:3	———
1:12	9:2	21:4	87:2
2:4B	12:2	26:2A	87:3
3:6B	12:13	27:2	89:2
4:5	20:2A	29:5	89:3
5:7A	21:2	30:2	

4. *Rabbi opened/commenced + citation of a verse + parsing and exegesis of the cited verse through citation of intersecting verses.* The key verse is not at hand and not cited, but it is subject to allusion through its topic or theme. There is then secondary expansion, general discourse without word-for-word citation of verses, often ending with citation of the key verse.

1:1	1:7	5:1B	9:1
1:2	3:2	6:1A	10:2
1:5	3:3	8:1	16:1
1:6	3:8	8:2	24:3

5. *Key verse not cited at all.* In these instances the passage at hand is left behind in the construction of a unit of discourse. The placing of the (already constructed) unit of discourse then is not because the composer of the chapter imagined the unit served for a close reading of the passage at hand, but because of an intersecting theme or conception.

1:3A	3:6C [from:	6:7	11:3
1:4A–C	Judah b.	6:8	11:4
1:8, 9	R. Simon]	7:2B	11:5
1:10B	3:9	8:5	11:6
[from: Bar	4:4	8:6	11:7
Qappara]	4:6B, C, D	8:7	11:8
1:11	5:3	8:10	12:7
1:13A	5:4	8:11B	12:8
1:13B	5:5	9:4	12:11
1:14	5:7B	9:5B, C	12:12
1:15	6:3B	10:5A	12:14
3:4	6:4	10:6	13:4
3:6A	6:5B, C	10:7	13:5

13:6	17:8	26:2C	28:3
13:11	19:4	26:6	28:7
13:13	19:9B	26:7	28:8A–B
13:15	22:6F–H	27:1	29:2
17:7	23:7	27:3	

The alternative taxonomy yields results strikingly close to those already presented. When we ask whether or not a verse or key word is cited, and, if so, where and for what purpose, we turn out to locate two main types of units of discourse: (1) a great number in which the key word or verse is cited, (2) a few in which the key verse is not cited. Among the former we find close counterparts to familiar taxa.

The taxon encompassing units of discourse in which a key verse is cited and then given *word-for-word exegesis* takes in precisely the same sorts of units of discourse as fall into the category of exegesis of Scripture (or the Mishnah).

The formal taxon composed of units of discourse in which there is a citation of the key verse followed by amplification or expansion on the *theme* of the verse, without word-for-word exegesis, corresponds to the substantive taxon of units of discourse presenting amplification on the meaning of a given verse of Scripture (or the Mishnah).

The third formal taxon normally constitutes a mere variation on the second. That is, the location of the key verse—fore or aft—makes no difference in the principle of cogency established within the unit of discourse. These entries normally serve a purpose no different from the one met by the foregoing.

The most interesting taxon is the one in which there is use of a key word, *opened*, followed by discussion along self-evidently conventional lines of structure. This so-called proem turns out to correspond exactly to our earlier, Talmudic taxon in which a unit of discourse expands on problems of Scripture (or the Mishnah pericope) through the composition of a well-conceived and cogent essay, framed of cited verses of Scripture (or passages of the Mishnah) and, sometimes, secondary expansion in more general, topical terms. So here the substantive or functional principle of taxonomy produced by the Talmud and the formal one in the present exercise produce virtually identical results.

To summarize: If we differentiate units of discourse through the use and placement of key verses or words we discover that that principle of taxonomy produces pretty much the same results as those attained when we ask about the purpose or function of a unit of discourse. That is to say, the real point of differentiation is not the position of the key verse, or even whether it is cited, but whether or not it is amplified in a direct way. The compositions that begin "Rabbi X opened" materials may or may not cite the key verse at the outset. They are distinctive because they ignore it and deal solely with its theme or topic—just as do the units of discourse we earlier called "expansion on problems of Scripture." Taxonomically the results are the same.

WAYS NOT TAKEN

Only when we compare to the choices made by others the work of the earliest rabbinic compilers of scriptural exegeses shall we appreciate their distinctiveness. That they clearly made choices, doing one thing and not some other, becomes evident when we see how others did the same sort of thing. The task at hand, once more, is in two parts: composing a thought, joining one thought to another, that is, in context, (1) making up an exegesis of a verse of Scripture, (2) collecting exegeses of Scripture into compositions or collections. We proceed very rapidly to review commonplace facts.

We remind ourselves, to begin with, that exegesis of Scripture was routine and ubiquitous even in the times in which various books of the Hebrew Bible were coming into being. A simple instance of the so-called "internal-biblical" exegetical mode, for example, is given by a contrast of Ps. 106:32–33 and Num. 20:2–13. The former of the two passages supplies a motive for the action described in the latter. We begin with the story, as narrated at Num. 20:10–13:

> And Moses and Aaron gathered the assembly together before the rock, and he said to them, "Hear now, you rebels; shall we bring forth water for you out of this rock?" And Moses lifted up his hand and struck the rock with his rod twice; and water came forth abundantly, and the congregation drank, and their cattle. And the Lord said to Moses and Aaron, "Because you did not believe in me, to sanctify me in the eyes of the people of Israel, therefore you shall not bring this assembly into the land which I have given them." These are the waters of Meribah, where the people of Israel contended with the Lord, and he showed himself holy among them.

Why then did Moses strike the rock? The foregoing account at best suggests an implicit motive for his action. The author of Ps. 106:32–33 makes it explicit: "They angered him at the waters of Meribah, and it went ill with Moses on their account; for they made his spirit bitter, and he spoke words that were rash." Now what is important in this instance is simply the evidence of how, within the pages of the Hebrew Scriptures themselves, a program of exegesis people call *midrash* reaches full exposure. Furthermore, we need not hunt at length for evidence of the work of collecting such exercises in exegesis—of rewriting an old text in light of new considerations or values. Such a vast enterprise is handsomely exemplified by the book of Chronicles which, instead of merely commenting on verses, actually rewrites the stories of Samuel and Kings. Obviously, neither of these two biblical cases—the one of exegesis, the other of composition or compilation of exegeses—bears any close relationship to the problem at hand. Both serve merely to provide instances of the antiquity of both making up and also purposefully compiling exegeses of Scripture.

To gain perspective on the present materials, we turn to two fairly systematic efforts at compiling exegeses of Scripture specifically in order to make some polemical point. These present us with parallels to what is at hand in the work of the earliest composers of exegeses within the rabbinic movement. In both cases we see how things *were* done. These instances therefore demonstrate how exegetes and compilers *might* have carried out their work. Recalling the exercises already completed, we ask two questions. First, what is the character of the unit of discourse? Second, how are the units of discourse put together into a large-scale composition? For the answers to both of these questions pertinent to Genesis Rabbah may be simply stated. Units of discourse are framed so as either (1) to explain or (2) to amplify verses of Scripture. They are compiled in the order of the verses as they occur in the biblical passage at hand—two simple facts. Shall we now dismiss them as obvious, concluding this was the natural way to do things? Or shall we regard as reflective and deliberate the ways in which the framers of units of discourse of Genesis Rabbah composed their ideas, and the ways in which the redactors then put the units together, following the order of verses of Genesis itself? These questions find answers only in the comparisons now quickly to be carried out.

We turn first to two passages of exegesis, one of Hosea, the other of Nahum, found in the Essene Library of Qumran. As presented by Geza Vermes (*The Dead Sea Scrolls in English* [Harmondsworth, 1975], 230–33), the exegeses do form something we might call a collection, or at least a chapter, that is, a systematic treatment of a number of verses in sequence. Vermes's presentation is as follows:

Commentary on Hosea

In this interpretation, the unfaithful wife is the Jewish people, and her lovers are the Gentiles who have led the nation astray.

"[She knew not that] it was I who gave her [the new wine and oil], who lavished [upon her silver] and gold which they [used for Baal]" (2:8).

Interpreted, this means that [they ate and] were filled, but they forgot God who. . . . They cast His commandments behind them which He had sent [by the hand of] His servants the Prophets, and they listened to those who led them astray. They revered them, and in their blindness they feared them as though they were gods.

"Therefore I will take back my corn in its time and my wine [in its season]. I will take away my wool and my flax lest they cover [her nakedness]. I will uncover her shame before the eyes of [her] lovers [and] no man shall deliver her from out of my hand" (2:9–10).

Interpreted, this means that He smote them with hunger and nakedness that they might be shamed and disgraced in the sight of the nations on which they relied. They will not deliver them from their miseries.

"I will put an end to her rejoicing, [her feasts], her [new] moons, her Sabbaths, and all her festivals" (2:11).

Interpreted, this means that [they have rejected the ruling of the law, and have] followed the festivals of the nations. But [their rejoicing shall come to an end and] shall be changed into mourning.

"I will ravage [her vines and her fig trees], of which she said, 'They are my wage [which my lovers have given me]'. I will make of them a thicket and the [wild beasts] shall eat them. . . ." (2:12).

Commentary on Nahum

For a correct understanding of the interpretation of Nahum 2:12, the reader should bear in mind the biblical order that only the corpses of

95

executed criminals should be hanged (Deut. 21:21). Hanging men alive, i.e., crucifixion, was a sacrilegious novelty. Some translators consider the mutilated final sentence unfinished, and render it: "For a man hanged alive on a tree shall be called. . . ." The version given here seems more reasonable.

"[Where is the lions' den and the cave of the young lions?]" (2:11).

[Interpreted, this concerns] . . . a dwelling-place for the ungodly of the nations.

"Whither the lion goes, there is the lion's cub, [with none to disturb it]" (2:11b).

[Interpreted, this concerns Deme]trius king of Greece who sought, on the counsel of those who seek smooth things, to enter Jerusalem. [But God did not permit the city to be delivered] into the hands of the kings of Greece, from the time of Antiochus until the coming of the rulers of the Kittim. But then she shall be trampled under their feet. . . .

"The lion tears enough for its cubs and it chokes prey for its lionesses" (2:12a).

[Interpreted, this] concerns the furious young lion who strikes by means of his great men, and by means of the men of his council.

"[And chokes prey for its lionesses; and it fills] its caves [with prey] and its dens with victims" (2:12a–b).

Interpreted, this concerns the furious young lion [who executes revenge] on those who seek smooth things and hangs men alive, [a thing never done] formerly in Israel. Because of a man hanged alive on [the] tree, He proclaims, "Behold I am against [you, says the Lord of Hosts]."

"[I will burn up your multitude in smoke], and the sword shall devour your young lions. I will [cut off] your prey [from the earth]" (2:13):

[Interpreted] . . . "your multitude" is the bands of his army . . . and his "young lions" are . . . his "prey" is the wealth which [the priests] of Jerusalem have [amassed], which . . . Israel shall be delivered. . . .

"[And the voice of your messengers shall no more be heard]" (2:13b).

[Interpreted] . . . his "messengers" are his envoys whose voice shall no more be heard among the nations.

We simply cannot categorize these several "units of discourse" within the established framework of taxonomy suitable for the Talmud and Genesis Rabbah. For we do not have (1) a word-for-word or point-by-point reading, in light of other verses of Scripture, of the verses that are cited, let alone (2) an expansion on the topics of the verses. What we have is an entirely different sort of exegesis, namely, a reading of the verses of Scripture in light of an available scheme of concrete events. The exegete wishes to place into relationship to Scripture things that have happened in his own day.

If the generative principle of exegesis seems alien, the criterion of composition as a whole is entirely familiar. It falls within the second Yerushalmi taxon given above (84). The composer wished to present amplifications of the meaning of a verse of Scripture, not word-for-word or phrase-for-phrase interpretations. He also has not constructed a wide-ranging discussion of the theme of the verse such as we noted in the more philosophical taxon (86), let alone a mere anthology (87).

This is the main point: the framer of the passage selected a mode of constructing his unit of discourse wholly congruent with the purpose for which, to begin with, he undertook the exegesis of the passage. He wished to read the verses of Scripture in light of events. So he organized his unit of discourse around the sequence of verses of Scripture under analysis. Had he wanted, he might have provided a sequential narrative of what happened, then inserting the verse he found pertinent, thus: "X happened, and that is the meaning of (biblical verse) Y." Such a mode of organizing exegeses served the school of Matthew, but not the framer of the text at hand. I do not know why, except that everything done in early circles of Christian Jews lacks precedent in antecedent cultural-religious conventions. In any event the construction at hand is rather simple. The far more complex modes of constructing units of discourse in Genesis Rabbah serve a different purpose. They are made up, moreover, of different approaches to the exegesis of Scripture. So we see that the purpose of exegesis makes a deep impact upon not only the substance of the exegesis, but also, and especially, upon the mode of organizing the consequent collection of exegeses.

Obviously, there were diverse ways both of undertaking scriptural exegesis and of organizing the collections of such exegeses. In the setting of examples of these other ways in which earlier Jews had responded to verses of Scripture and then collected and organized their responses, we see that there was more than a single compelling way in which to do the work. It follows that the way in which the framers of Genesis Rabbah did the work was not predictable. Their mode of organization and composition therefore is not to be taken for granted. It represented a distinctive choice among available possibilities. Whether or not the people who did things this way rather than in some other had self-consciously examined the possibilities before them—knowing, for instance, what had been done, not only by the Essenes of Qumran but also by others in their scriptural community—is inconsequential. That our sages could have done things in other ways is demonstrated by the simple fact that others did things differently from them.

It may now be fairly argued that the rather episodic sets of exegeses presented to us by the Essene library of Qumran cannot be compared to the sustained and purposeful labor of both exegesis and composition revealed in the earliest rabbinic collection. Accordingly, let us turn, for a second exercise of comparison, to an exegetical passage exhibiting clear-cut and fixed forms of rhetoric, both of the exegetical passage itself, and of the composition of several exegetical passages into a large-scale discourse—hence, units of discourse to be compared with units of discourse of Genesis Rabbah. We find in the literary composition of the school of Matthew a powerful effort to provide an interpretation of verses of Scripture in line with a distinct program of interpretation. Furthermore, the selection and arrangement of these scriptural exegeses turn out to be governed by the large-scale purpose of the framers of the document as a whole.

To illustrate these two facts, I present four parallel passages, in which we find a narrative, culminating in the citation of a verse of Scripture, hence a convention of formal presentation of ideas, style and composition alike. In each case, the purpose of the narrative is not only fulfilled in itself, but also in a subscription linking the narrative to the cited verse and stating explicitly that the antecedent narrative serves to fulfill the prediction contained in the cited verse, hence a convention of theological substance. We deal with Matthew 1:18–23, 2:1–6, 2:16–18, and 3:1–3.

MT. 1:18–23

Now the birth of Jesus Christ took place in this way. When his mother Mary had been betrothed to Joseph, before they came together she was found to be with child of the Holy Spirit; and her husband Joseph, being a just man and unwilling to put her to shame, resolved to divorce her quietly. But as he considered this, behold, an angel of the Lord appeared to him in a dream, saying, "Joseph, son of David, do not fear to take Mary your wife, for that which is conceived in her is of the Holy Spirit; she will bear a son, and you shall call his name Jesus, for he will save his people from their sins." All this took place to fulfill what the Lord had spoken by the prophet: "Behold, a virgin shall conceive and bear a son, and his name shall be called Emmanuel" (which means, God with us).

MT. 2:1–6

Now when Jesus was born in Bethlehem of Judea in the days of Herod the king, behold, wise men from the East came to Jerusalem, saying, "Where is he who has been born king of the Jews? For we have seen his star in the East, and have come to worship him." When Herod the king heard this, he was troubled, and all Jerusalem with him; and assembling all the chief priests and scribes of the people, he inquired of them where the Christ was to be born. They told him, "In Bethlehem of Judea; for so it is written by the prophet: 'And you, O Bethlehem, in the land of Judah, are by no means least among the rulers of Judah; for from you shall come a ruler who will govern my people Israel.'"

MT. 2:16–18

Then Herod, when he saw that he had been tricked by the wise men, was in a furious rage, and he sent and killed all the male children in Bethlehem and in all that region who were two years old or under, according to the time which he had ascertained from the wise men. Then was fulfilled what was spoken by the prophet Jeremiah: "A voice was heard in Ramah, wailing and loud lamentation, Rachel weeping for her children; she refused to be consoled, because they were no more."

MT. 3:1–3

In those days came John the Baptist, preaching in the wilderness of Judea, "Repent, for the kingdom of heaven is at hand." For this is he who was spoken of by the prophet Isaiah when he said, "The voice of one crying in the wilderness: Prepare the way of the Lord, make his paths straight."

The four passages, as I said, show us a stunningly original mode of linking exegeses. The organizing principle derives from the sequence of events of a particular biography, rather than the sequence of verses in a given book of Scripture or of sentences of the Mishnah. The biography of the person under discussion serves as the architectonic of the composition of exegeses into a single statement of meaning. This mode of linking exegeses—that is, composing them into a large-scale collection, such as we have at hand in the earliest rabbinic compilations—shows us another way than the way taken at Qumran, on the one side, and among the fifth and sixth centuries' compilers of rabbinic collections of exegeses, on the other. Elsewhere (*Journal of Jewish Studies* 25 [1974]:263) I have shown that a few stories about the life of Hillel were linked to a sequential set of verses of Deut. 15:1ff. Perhaps someone may have thought of linking events of Hillel's life to a contiguous group of verses. But no "life" of a sage of antiquity forms the base line for a composition, whether made up of exegeses, or (more likely) of legal opinions. There are a few chapters in the Mishnah, e.g., M. Kelim chapter 24, that systematically express the generative principle of a single authority; there are many pericopes (units of discourse) framed around opinions of a single authority, and a great many around disagreements between two or more fixed names. But these are not comparable.

The passages of Matthew, therefore, indicate a clear-cut, distinctive choice on how to compose a "unit of discourse." The choice is dictated by the character and purpose of the composition at hand. Since the life of a particular person—as distinct from events of a particular character—forms the focus of discourse, telling a story connected with that life and following this with a citation of the biblical verse illustrated in the foregoing story constitutes the generative and organizing principle of the several units of discourse, all of them within a single taxon. The taxon is not only one-dimensional. It also is rather simple in both its literary traits and its organizing principle. We discern extremely tight narration of a tale, followed by a citation of a verse of Scripture, interpreted only through the device of the explicit joining language: *this (1) is what that (2) means*.

What we see so clearly in the work of the school of Matthew is a simple fact. The work of making up units of discourse and the labor of collecting these units of discourse together express a single principle, make a single statement, carry out the purposes of a single polemic. Let me give proper emphasis to this simple result.

Three things go together: (1) the principles of exegeses, (2) the purposes of exegeses, and (3) the program of collecting and arranging exegeses.

That is the fact of Matthew. It is true of Sifra. In time to come, detailed analysis of the various compilations of biblical exegeses produced at diverse places and times within Judaism, from the fifth century to the eighteenth, will tell us whether or not it is so later on as well. Meanwhile it suffices to observe that, in the present instance, what people wished to say about the meaning of a verse of Scripture and why they then proposed to collect what they had said into cogent compositions cohere. When we can say in connection with other compilations of scriptural exegeses what we think generated comments on biblical verses, and how composing these particular comments on these selected verses into compilations or compositions made sense to composers, we shall be well on the way to describing, analyzing, and interpreting the context—the life-situation—of those documents.

At this elementary stage in our work, I claim to explain only the original context in which sages first compiled collections of scriptural exegeses: *midrash* (of the rabbinical sort) in context. That is the program of the concluding chapter. But before we proceed to the final element in this account, let us stand aside and ask one further question on the traits of collections of scriptural exegeses accomplished by rabbis. It concerns those compilations other than Genesis Rabbah, with which we have dealt in detail. I refer specifically to the collections of exegeses generally supposed to have been worked out later than Genesis Rabbah, in the fifth and sixth centuries. I now shall offer an encompassing typology of all of the compositions scholars agree belong to the period of late antiquity, before the rise of Islam. In this way I place into a single taxonomic pattern the entire repertoire of compilations, and not only the exegetical collections, the context of which is here shown to be defined by the work on the Mishnah accomplished by the Talmud of the Land of Israel.

THE THREE TYPES OF COMPILATIONS
OF EXEGESES OF SCRIPTURE

Once a new kind of composition came into being, its own conventions and aesthetic were bound to undergo development in fresh ways, not limited by the ones established at the outset. The mode of compiling biblical exegeses, to be sure, would persist along the lines originally laid out in Genesis Rabbah. Accordingly, the redaction of exegeses in accord with the layout of a book of Scripture established a permanent editorial convention. But the sorts of materials gathered and, more important, the way in which units of discourse were composed to begin with would move in quite novel directions. The taxonomy established for the Talmud of the Land of Israel and Genesis Rabbah therefore proves of little use in analyzing further compilations. It is the point of origin alone, the original context of composing a book of exegeses of a book, that comes under the illumination of a shared taxonomy. From that moment, the Talmud of the Land of Israel went one way, in the direction of growth and expansion solely through commentary. The making of collections of exegeses, beginning with Genesis Rabbah, went quite a different way. Later compilers indeed took the direction of imitation and replication of the original editorial genre. But they laid emphasis upon the utilization of units of discourse of a type strikingly remote from the narrowly exegetical ones familiar to us from Genesis Rabbah. When, therefore, we reach the further compilations of exegeses generally assigned to the last two centuries of late antiquity, that is, the two hundred years prior to the Moslem conquest of the Middle East, including the Land of Israel, our original thesis reaches the end of its usefulness. The history of the formation of compositions of biblical exegeses moves forward—I should imagine—along lines dictated by its own inner logic, whether literary, aesthetic, apologetic, or theological. But I cannot say what that logic may have been.

As I said, the task before us is rapidly to bring into relationship with the taxonomy suitable for Genesis Rabbah all of those other compilations of biblical exegeses produced by the rabbinical sages in the fifth and sixth centuries. These fall into three groups, each one defined by the type of unit of discourse favored by its compilers. We differentiate among the collections in a very simple way. We know that, in the exegetical compilations in general, there are two types of units of discourse: (1) exegetical and (2) discursive. The former work through the words or phrases of a verse of Scripture. The latter take up and present wide-ranging and speculative essays on a theme. Only incidentally, if at all, do they intersect with the particular verse of Scripture that serves to link the entire construction to its larger redactional context as a collection of exegeses organized around a particular book.

For the reader's convenience, let me first list the three types of compilations of exegeses of Scripture, in accord with the present system of classification. (The appendix presents sample chapters of each).

1. *Compositions based on close reading and interpretation of verses of Scripture, one after the other:*
   Mekhilta (to parts of Exodus)
   Sifra (to Leviticus)
   Sifre Numbers
   Sifre Deuteronomy

2. *Compositions made up of both close reading of verses of Scripture and also speculative discourse on scriptural themes, not merely specific verses:*
   Genesis Rabbah
   Leviticus Rabbah

3. *Compositions made up mainly of speculative discourse on scriptural themes, rather than close reading of specific verses of Scripture:*
   Lamentations Rabbah
   Esther Rabbah I
   Pesikta de Rab Kahana
   Songs Rabbah
   Ruth Rabbah

The eleven compilations of scriptural exegeses generally supposed to have been produced by the end of the sixth century may be divided into three groups in accord with the two types of units of discourse their respective composers drew together. (1) One group consists of collections of comments upon Scripture that are narrowly exegetical. These deal with words and phrases, at most with complete verses. Rarely, if ever, do they generalize or expand discourse to encompass a single theme as unpacked in numerous verses of Scripture. (3) The opposite extreme is marked by collections of exegeses of verses of Scripture that are topical. These units of discourse are focused upon the exposition of a given theme through wide-ranging allusions to a great variety of verses. (2) The middle range of compilations is made up of collections of both types of material.

In the appendix I give a sample chapter of each of the eleven compilations of exegeses of Scripture believed to have come to closure before the end of the sixth century. The reader will readily observe that the first four, centered on Pentateuchal books, fall into the category of predominantly exegetical compilations. I shall have more to say about this group in the concluding section.

The next two form a middle group. Genesis Rabbah, we know, presents a fair balance between the two types of units of discourse, with a tendency toward the narrowly exegetical. Leviticus Rabbah favors the more broadly discursive sort of unit of discourse, though it does contain the other kind.

The remaining five compilations exhibit only passing connections to particular verses of Scripture. They are made up of units of discourse of a quite different sort from those that predominate in the collections of Pentateuchal exegeses, inclusive of Genesis Rabbah and Leviticus Rabbah.

The setting and purpose for which these sorts of units of wide-ranging discourse—general rather than narrowly exegetical—were made up and then composed into large-scale collections define problems for future investigation. The simple equation on which this chapter rests simply is not relevant to them. They are in no way like the Talmud of the Land of Israel in their approach to the problem of Scripture. But they are very much like Genesis Rabbah, the center of our interest, in *its* approach to the problem of Scripture. That is to say, they take as a critical mode of discourse saying things through incessant, indeed obsessive, citation of biblical verses. And that is the critical definition of a compilation of exegeses of Scripture.

We now have no tested means of dating the various compilations before us. The most recent systematic discussion of all of them, the several articles by M. D. Heer in *Encyclopaedia Judaica*, takes the plausible position that the Talmud of the Land of Israel stands aloof from the materials of these compilations in general. Hence, Heer generally holds, they all come after the closure of that document. The order in which Heer lists them, which I follow, is to start with type 1, the compositions made up almost entirely of narrowly exegetical units of discourse and to end up with type 3, the compilations of almost entirely discursive ones. We cannot demonstrate that that is the chronological order in which the documents reached their present condition. To be sure, it may be regarded as more "reasonable" to approach them in this order. But we cannot show that it is the order in which the collections actually reached closure.

Accordingly, the classification of the documents on the face of it rests on no historical evidence. It is a classification based on timeless traits of preferences among types of materials to be collected and arranged. We do not know when those various units of discourse themselves were composed. Nor can we say that people thought it better to do one kind before they chose to make up the other. It is not to be taken for granted that people who did the one would not do the other. I emphasize the simple proposition that the sort of unit of discourse that is used bears remarkable correspondence to the purpose for which units of discourse are collected and strung together. Would that we could state the reasons why people made up the collections of exegeses at hand—their points of emphasis and insistence, recurrent issues, restated propositions, persistent and obsessive concerns! Then we should have a measure of insight into the problems that might have generated both the gathering of units of discourse and—in the nature of things—and also the making up of units of discourse to register the besought propositions. But at this time we have no knowledge whatsoever of the large and unifying traits, the evident polemic of the composers or collectors, revealed throughout a document. So these indicators to define a single compilation of exegeses remain for future inquiry.

I proposed earlier that the authors of the Sifra wished to make quite specific statements about the appropriate origin of the laws contained (also) in the Mishnah. But my judgment of the matter rests upon an analysis of less than a third of the entire document. The pertinent evidence, moreover, by no means covers the surface of the Sifra, but only a part of it. Accordingly, at best I could suggest, on the basis of a sample, what I thought collectors and framers of the entirety of the document wished to say. It remains to be demonstrated through a complete analysis of the whole. And for all the other compilations, we do not even have so much as a thesis worthy of inquiry—even impressions or intelligent guesses.

Let me give a second instance of a sort of question awaiting inquiry. We begin with the simple fact that framers of collections of exegeses of Scripture ordinarily selected as the framework of organizing units of discourse (whatever the characteristics of the units of discourse) the order of the verses of a book of Scripture. That was the self-evident mode of organizing discourse for the Essene exegete at Qumran, working on Hosea and Nahum (among other books). It seems the obvious way to the composer of all the Pentateuchal compilations of exegeses as well. That choice might appear to us natural and predictable—if we did not find a document the organizer of which rejected that principle in favor of some other. Now we have a compilation, Pesikta de Rab Kahana, that rejects the mode of organizing units of discourse in accord with the order of verses of Scripture, which is characteristic of the other ten collections. The framer of Pesikta de Rab Kahana instead arranged materials as he thought they pertained to the sacred calendar. Perhaps what this represents is a logical third step in the unfolding of redactional principles. First comes a close reading of a verse of Scripture, arranged in accord with the order of verses of Scripture. Then comes a discursive treatment of a general theme of Scripture, no longer bound to the limits of a particular verse, yet organized in line with the order of verses. Why stick so close to the order of verses, if discourse moves far beyond the bounds of any one verse? Once the substance broadens, the principle of organizing units of discourse may shift away from particular verses of Scripture altogether. That is a natural third step. For aggregates of materials around a given theme or topic, rather than around a given verse of Scripture, may just as well be combined in accord with schema quite separate from the order of verses of a given book of the Hebrew Scriptures. In such a case, what does it matter whether the schema derives from the holy days of the year or from some other construct altogether?

To conclude: if, as I imagine, there are points of insistence, if the compilers of the materials wished to make particular points or statements by collecting units of discourse serviceable to make these statements, if the writers of units of discourse furthermore had in mind laying emphasis upon a given proposition rather than some other—if all of these things are so, not a single one of them has yet sustained investigation. Nor do the purposes of my argument in this book require that we do more than point toward the vast, as yet unexplored, territory of darkness lying beyond the illuminated boundaries of the present argument and its requirements. The allusions to the probable polemic of the Sifra and to the likely problematic represented by the (in context) odd mode of organization chosen for Pesikta de Rab Kahana therefore serve only a modest purpose. I mean to point out that the framing of the compilations of exegeses, and, we now surmise, the making up of what is to be collected and organized—the unit of discourse itself—present occasions for analysis of each of the compilations in its own terms. What I think I have shown for Genesis Rabbah suggests points of entry into the study of other compilations of exegeses. But the traits of all compilations await description, analysis, and interpretation. It is sufficient to point to some definitive qualities awaiting closer attention than has yet gone to them. I refer, first, to traits of comparison and contrast between one compilation and another, affording the possibility of large-scale taxonomy. I mean, second, traits of insistence and emphasis, making likely further inquiry into the interplay between exegeses and contexts. That is the main point of interest to me, the encounter between the story of the rabbinic exegesis of Scripture and the history of the Jewish people. Those intellectuals among the Jewish people who undertook the exegesis and proposed therefore to make sense of that history form the point of interest. For they made Judaism.

. . . AS COMPILATIONS OF EXEGESES
ARE TO SCRIPTURE

The equation that forms the center of inquiry thus far has served for analysis of the types of units of discourse in Genesis Rabbah. The reason is that that compilation presents a striking balance between the two types of units of discourse. We may now take one step further, however, guided by two important facts. First, one of the principal exegetical interests of the Talmud of the Land of Israel focuses upon finding biblical foundations for Mishnaic rules. Associated with this interest, second, is the determination to supply a close reading of the sentences of the Mishnah paragraph itself. These are striking decisions, in light of the indifference to the same issues and exegetical style of other framers of units of discourse and other composers of such units into compilations. Accordingly, we note that a persistent trait of units of discourse of the Talmud of the Land of Israel is a close reading of one text in light of the other, of the Mishnah in light of Scripture.

Now when we review the repertoire of units of discourse of the Sifra, Sifre Numbers, and Sifre Deuteronomy, compilations of exegeses of Leviticus, Numbers, and Deuteronomy, we are struck, first of all, by their taxonomical uniformity. Nearly all units of discourse fall into the same taxon, for they take up a single issue, the close reading of a verse of Scripture. A fair portion of them, moreover, belongs within a single sub-classification, for they examine the relationship of that verse to laws (also) found in the Mishnah. These three collections, overall, may therefore serve as a mirror image and counterpart of the numerous units of discourse of the Talmud of the Land of Israel which do the same thing in reverse: close reading of a passage of the Mishnah, with attention to the relationship of that passage to a verse of Scripture.

In a rather general way, therefore, we observe that the equation at hand holds for the other compilations of exegeses on Pentateuchal books, that is, Sifra and the two Sifres, for Leviticus, Numbers, and Deuteronomy, just as it does for Genesis and, in diminished measure, Leviticus, in Genesis Rabbah and Leviticus Rabbah, respectively.

If Mekhilta de R. Ishmael could be shown to derive from the period at hand, the Pentateuchal repertoire would be complete. Most authorities maintain that Mekhilta indeed is contemporary with Sifra and the two Sifres. But sufficient grounds for doubt exist to prevent further discussion of that collection in this context. Specifically, Ben Zion Wacholder, "The Date of the Mekilta de-Rabbi Ishmael," *Hebrew Union College Annul* 39 (1968), 117, calls into question the assumption that that composition derives from the authorities behind the Mishnah cited therein by name and maintains that the composition is pseudepigraphic and "may not be dated much later than the year 800." While I am puzzled by some of Wacholder's procedures (see my *Development of a Legend* [Leiden: Brill, 1970], xiii–xiv, n. 1), I believe the question long settled has been reopened by him. But so far as I know, no one has yet questioned the prevailing assumption that Sifra, Sifre Numbers, and Sifre Deuteronomy derive from the period at hand, though opinion is divided on what part of the period (we speak, after all, of five hundred years!). Still, it would appear that one phase in compiling exegeses of Scripture saw the provision of such collections for most, or possibly all, of the Torah of Moses, the Pentateuch.

We may now take yet one step further. The compilations of exegeses subjecting sequences of particular verses of Scripture to close reading—Sifra, Sifre Numbers, Sifre Deuteronomy, in particular—bear comparison to a very particular part of the Talmud of the Land of Israel. In a landmark monograph, *The Talmud of Caesarea, Supplement to Tarbiz 2* (Jerusalem, 1931, in Hebrew), Saul Lieberman demonstrated that three Talmudic tractates, the ones devoted to civil law, Baba Qamma, Baba Mesia, and Baba Batra, are different from the other thirty-six of the Yerushalmi. The code of civil law reached closure in Caesarea, ca. 350, that is, about a half-century before the other thirty-six tractates were finished. Study of these three tractates shows that they differ from all the others not only in the many ways outlined by Lieberman, but in an aspect strikingly relevant to our inquiry.

Specifically, the tractates of Caesarea are made up of only two sorts of material. These are, first, units of discourse that take up the language of the Mishnah passage at hand and subject it to a close and careful reading, and, second, units of discourse that cite pertinent complementary materials of the Tosefta and do the same to those passages. Accordingly, the tractates of Caesarea are composed of units of discourse of a narrowly exegetical character, and of such units of discourse alone. (The exceptions to the rule are statistically negligible.) In this context we observe that the composers of the exegetical compilations, on Pentateuchal law, the aforementioned Sifra for Leviticus, Sifres for Numbers and Deuteronomy, respectively, exhibit a similar preference for units of discourse of one kind—that same kind only. That point of preference is such as to suggest an equation along the lines of the one under investigation:

$$\frac{\text{Caesarean tractates of Yerushalmi}}{\text{The Mishnah (of those tractates)}} = \frac{\text{Sifra and Sifre}}{\text{Scripture (Lev., Num., Deut.)}}$$

We have traveled so far from our original point of departure that it again is time to recapitulate the main argument. This may be done with appropriate economy.

First, types of units of discourse that we find in the Talmud of the Land of Israel and the ones that comprise Genesis Rabbah fall into precisely the same categories and only into those categories. As just now noted, types of units of discourse in tractates of the civil law and those that make up Sifra and the two Sifres likewise exhibit the same monothetic taxonomical traits.

Second, these simple facts of taxonomy then are to be joined to a further datum. It is generally supposed that the work of composing the first rabbinic collection of exegeses of Scripture to take up non-legal portions of the Pentateuch (or any other part of the Hebrew Bible), Genesis Rabbah, came at about the same time as the labor of composing the Talmud of the Land of Israel. Whatever the origin of the materials brought together and formed into a composition, the final composition turns out to be made up of materials framed in accord with the same principles of cogent discourse and, hence, for the purpose of the same sort of exegesis, as the ones in the Talmud of the Land of Israel. Taxonomically, all that changes is the document subjected to exegesis (as well, of course, as what is said about it). Because the modes of thought and discourse turn out to exhibit precisely the same definitive traits and only those traits, they sustain a remarkably monothetic taxonomy. Third, that is why I propose the simple equation:

The Talmud of the Land of Israel is to the Mishnah as compilations of exegesis are to Scripture.

Now that that fact has been shown to be sound, we explore its consequences for the interpretation of the shared context of both the Talmud of the Land of Israel and books made up of compositions of exegeses. To state the ultimate question simply: we now wish to ask about the historical circumstances in which the work of creating both the larger part of the Talmud of the Land of Israel and some of the collections of scriptural exegeses took place. The inquiry into context turns to the rapid description of social and political, intellectual (that is, theological), literary, and religious dimensions of the national life of Israel in the Land of Israel. For the life of the nation is lived in many dimensions: in society, in mind, in imagination, in the heart and soul. Among them all we seek the measure of *midrash*.

5

Revelation, Canon, and Scriptural Authority

NATIONAL CONTEXT: ISRAEL IN THE
LAND OF ISRAEL IN THE AGE OF
THE MAKING OF THE TALMUD
AND COMPILATIONS OF
SCRIPTURAL EXEGESES

The path from literary analysis to religious insight leads through the history of the community. The context addressed by the sacred writings, old and new, and sustained by the theological convictions and religious experience contained in them, defines the issues, so governs the content of the faith. To speak of the Torah of Israel, therefore, we have first to address the condition of the nation of Israel, the Jewish people. Accordingly, to interpret conviction, we begin with a description of context. True, conviction resists reduction to the status of a mere function of circumstance. Truth is truth. Revelation is not contained in what merely takes place by accident in time. But the believing community wrote books in some one place, at some specific time, not elsewhere and on another day. So we have to ask ourselves, why at just this time and in just this place did sages (or some of them) think it important to say just what they said to Israel? And first we have to speak of who the people of Israel were, and what was happening to them, in that place and in that day, in which rabbis made the statements now before us.

For nearly everyone in the Roman world the most important events of the fourth and fifth centuries, the period in which the Talmud of the Land of Israel and collections of exegeses were coming into being, were, first, the legalization of Christianity, followed very rapidly by the adoption of Christianity as the state's most favored religion, and then by the delegitimization of paganism (and systematic degradation of Judaism). The astonishing advent of legitimacy and even power provoked Christian intellectuals to rewrite Christian and world history and work out theology in reflection on this new polity and its meaning in the unfolding of human history. A new commonwealth was coming into being, taking over the old and reshaping it for the new age. In 312 C.E. Constantine achieved power in the West. In 323 he took the government of the entire Roman empire into his own hands. He had promulgated the edict of Milan in 313, whereby Christianity attained the status of toleration. Christians and all others were given "the free power to follow the religion of their choice." In the next decade Christianity became the most favored religion. Converts from Judaism were protected and could not be punished by Jews. Christians were freed of the obligation to perform pagan sacrifices. Priests were exempted from certain taxes. Sunday became an obligatory day of rest. Celibacy was permitted. From 324 onward Constantine ceased to maintain a formal impartiality, now intervening in the affairs of the Church, settling quarrels among believers, and calling the Church Council at Nicaea (325) to settle issues of the faith. He was baptized only on the eve of his death in 337. Over the next century the pagan cults were destroyed, their priests deprived of support, their intellectuals bereft of standing.

So far as the Jews of the Land of Israel were concerned, not much changed at the Milvian Bridge in 312, when Constantine conquered in the sign of Christ. The sages' writings nowhere refer explicitly to that event. They scarcely gave testimony to its consequences for the Jews, and continued to harp upon prohibited relationships with "pagans" in general, as though nothing had changed from the third century to the fourth and fifth. Legal changes affecting the Jews under Constantine's rule indeed were not substantial. Jews could not proselytize; they could not circumcise slaves when they bought them; Jews could not punish other Jews who became Christians. Jews, finally, were required to serve on municipal councils wherever they lived, an onerous task involving responsibility for collecting taxes. But those who served synagogues, and patriarchs and priests, were still exempted from civil and personal obligations. In the reign of Constantius III (337–361), further laws aimed at separating Jews from Christians were enacted, in the Canons of Elvira of 339. These forbade intermarriage between Jews and Christians, further protected converts, and forbade Jews to hold slaves of Christian or other gentile origin.

The reversion to paganism on the part of the emperor Julian, ca. 360, brought a measure of favor to Jews and Judaism. To embarrass Christianity, he permitted the rebuilding of the Temple at Jerusalem. But he died before much progress could be made. In the aftermath of the fiasco of Julian's reversion to paganism, the Christians, returning to power, determined to make certain such a calamity would never recur. Accordingly, over the next century they undertook a sustained attack on the institutions and personnel of paganism in all its expressions. The long-term and systematic effort eventually overspread Judaism as well. From the accession of Theodosius II in 383 to the death of his son, Arcadius, in 408, Judaism came under attack. In the earlier part of the fifth century, Jews' rights and the standing of their corporate communities were substantially affected. The patriarchate of the Jews of the Land of Israel, the ethnarch and his administration, was abolished. So from the turn of the fifth century, the government policy meant to isolate Jews, lower their status, and suppress their agencies of self-rule.

Laws against intermarriage posed no problem to the Jews. The ones limiting proselytism and those protecting converts from Judaism did not affect many people. But the edicts that reduced Jews to second-class citizenship did matter. They were not to hold public office, but still had to sit on city councils responsible for the payment of taxes. Later, they were removed from the councils, though remaining obligated, of course, for taxes. Between 404 and 438 Jews were forbidden to hold office in the civil service, represent cities, serve in the army or at the bar, and ultimately were evicted from every public office. In all, the later fourth and fifth centuries for Israel in its land marked a time of significant change. Once a mere competing faith, Christianity now became paramount. The period from Julian's fall onward, moreover, presented to Israel problems of a profoundly religious character. To these we now turn.

RELIGIOUS CONTEXT: THE CRISIS OF TRIUMPHANT CHRISTIANITY AND THE APOLOGETIC TASK

There were five events of fundamental importance for the history of Judaism in the fourth and fifth centuries. All of them but the last were well-known in their own day. These were as follows: (1) the conversion of Constantine, (2) the fiasco of Julian's plan to rebuild the temple of Jerusalem, (3) the depaganization of the Roman empire, a program of attacks on pagan temples and, along the way, synagogues, (4) the Christianization of the majority of the population of Palestine, and (5) the creation of the Talmud of the Land of Israel and of compositions of scriptural exegeses. The Talmud and the exegetical compilations came into being in an age of high crisis, hope, and then disaster. Vast numbers of Jews now found chimerical the messianic expectation, as they had framed it around Julian's plan to rebuild the Temple. So it was a time of boundless expectations followed by bottomless despair.

Let us briefly review from the present perspective the four events that framed the setting for the fifth, starting with Constantine's conversion. The first point is that we do not know how Jews responded to Constantine's establishment of Christianity as the most favored religion. But in the Land of Israel itself his works were well-known, since he and his mother purchased many sites believed connected with Israel's sacred history and built churches and shrines at them. They rewrote the map of the Land of Israel. Every time they handled a coin, moreover, Jews had to recognize that something of fundamental importance had shifted, for the old pagan images were blotted out as Christian symbols took their place—public events indeed!

A move of the empire from reverence of Zeus to adoration of Mithra meant nothing; paganism was what it was, lacking all differentiation in the Jewish eye. Christianity was something else. It was different. It was like Judaism. Christians read the Torah and claimed to declare its meaning. Accordingly, the trend of sages' speculation cannot have avoided the issue of the place, within the Torah's messianic pattern, of the remarkable turn in world history represented by the triumph of Christianity. Since the Christians now celebrated confirmation of their faith in Christ's messiahship, and, at the moment, Jews were hardly prepared to concur, it falls surely within known patterns for us to suppose that Constantine's conversion would have been identified with some dark moment to prefigure the dawning of the messianic age.

If, second, people were then looking for a brief dawn, the emperor Julian's plan to rebuild the ruined Temple in Jerusalem must have dazzled their eyes. For while Constantine surely raised the messianic question, for a brief hour Emperor Julian appeared decisively to answer it. In 361 the now-pagan Julian gave permission to rebuild the Temple. Work briefly got underway, but stopped because of an earthquake. The intention of Julian's plan was quite explicit. Julian had had in mind to falsify the prophecy of Jesus that not one stone of the temple would be left upon another. We may take for granted that, since Christ's prophecy had not been proven false, many surely concluded that it indeed had now been shown true. We do not know that Jews in numbers drew the conclusion that, after all, Jesus really was the Christ. Many Christians said so. In the next half-century, Palestine gained a Christian majority. Christians were not slow to claim their faith had been proved right. We need not speculate on the depth of disappointment felt by those Jews who had hoped that the project would come to fruition and herald, instead of the Christian one, the Messiah they awaited.

Third, as we noted above, the last pagan emperor's threat to Christianity made urgent the delegitimization of paganism. The formation of a new and aggressive policy toward outsiders caught Judaism in the net too. To be sure, Jews were to be protected. But the sword unsheathed against the pagan cult places, if sharp, was untutored. It was not capable of discriminating among non-Christian centers of divine service. Nor could those who wielded it, zealots of the faith in church and street, have been expected to. The non-Christian Roman government protected synagogues and punished those who damaged them. Its policy was to extirpate paganism but protect a degraded Judaism. But the faithful of the church had their own ideas. The assault against pagan temples spilled over into an ongoing program of attacking synagogue property.

Still worse from the Jews' viewpoint, a phenomenon lacking much precedent over the antecedent thousand years now came into view: random attacks on Jews by reason of their faith, as distinct from organized struggles among contending and equal forces, Jewish and other mobs. The long-established Roman tradition of toleration of Judaism and of Jews, extending back to the time of Julius Caesar and applying both in law and in custom, now drew to a close. A new fact, at this time lacking all basis in custom and in the policy of state and Church alike, faced Jews: physical insecurity in their own villages and towns. So Jews' synagogues and their homes housed the same thing, which was to be eradicated: Judaism. A mark of exceptional piety came to consist in violence against Jews' holy places, their property and persons. Coming in the aftermath of the triumph of Christianity, on the one side, and the decisive disproof of the Jews' hope for the rebuilding of the Temple, on the other, was the hitherto-unimagined war against the Jews. In the last third of the fourth century and the beginning of the fifth, this war raised once again those questions about the meaning and end of history that Constantine, at the beginning of the age at hand, had forced upon Israel's consciousness.

Fourth, at this time there seems to have been a sharp rise in the numbers of Christians in the Holy Land. Christian refugees from the West accounted for part of the growth. But we have stories about how Jews converted as well. The number of Christian towns and villages dramatically increased. If Jews did convert in sizable numbers, then we should have to point to the events of the preceding decades as ample validation in their eyes for the Christian interpretation of history. Jews had waited nearly three hundred years, from the destruction in 70 C.E. to the promise of Julian. Instead of being falsified, Jesus' prophecy had been validated. No stone had been left on stone in the Temple, not after 70, not after 361, just as Jesus had said. Instead of a rebuilt Temple, the Jews looked out on a world in which now even their synagogues came under threat, and, along with them, their own homes and persons. What could be more ample proof of the truth of the Christians' claim than the worldly triumph of their Church? Resisted for so long, that claim called into question, as in the time of Bar Kokhba, whether it was worth waiting any longer for a messiah that had not come when he was most needed. With followers proclaiming the messiah who *had* come now possessing the world, the question could hardly be avoided.

No one may argue that, because a fair part of the population of the Land of Israel, possibly including numbers of Jews, evidently adopted Christianity after the conversion of Constantine, (particularly in the aftermath of the failure of Julian's plan to build the Temple, and the beginning of the Christian war against synagogue buildings and the start of chronic Jewish insecurity) the population that converted did so on account of the cumulative effect of these events. Why claim *post hoc, ergo propter hoc*? We merely observe a familiar pattern: (1) messianic hope, (2) post-messianic disillusion, (3) book. This pattern had played itself out two hundred years earlier, in the second century, the time of the Bar Kokhba war, messianic war, post-war disillusion, the Mishnah. Along these same lines, we notice in the later fourth and fifth centuries, (1) the messianic hope, aroused by Julian, (2) the deep disappointment consequent upon the failure to rebuild the Temple, and (3) the composition of both the Talmud of the Land of Israel and also important collections of scriptural exegeses, particularly including Genesis Rabbah, constructed of materials of essentially the same intellectual fabric. It is in this context that we interpret the formation of these fundamental documents of Judaism in the Land of Israel.

What were the tasks to be carried out through the writing of these books in behalf of, and within, the Jewish community, to which the framers addressed their work? First and foremost, there was the one brought to the forefront by the calamities of the later fourth and fifth centuries: apologetics. Whether or not the Christians now pointed to historical events as proof that Jesus indeed had been Christ, and that Israel-after-the-flesh had been punished for rejecting him as the Messiah, we do not know. These messages to be sure were standard. But we cannot demonstrate that, in just these decades, Jews paid attention to them. Still, they did not have to turn to Christian critics to tell them what they surely recognized on their own. Israel's condition in its own land proved ever more parlous. The status of "the Torah" declined, and, with it, the standing and security of Israel. Whatever the world may have said, Jews themselves surely had to wonder whether history was headed in the right direction, and whether indeed the Christians, emerging from within Israel itself, may not initially have been right. For the Empire now was Christian. Israel's most recent bout with the messianic fever had proved disastrous. Julian's Temple had not been built. If, as is surely likely, some Jews thought that the building of that Temple would mean the Messiah was near at hand—or in fact had come —then the failure to build the Temple meant the Messiah was not near, or never would come in the way Jews expected. The requirement to construct an apologetics therefore emerged from the condition of Israel, whether or not, in addition, Christian polemicists had a hearing among Jews.

If, now, we inquire into what in fact sages did at that time, the answer is clear. They composed the Talmud of the Land of Israel as we know it. They collected exegeses of Scripture and made them into systematic and sustained accounts of, initially, the meaning of the Pentateuch (assuming dates in these centuries for Sifra, the two Sifres, Genesis Rabbah and Leviticus Rabbah). So on the face of it we have to ask about the utility, for the larger apologetic exercise, of the editorial work done at that time.

When we recall what Christians had to say to Israel, we may find entirely reasonable the view that compiling scriptural exegeses constituted part of a Jewish apologetic response. For one Christian message had been that Israel "after the flesh" had distorted and continually misunderstood the meaning of what had been its own Scripture. Failing to read the Old Testament in the light of the New, the prophetic promises in the perspective of Christ's fulfillment of those promises, Israel "after the flesh" had lost access to God's revelation to Moses at Sinai. If we were to propose a suitably powerful, yet appropriately proud, response, it would have two qualities. First, it would supply a complete account of what Scripture had meant, and always must mean, as Israel read it. Second, it would do so in such a way as not to dignify the position of the other side with the grace of an explicit reply at all.

The compilations of exegeses accomplished at this time assuredly take up the challenge of restating the meaning of the Torah revealed by God to Moses at Mount Sinai. This the sages did in a systematic and thorough way. At the same time, if the charges of the other side precipitated the work of compilation and composition, the consequent collections in no way suggest so. The issues of the documents are made always to emerge from the inner life not even of Israel in general, but of the sages' estate in particular. Scripture was thoroughly rabbinized, as earlier it had been Christianized. None of this suggests the other side had won a response for itself. Only the net effect—a complete picture of the whole, as Israel must perceive the whole of revelation—suggests the extraordinary utility for apologetics, outside as much as inside the faith, served by these same compilations. And that utility is discerned only by us, long after the fact and only in general.

In this same context we also observe that the rabbis' insistence on the authority of traditions in addition to Scripture, laws contained then in the Mishnah and whatever other documents sages treasured, had long provoked a further polemic. The other side held that Israel not only could not read and understand the ancient revelation of God to Moses at Mount Sinai. Israel furthermore had changed and falsified that revelation. This was by adding things not in the Old Testament or by changing the substance of the law through appeal to other sources of truth than Sinai. A ready answer to this critique, surely deriving from within Israel, emerged from the systematic provision of biblical proof-texts for the Mishnah. To claim that people looked for proof-texts for the Mishnah in order to know what to answer the other side is excessive. Ample motivation for undertaking the same search was simply that Jews, as much as outsiders within the larger scriptural commonwealth, were asking the same questions. So in doing what they did for the Mishnah, sages indeed provided a suitable reply, at least for themselves.

A still more powerful apologetic for Judaism emerged from the implicit conviction, everywhere present and always taken for granted in sages' writings, that things in ancient times were precisely as they had emerged in the life of present-day Israel. The insistence of all compilations of scriptural exegeses as much as of the Talmud was that ancient Israel had always lived in accord with the rabbis' vision of Israel. The innocent anachronism, projecting backward patterns of belief and behavior of sages' own world and time, of course is to be expected. Any other conception in context was unthinkable. But the uses of anachronism are many. One important instance, in the present argument, as we shall see, turns out to be the identification of David, in particular, as a rabbi and as the model for the rabbis of the later age as well. But David was also the Messiah's progenitor, so the Messiah would be like a rabbi. Given the crisis of faith precipitated by the triumph of Christianity and the disappointment of the messianic hope of Judaism, we may hardly wonder at the uses to which this particular expression of the prevailing anachronism might be put in the salvific debates of the age.

The framers of both the Talmud and collections of scriptural exegeses naturally took for granted that the world they knew in the fourth and fifth centuries had flourished a thousand and more years earlier. The values they embodied and the supernatural powers they fantasized for themselves were predictably projected backward onto biblical figures. The ubiquitous citation of biblical proof-texts in support of both legal and theological statements shows the mentality of the sages. In their imagination, everything they said stood in direct continuity with what Scripture had stated. Biblical and rabbinical authorities lived on a single plane of being, in a single age of shared discourse.

Now to proceed to interpret the matter at hand, we have to step aside for a moment and review the point of emphasis of the Mishnah's system. Only then do we see the transformation effected over two hundred years. The Mishnah had presented a system of sanctification. Its emphasis lay upon the creation of a world of order and stability, perfected as the world had been at the moment of its original creation. When the world was wholly in place, then, as when God had made the world, God would finish the world and sanctify it. Now when we address the questions of Messiah, the meaning and end of history, the rescue of Israel from its political circumstance, we deal not with *sanctification* but with the *salvation* of Israel—a different dimension of being and of meaning altogether. Sanctification constitutes a category of ontology; salvation, an issue of eschatology and so of ongoing history. To be holy is to *be*. To be saved is to be saved *from* something and *for* something. The language of the Mishnah is a language of holiness, and the language at hand, with its interest in events and their meaning, with history and eschatology, is a language of salvation. So we have to recognize that the issues, at least as I attempt to outline them, testify to a massive shift, from a system of stasis and sanctification, with slight interest in historical events, to a system of movement toward salvation, with intense attention to what was happening.

If, then, we speak no longer of sanctification but rather of salvation, we now recognize what has changed. Exegesis of Scripture, with attention to the particular, Messianic (Davidic) passages at hand, signals a shift in the depths of sages' conception of what is important. That is why what is consequential in this emphasis upon (to us) anachronistic exegesis is the theory of salvation thereby given its clearest statement. What was the rabbis' view of salvation? Seeing Scripture in their own model, they took the position that the Torah of old, its supernatural power and salvific promise, in their own day continued to endure among themselves. In consequence, the promise of salvation contained in every line of Scripture was to be kept in every deed of learning and obedience to the law effected under their auspices. To be sure they projected backward the things they cherished in an act of (to us) extraordinary anachronism. But in their eyes they carried forward, to their own time, and themselves embodied the promise of salvation for Israel contained within the written Torah of old.

In this aspect the mode of thought and the consequent salvific proposition conformed to the model revealed likewise in the Gospel of Matthew. The reason Scripture was cited, for both statements on Israel's salvation—that of Matthew, that of the exegetical compositions—was not to establish or validate authority alone. Rather, it was to identify what was happening at just that time with what had happened long ago. The purpose then was not merely to demonstrate and authenticate the *bona fide* character of a new figure of salvation. It was to show the continuity of the salvific process. The point is that the figure at hand was not new at all. He stood as a renewed exemplar and avatar of Israel's eternal hope, now come to full realization—a very different thing. Authenticity hardly demanded demonstration of scriptural origin. That was the datum of the more extreme claim laid down in the profoundly anachronistic reading accorded to Scripture. In finding *sages* in the (written) Torah, therefore, the sages of the exegetical compositions and the Talmud implicitly stated a view of themselves as the continuation and model of the sanctified way of life of the written Torah. It followed that the pattern and promise of salvation contained therein found full embodiment in their teachings and way of life. That is the meaning of the explicit reading of the present into the past. It is the implicit arrogation of the hope of the past to the salvific heroes of the present: themselves.

Who can imagine, therefore, a more powerful apologetic to offer the disappointed, indeed despairing community of Israel than the simple one contained in the sages' systematic reading and exposition of the meaning of the ancient Scriptures of Israel? To be sure, we do not know who listened to the apologetic. But the Jewish nation indeed continued in its land down to the Sasanian Persian and later Arab conquests and beyond. The nation took an active part in the wars of the early seventh century; it remained numerous and effective, So someone must have heard the sages' message, or the nation surely would have disintegrated and amalgamated into the new Israel, now everywhere triumphant.

The labor of exegesis takes on still more concrete interest when we make explicit the salvific message contained within the method itself, I mean, the methodical reading of the old in terms of the new life of Israel, the Jewish nation. To state matters simply, if Moses, "our rabbi," and David, King of Israel, were (as sages everywhere

121

claimed) like a rabbi today, then a rabbi today stood as successor to the throne of Moses, our rabbi, and reveal God's will. A rabbi today could be the son of David who was to come as King of Israel. It is not surprising, therefore, that among the many biblical heroes whom the rabbis treated as sages, principal and foremost was Moses, treated as the model of the rabbi, and David, made into a messianic rabbi or a rabbinical Messiah. David as the sage of the Torah served as avatar and model for the sages of their own time. That view was made explicit in detail. If, for instance, a rabbi was jealous to have his traditions cited in his own name, it was because that was David's stated view as well. In more general terms, both David and Moses are represented as students of Torah, just like the disciples and sages of the current time. Here is one minor example.

> Y. Sanhedrin 2:6. [IV.A] It is written, "And David said longingly, 'O that someone would give me water to drink from the well of Bethlehem [which is by the gate]'" (1 Chron. 11:17).
> [B] R. Hiyya bar Ba said, "He required a teaching of law."
> [C] "Then the three mighty men broke through [the camp of the Philistines]" (1 Chron. 11:18).
> [D] Why three? Because the law is not decisively laid down by fewer than three.

The triviality of the foregoing instance of the rabbinization of scriptural heroes, including David himself, should underline the larger importance of the process. It is simply taken for granted that David was a rabbi. If he wanted water, it could only mean, the "water of the Torah." If he sent three soldiers, it was because three judges were needed. So the military tale is turned into a Torah story. Every detail of the verses of Scripture is read in the light of a totally alien program.

This sort of rereading of Scripture encompassed a vast number of passages. What is important for our argument is that, in particular, Moses and David were turned into principal rabbis and models for the rabbis of the new age. No one could miss the deep meaning. Through representing Moses, David, and other biblical heroes as they did, the framers of the exegetical compilations and of the Talmud provided a considerable body of evidence of Israel's continuing hope. For, through the labor of exegesis of Mishnah and Scripture alike, sages themselves turned out to do those very things that the ancient, and coming, saviors of Israel had done, and would again do in time to come. Moses and David in the long-ago past and in the age to come, and sages here and now—all formed part of the supernatural basis for the single, certain hope for Israel. In this context, the framing of exegeses of Scriptures and the collection of such exegeses into holy books constituted an act heavy with salvific meaning and promise.

We note, finally, one further aspect of the utility of the resort to exegesis of Scripture in the apologetic venture. In addition to endemic anachronism, we observe something far more accessible, both then and now, to us as outsiders to the rabbinic system: a concern for the close and careful explanation of words and phrases. We may well be struck by the interest in the mere facts of the meaning of words and phrases, proved by perfectly reasonable resort to data made available by other words and phrases, the meaning of which was already known. The very facticity of discourse should not be missed. It too bears meaning. For the numerous passages in the collections of exegeses in which theological exegeses—through apologetics, dogmatics, mere homiletics, or historical anachronism— dominate are outweighed by the still more numerous ones of a different sort. In these more common exegeses there is a clear claim that any reasonable and informed person must read things in this way and not in some other. What is particular to the rabbinic perspective thus competes with what may prove acceptable to outsiders as well.

The apologetic use of this second sort of reading of the ancient verses of Scripture, the one we may characterize as philological or, at least, other-than-theological, is now to be specified. It makes possible a second sort of discourse. If the theological passage is to address the insider, the philological kind (in the mind of the insider at least) speaks to the world at large. This other, general mode of discourse about Scripture serves to persuade the insider that outsiders, reasonable and informed people, may well accept what the exegete has to say. A powerful apologetic—addressed, self-evidently, to the believer—thereby emerges. What *we* say about Scripture's meanings is reasonable and demonstrable, not merely to be believed by a private act of faith. It is to be critically examined, assented to by shared reason. So the claim of the exegete to provide mere facts supplies the most powerful apologetic. Transforming convictions into (mere) facts serves to reenforce the faith of the believer, beyond all argument from revelation, let alone historical confirmation. How better to do this than work out exegeses serving to clarify, demonstrating through the appeal to self-evident proofs and incontrovertible data of language.

To whom is such exegesis serviceable in apologetics? The appeal to the plain meaning of Scripture and how it coincides with the particular position, on the meaning of Scripture, taken by the apologist, serves in particular not the dominant but the subordinate party to the debate. The winning side may rearrange things, appropriate proof for their convictions as compelling as the very topography of the land and geography of the world. What better proof did Christianity's exponents have to offer than the argument from history? Look at any coin, with its Christian symbol, and the facts come clear. Everything Christ had said was proved true. Reconstructing the geography of the Holy Land made the same point. Anything Israel (after the flesh) had hoped to see had turned out ashes and dust. Lacking access to, unable to change, the facts of reality, the rabbinical apologists through their approach to the reading of Scripture could appeal only to the facts of revelation, as (rightly) construed by them. These too, in the nature of things, constituted facts. They were, moreover, the only palatable facts left for the subordinate side.

A glance backward at the way in which Aphrahat, sage of the oppressed Christian Church of Iranian Babylonia not even a century earlier, had conducted his debate with the dominant Judaism of his locale provides a striking parallel. Writing ca. 330, during a time of severe Iranian persecution of Christianity, Aphrahat addressed the Jewish critics of the Church. If their arguments tempted the faithful, the Jews who pointed to the calamity affecting Christianity as evidence of the falsity of the claim of Christ to be Messiah only said out loud what some within the Church were thinking. Aphrahat's mode of argument took the form of a stunningly reasonable reading of the shared statements—facts—of Scripture. He adduced the scriptural facts, on which all parties agreed, to prove that, despite the events of the hour, the Christians, not the Jews, truly understood and lived by the faith of Sinai. Appeal to facts shared by all parties, the claim to speak in accord with the canons of reason universally compelling for every side—these serve in particular the polemical requirements of the weak. The strong define logic for themselves and declare what is reasonable.

I need hardly point out that this perspective on the compilations of scriptural exegeses composed in the trying times of the fifth and sixth centuries is gained only by viewing them from very far away. It is not only *post facto*. Comparing two different sources of exegeses—Aphrahat's and the sages'—centered on establishing facts and finding shared bases for difference is a very general argument indeed. Still, when we consider that, from the fifth century onward, Jewish participants in the Jewish-Christian argument invariably conducted the debate through reference to Scripture, its language and facts, normally avoiding the confrontation with the miserable condition of Israel in contrast to the triumphant success of Christianity, the comparison becomes compelling. For it is a commonplace to observe that the institutions of the fourth, fifth, and sixth centuries form the bridge from Middle Eastern antiquity to the medieval, hence modern, West. To that commonplace, I may add the suggestion that the main outlines of the Jewish-Christian argument of medieval and early modern times may be discerned in the form of the scriptural studies taken by the fifth- and sixth-century sages. These were (1) close reading of verses of the Scripture, (2) composition of exegeses into large collections, (3) all the time pretending to no apologetic motive, but (4) claiming only to say what things really meant.

That was, and would remain, the Jewish position, because, in the nature of things, the Jews, being weak, would always resort to the weapons of the weak: denial of the strength of the strong through exaggeration of the power of (shared) reason to coerce the strong to accommodate the weak. That position emerges less in the detail of what was said about Scripture than from two simple facts: first, how much was said about Scripture, and, second, how much effort would go into compiling and preserving what was said as a statement of what God had said, of what therefore was so.

THEOLOGICAL AND CANONICAL CONTEXT:
THE SAGE'S EXEGESIS
AND THE TORAH

While framing collections of scriptural exegeses may have served a (to us) blatant apologetic purpose, the character of the collections themselves hardly suggests that that was the reason rabbis made them. It follows that the crisis for Judaism presented by the political triumph of Christianity cannot define the context or generative considerations in which the documents came to formation. Nor may we claim that the documents were held authoritative within Judaism merely because we see in them the utility of having something to say to the wavering faithful. The exegetical documents were composed of statements on the meaning of Scripture. Where did these statements come from? Were they revealed? The framers of the documents collected and presented as authoritative books these sets of statements on the meaning of Scripture. What status then did the composers of the collections claim for their books? Were they *torah* (revelation) and part of the Torah? Accordingly, both the contents of the compilations of scriptural exegeses and the collections themselves make necessary an inquiry into the complementary contexts of a theological and canonical character, in which *midrash* as a mode of writing and of compiling a holy book took place. Let me now unpack the two questions at hand.

When a sage had framed an opinion on the meaning of a verse, whether supplying a close exegesis or constructing a wide-ranging discourse, and that sage, or others, had collected numerous exegeses and strung them together into a collection, the status of the book surely had to be determined. Clearly, the authors or compilers claimed to state the meaning of Scripture. Was that book of imputed meanings—exegeses—held to be the same as Scripture, that is, a book of *torah* or revelation? The collection contained statements of the Torah, that is, citations of Pentateuchal writings, as well as authoritative judgments on the meanings of those statements. As such, the author, or the people who received the work and venerated it, may have regarded the whole as equivalent to the Torah. On the other hand, people knew the difference between the text of Scripture, written down in a sacred scroll, and what authorities of their own day and age had to say about the meaning of the text. Did the distinction between media make a difference? The issue of the relationship between collections of exegeses of Scripture and Scripture itself requires attention. The latter was revealed. What was the source of the former? The latter enjoyed the status of the word and will of God for Israel. Why pay attention to the former? At issue was the standing of the sage who made up the exegeses and collected them.

The source and authority of the compilations of biblical exegeses

—revealed by God along with the Scripture subjected to exegesis, or made up by men and in no way part of revelation—furthermore governed the complementary question of the status and authority of the collections of exegeses in relationship to the established "canon" of the Hebrew Scriptures—if there really was one. On the one side, if people conceded that the collections of exegeses derived from God's word and expressed God's meaning in Scripture, then the compositions of exegeses demanded a place within the canon of authoritative sacred writings of Israel. On the other, if the collections of exegeses preserved the opinions of ordinary men, albeit sages of exceptional learning, then the canon need not open up to accommodate them. The issue of the source and authority of the exegeses, hence of the compositions made up of them, drew in its wake the closely related question of the place and standing of the documents that contained and preserved these exegetical writings. Once more, the heart of the matter was the standing of the sage.

The compilations before us present no answers to the questions at hand. Like other rabbinic documents, they do their business with remarkably little explanation implying self-consciousness. Within the bounds of the document itself, no effort goes into identifying the author and his authority, defining the nature of the work and its purpose, indicating the prospective audience for discourse and its desired response. Obviously, to the framers of the collections, the answers to these questions must have been obvious. But they do not tell us what they were. The reason, I think, is that all rabbinic documents came to fullness within an established matrix of mind and imagination. Since everyone engaged in the work of formation and composition knew the meaning of the creation of any document, no one found it necessary to explain what he was doing. That is why, after the Mishnah itself, no document of formative Judaism—the writings of sages from the second through the seventh centuries—contains a full and complete account of itself, its context and intent. Except for the Mishnah, all rabbinic writings form fragments of a complete system, itself nowhere fully exposed in a single document.

What then defines that matrix into which the collections of exegeses of Scripture were born, and to the configuration of which they too give evidence? Since these collections point elsewhere, they depend upon facts outside of their own compositions for definition of what is collected within them. We turn forthwith to the ubiquitous figure everywhere in the wings. We now call to center-stage him who speaks in these collections: the rabbi himself. The issues of the status of the exegeses of Scripture collected in the documents at hand, the relationship of the collections themselves to the "established canon" the issue of revelation after Scripture—these are to be resolved only when we know the status, in Heaven and on earth, and the standing, in the context of Torah, of the sage.

SCRIPTURE AND MISHNAH, MIDRASH
AND TALMUD: THE CONTEXT

No rabbinic document presents a complete account of the system of Rabbinic Judaism, and every rabbinic document presupposes a fully developed system. But if no book tells us how to grasp the system as a whole, then where shall we find it? The obvious locus for the discovery of the encompassing and definitive category, within which all else will find proper location and definition, surely lies in the name by which we call the thing itself. Since we speak of Rabbinic Judaism, we have ample reason to turn to the figure of the rabbi. In that figure we should find the center of gravity, the force that holds the whole together. In the authority of the rabbi we should uncover warrant for the inclusion of the compilations of exegeses of Scripture into the Torah's canon. In the supernatural standing of the rabbi, we should perceive grounds for regarding the exegeses themselves as *torah*, revelation, within the Torah.

If, in the figure of the rabbi as he emerges in diverse rabbinic texts, we do not uncover answers to the questions about the status and authority of things rabbis wrote, we are not apt to find out elsewhere. For, as I said, the texts themselves presuppose that everyone knows what, in fact, lies wholly beyond demonstration within the body of any one of the various texts. All we have as fact is that rabbis claimed to enjoy full authority to declare the meaning of both Scripture and the Mishnah. This they did in massive and authoritative works, of *midrash* and Talmud alike. What we want to ask then is whether sages held God had told them what to say in these writings. If so, did they claim their books consequently belonged to the

Torah? When we know who and what the rabbi said he was, we also shall turn up clear responses to the issues of revelation and canon as I just now suggested that these pertain to collections of scriptural exegeses.

The strategy of argument requires that we repeat the simple exercise on which this entire account of the context of *midrash* rests: taxonomy. We compare what people did in one, known context with what they did in another, unknown one. So we establish lines of comparison and contrast from the one to the other, applying to the unknown the facts revealed by the known. We have now to repeat the same procedure. For we do know how, in the Talmud, the rabbis related what they had to say about their authority vis-à-vis the two sources of truth in their hands, the Scripture and the Mishnah. Accordingly, when we see how, in the Talmud, the rabbis treated their own views in the setting of the exegesis of the Mishnah and Scripture alike, we shall understand the status they likely accorded to their exegeses of Scripture. At that point we shall have whatever answer we are apt to find, generated solely within the limits of the documents in hand, to the questions raised in the preceding sections.

Once more, therefore, a simple equation, now established as fact, guides us: the Talmud is to the Mishnah as the collections of scriptural exegeses are to Scripture. Hence, when we know the status in the Talmud of rabbinical statements about the Mishnah and about Scripture, we shall reach proper conclusions about the status accorded to those same statements in the compilations of scriptural exegeses.

Let me state the result at the outset. Sages' Talmudic statements about the Mishnah are treated precisely as are statements found both *in* the Mishnah and *in* Scripture itself. Thus, Talmudic statements either form part of *torah*, or are wholly derivative from the Torah and hence of the same status and standing as Torah. Likewise, statements in the compositions of scriptural exegeses about the meaning of Scripture, and, by extension, the collections themselves enjoy the status of revelation and form part of the canon of Torah, of Judaism. The upshot is that what the rabbi says is *torah*. The collections of exegeses were received in revelation and belong in the canon as part of the Torah.

Let us now examine in a few examples exactly how the Talmud proposes to analyze opinions of its own authorities, the rabbis of the third and fourth centuries themselves. Then the preceding statements will find ample justification in sources.

Proof-texts

We began our inquiry by pointing out that a principal mode of the exegesis of the Mishnah was to supply proof-texts for the Mishnah's various statements. This served to link what the Mishnah said to principles and rules of Scripture. What we shall now again observe, through a single interesting instance, is that the same inquiry pertaining to the Mishnah applies without variation to statements made by rabbis of the contemporary period themselves. Indeed, precisely the same theological and exegetical considerations came to bear upon both the Mishnah's statements and opinions expressed by Talmudic rabbis. Since these were not to be distinguished from one another in the requirement that opinion be suitably grounded in Scripture, they also should be understood to have formed part of precisely the same corpus of (scriptural) truths. What the Mishnah and the later rabbi said further expressed precisely the same kind of truth: revelation, through the medium of Scripture, whether contained in the Mishnah or in the opinion of the sage himself. While this matter is familiar from our interest in the role of Scripture in the exegesis of the Mishnah, we review it to establish the main point of the argument: the context in which all exegesis took place, the polemic which, by indirection, exegesis served.

The way in which this search for proof-texts applies equally to the Mishnah and to the rabbi's opinion is illustrated in the following passage.

Yerushalmi Sanhedrin 10:4: [A] *The party of Korah has no portion in the world to come, and will not live in the world to come [Mishnah Sanhedrin 10:4].*

[B] What is the Scriptural basis for this view?

[C] "So they and all that belonged to them went down alive into Sheol; and the earth closed over them, and they perished from the midst of the assembly" (Num. 16:33).

[D] *"The earth closed over them"—in this world.*

[E] *"And they perished from the midst of the assembly"*—*in the world to come [Mishnah Sanhedrin 10:4D–F]*.

[F] It was taught: R. Judah b. Batera says, "The contrary view is to be derived from the implication of the following verse:

[G] "'I have gone astray like a lost sheep; seek thy servant and do not forget thy commandments' (Ps. 119:176).

[H] "Just as the lost object which is mentioned later on in the end is going to be searched for, so the lost object which is stated herein is destined to be searched for" [Tosefta Sanhedrin 13:9].

[I] Who will pray for them?

[J] R. Samuel bar Nahman said, "Moses will pray for them.

[K] [This is proved from the following verse:] "'Let Reuben live, and not die, [nor let his men be few]' (Deut. 33:6)."

[L] R. Joshua b. Levi said, "Hannah will pray for them."

[M] This is the view of R. Joshua b. Levi, for R. Joshua b. Levi said, "Thus did the party of Korah sink ever downward, until Hannah went and prayed for them and said, 'The Lord kills and brings to life; he brings down to Sheol and raises up' (1 Sam. 2:6)."

We have a striking sequence of proof-texts, serving (1) the cited statement of the Mishnah, A–C, then (2) an opinion of a rabbi in the Tosefta, F–H, then (3) the position of a rabbi, J–K, L–M. The process of providing proof-texts therefore is central, the nature of the passages requiring the proof-texts a matter of indifference. We see that the search for appropriate verses of Scripture vastly transcends the purpose of study of the Mishnah and Scripture, exegesis of their rules, or provision of adequate authority for the Mishnah and its laws. In fact, any proposition that is to be taken seriously, whether in the Mishnah, in the Tosefta, or in the mouth of a Talmudic sage himself, will elicit interest in scriptural support.

This quest in Scripture thus extended beyond the interest in supplying the Mishnah's rules with proof-texts. On the contrary, the real issue turns out to have been not the Mishnah at all, nor even the vindication of its diverse sayings, one by one. Once the words of a *sage*, not merely a rule of the Mishnah, are made to refer to Scripture for proof, it must follow that, in the natural course of things, a rule of the Mishnah or of the Tosefta will likewise be asked to refer to Scripture. The fact that the living sage validated his own words through Scripture explains why the sage in the fourth century validated also the words of the (then) ancient sages of the Mishnah and Tosefta through verses of Scripture. It is one, undivided phenomenon. Distinctions are not made among media—oral, written, living, book—of *torah*.

The Consensus of Sages.
Resolving Disputes

We turn to the way in which the rabbis of the Talmud proposed to resolve differences of opinion. This is important, because the Mishnah presents a mass of disputes. Turning speculation about principles into practical law required resolving them. Precisely in the same way in which Talmudic rabbis settled disputes in the Mishnah and so attained a consensus about the law of the Mishnah, they handled disputes among themselves. The importance of that fact for our argument is simple. Once more we see that the rabbis of the third and fourth centuries, represented in the Talmud, treated their own contemporaries exactly as they treated the then-ancient authorities of the Mishnah. In their minds the status accorded to the Mishnah, as a derivative of the Torah, applies equally to the Talmudic sages' teachings. In the following instance we see how the same discourse attached to (1) a Mishnah rule is assigned as well to one in (2) the Tosefta and, at the end, to differences among (3) the Talmudic authorities.

Yerushalmi Ketubot 5:1: [VI.A] R. Jacob bar Aha, R. Alexa in the name of Hezekiah: "The law accords with the view of R. Eleazar b. Azariah, who stated, *If she was widowed or divorced at the stage of betrothal, the virgin collects only two hundred zuz and the widow, a maneh. If she was widowed or divorced at the stage of a consummated marriage, she collects the full amount [M. Ket. 5:1E, D]."*
[B] R. Hananiah said, "The law accords with the view of R. Eleazar b. Azariah."
[C] Said Abayye, "They said to R. Hananiah, 'Go and shout [outside whatever opinion you like.' But] R. Jonah, R. Zeira in the name of R. Jonathan said, 'The law accords with the view of R. Eleazar b. Azariah.' [Yet] R. Yosa bar Zeira in the name of R. Jonathan said, 'The law does not accord with the view of R. Eleazar b. Azariah.' [So we do not in fact know the decision.]"

[D] Said R. Yose, "We had a mnemonic. Hezekiah and R. Jonathan both say one thing."

[E] For it has been taught:

[F] He whose son went abroad, and whom they told, "Your son has died,"

[G] and who went and wrote over all his property to someone else as a gift,

[H] and whom they afterward informed that his son was yet alive—

[I] his deed of gift remains valid.

[J] R. Simeon b. Menassia says, "His deed of gift is not valid, for if he had known that his son was alive, he would never have made such a gift" [T. Ket. 4:14E–H].

[K] Now R. Jacob bar Aha [= A] said, "The law is in accord with the view of R. Eleazar b. Azariah, and the opinion of R. Eleazar b. Azariah is the same in essence as that of R. Simeon b. Menassia."

[L] Now R. Yannai said to R. Hananiah, "Go and shout [outside whatever you want].

[M] "But, said R. Yose bar Zeira in the name of R. Jonathan, 'The law is not in accord with R. Eleazar b. Azariah.'"

[N] But in fact the case was to be decided in accord with the view of R. Eleazar b. Azariah.

What is important here is that the Talmud makes no distinction whatever when deciding the law of disputes (1) in the Mishnah, (2) in the Tosefta, and (3) among Talmudic rabbis. The same already-formed colloquy that is applied at the outset to the Mishnah's dispute is then held equally applicable to the Tosefta's. The process of thought is the main thing, without regard to the document to which the process applies.

The Rabbi as Law-Giver

Still more important than the persistence of a given mode of thought applicable to Scripture, to the Mishnah, and to the sayings of Talmudic rabbis themselves is the presentation of the rabbi as a lawgiver in the model of Moses. The capacity of the sage himself to participate in the process of revelation is illustrated in two types of materials. First of all, tales told about rabbis' behavior on specific occasions immediately were translated into rules for the entire community to keep. Accordingly, he was a source not merely of good example but of prescriptive law:

Y. Abodah Zarah 5:4: [III.X] R. Aha went to Emmaus, and he ate dumpling [prepared by Samaritans].
[Y] R. Jeremiah ate leavened bread prepared by them.
[Z] R. Hezekiah ate their locusts prepared by them.
[AA] R. Abbahu prohibited Israelite use of wine prepared by them.

These reports of what rabbis had done enjoyed the same authority as statements of the law on eating what Samaritans cooked, as did citations of traditions in the names of the great authorities of old. What someone did served as a norm, if he was a sage of sufficient standing.

Second, and far more common, are instances in which the deed of a rabbi is adduced as an authoritative precedent for the law under discussion. It was everywhere taken for granted that what a rabbi did he did because of his mastery of the law. Even though a formulation of the law was not in hand, a tale about what a rabbi actually did constituted adequate evidence on how to formulate the law itself. So on the basis of the action or practice of an authority, a law might be framed that was quite independent of the person of the sage. The sage then functioned as a lawgiver, like Moses. Among many instances of that mode of generating law are the following:

Y. Abodah Zarah 3:11: [II.A] Gamaliel Zuga was walking along, leaning on the shoulder of R. Simeon b. Laqish. They came across an image.
[B] He said to him, "What is the law as to passing before it?"
[C] He said to him, "Pass before it, but close [your] eyes."
[D] R. Isaac was walking along, leaning on the shoulder of R. Yohanan. They came across an idol before the council building.
[E] He said to him, "What is the law as to passing before it?"
[F] He said to him, "Pass before it, but close [your] eyes."
[G] R. Jacob bar Idi was walking along, leaning upon R. Joshua b. Levi. They came across a procession in which an idol was carried. He said to him, "Nahum, the most holy man, passed before this idol, and will you not pass by it? Pass before it but close your eyes."

Y. Abodah Zarah 2:2: [III.FF] R. Aha had chills and fever. [They brought him] a medicinal drink prepared from the phallus of Dionysian revelers [thus Jastrow, I 400 B]. But he would not drink it. They brought it to R. Jonah, and he did drink it. Said R. Mana, "Now if R.

Jonah, the patriarch, had known what it was, he would never have drunk it."
[GG] Said R. Huna, "That is to say, 'They do not accept healing from something that derives from an act of fornication.'"

The point of these stories requires no repetition. What is important is GG, the rewording of the point of the story as a law. Since the purpose of this exercise is clear, let us proceed in the last two sections directly to the conclusions to be drawn from it.

TORAH AND CANON

Having come this far, we must now wonder whether, any longer, we can distinguish between *torah*, as divine revelation, and "the canon of the Torah," a particular set of books deemed more authoritative than any other books. If what an authorized rabbi states must be received as *torah*, as divine revelation, then we face two possibilities. Either there is *torah* which is not part of the Torah, the canon of revelation. Or there is no such thing as a canon at all. That is to say, the conception that, at a given point, a particular set of books is declared to be the final and authoritative statement of God's will and word, in the present context seems to me puzzling. The entire thrust of the exegetical process is to link upon a single plane of authority and reliability what a rabbi now says with what the (written) Torah said, what the Mishnah says with what the (written) Torah said, or what the Tosefta says with what the (written) Torah said.

What that means is simple. The sages of the Talmud recognized no distinction in authority or standing—hence, in status as revelation—between what the Mishnah said and what the written Torah said. They also used the same processes of validation to demonstrate that what they themselves declared enjoyed the same standing and authority as what they found in the written Torah. So their intent always was to show there in fact were no gradations in revelation. God spoke in various ways and through diverse media: to prophets and to sages, in writing and in memorized sayings, to olden times and to the present day. We can discern no systematic effort to distinguish one kind of revelation from another—revelation transmitted in writing, that transmitted orally, revelation to an ancient prophet, an exegesis or a Torah-teaching of a contemporary sage. Then it must follow, as I now propose, that sages rejected the conception of layers and levels of revelations, of making distinctions between one medium and another, hence one book and another.

To state matters simply: either a teaching was true and authoritative, wherever it was found and however it had reached the living age, or a teaching was untrue and not authoritative. Scripture, the Mishnah, the sage—all three spoke with equal authority. True, one thing had to come into alignment with the other, the Mishnah with Scripture, the sage with the Mishnah. But it was not the case that one component of *torah*, of God's word to Israel, stood within the sacred circle, another beyond. Interpretation and what was interpreted, exegesis and text, belonged together. In so vivid a world of divine address, what place was there for the conception of canon? There was none. And how can we show the distinction between canonical and non-canonical? We cannot. The truth as God declared it was canon. Everything else was not. So, to conclude, the conception of canon contradicts the theory of *torah* revealed in the Talmud of the Land of Israel and in the earliest collections of biblical exegeses.

THE RABBI AS WORD MADE FLESH

Scripture and the Mishnah govern what the rabbi knows. But it is *the rabbi* who authoritatively speaks about them. The simple fact is that what rabbis were willing to do to the Mishnah is precisely what they were prepared to do to Scripture—impose upon it their own judgment of its meaning. This fact is the upshot of the inquiry now completed. It also is the sole fact we have in hand for the identification of the context of *midrash* in formative Judaism. But it suffices. Since we see that the question of locus and setting devolves upon several books at once—Scripture and the Mishnah equally, so far as the Talmud is concerned—the answer to the question of context must come from something other than a book or even a set of books. It is the source of the authority of the rabbi himself that turns out to pose the fundamental question. With the answer to that question, we also know, first, the status, as to revelation, of the things the rabbi says, whether he speaks of the Mishnah or of Scripture; and second, the standing of the books he writes, whether these are tractates of the Talmud or the compositions of exegeses of Scripture.

The reason why the collections of scriptural exegeses do not contain answers to our questions of their theological and canonical status is that these questions, in their setting, were impertinent. These questions had been answered before the books came to be written. The books could not have been written the way they were if the questions at hand had not been answered in a particular way and in a prior setting. So everything turns upon the figure of the rabbi.

The rabbi speaks with authority about the Mishnah and the Scripture. He therefore has authority deriving from revelation. He himself may participate in the processes of revelation (there is no material difference). Since that is so, the rabbi's book, whether Talmud to the Mishnah or *midrash* to Scripture, is *torah*, that is, revealed by God. It also forms part of the Torah, a fully "canonical" document. The reason, then, is that the rabbi is like Moses, "our rabbi," who received *torah* and wrote the Torah.

Since rabbinical documents repeatedly claim that, if you want to know the law, you should not only listen to what the rabbi says but also copy what he does, it follows that, in his person, the rabbi represents and embodies the Torah. God in the Torah revealed God's will and purpose for the world. So God had said what the human being should be. The rabbi was the human being in God's image. That, to be sure, is why (but merely by the way) what the rabbi said about the meaning of Scripture derived from revelation. Collections of the things he said about Scripture constituted compositions integral to the Torah.

So in the rabbi, the word of God was made flesh. And out of the union of man and Torah, producing the rabbi as Torah incarnate, was born Judaism, the faith of Torah: the ever-present revelation, the always-open canon. For fifteen hundred years, from the time of the first collections of scriptural exegeses to our own day, the enduring context for *midrash* remained the same: encounter with the living God.

The Three Types of Compilations of Exegeses of Scripture: Sample Chapters

Biblical verses are given in italics. Citations of passages of the Mishnah or Tosefta are given in boldface type. I have not revised the style of the various translators or tried to make the translations uniform.

COMPOSITIONS BASED ON CLOSE READING AND INTERPRETATION OF VERSES OF SCRIPTURE

Mekhilta of R. Ishmael

Translated by Jacob Z. Lauterbach (Philadelphia: Jewish Publication Society of America, 1933), 2:237–247.

BAHODESH VI, TO EXODUS 20:FF.

You Shall Not Have Other Gods Before Me (Ex. 20:3). Why is this said? Because it says: "I am the Lord your God." To give a parable: A king of flesh and blood entered a province. His attendants said to him: Issue some decrees upon the people. He, however, told them: No! When they will have accepted my reign I shall issue decrees upon them. For if they do not accept my reign how will they carry out my decrees? Likewise, God said to Israel: "I am the Lord your God, you shall not have other gods—I am He whose reign you have taken upon yourselves in Egypt." And when they said to Him: "Yes, yes," He continued: "Now, just as you accepted My reign, you must also accept My decrees: 'You shall not have other gods before Me.'"

R. Simon b. Yohai says: What is said further on: *"I am the Lord your God" (Lev. 18:2),* means: "I am He whose reign you have taken upon yourselves at Sinai," and when they said: "Yes, yes," He continued: "Well, you have accepted My reign, now accept My decrees: *'After the doings of the land of Egypt,' etc." (ibid, v. 3).* What is said here: "I am the Lord your God who brought you out from the land of Egypt," means: "I am He whose reign you have taken upon yourselves," and when they said to Him: "Yes, yes," He continued: "You have accepted My reign, now accept My decrees: *'You shall not have other gods.'"*

You Shall Not Have. Why is this said? Because when it says: *"You shall not make for yourself a graven image,"* etc. *(Ex. 20:4),* I know only that it is forbidden to make any. But how do I know that it is forbidden to keep one that has already been made? Scripture says, *"You shall not have other gods,"* etc.

Other Gods. But are they gods? Has it not been said: *"And have cast their gods into the fire; for they were no gods"* *(Isa. 37:19)*? What then does Scripture mean when it says: *"Other gods"*? Merely those which others called gods. Another interpretation is: Gods that are backward ("Aharim"). For they hold back the coming of goodness into the world. Another interpretation: *Other Gods.* Who turn those who worship them into others. Another interpretation: *Other Gods.* Who act like strangers towards those who worship them. And thus it says: *"Yea, though one cry unto him, he cannot answer, nor save him out of his trouble"* *(Isa. 46:7).* R. Yose says: *Other Gods.* Why is this said? In order not to give the nations of the world an excuse for saying: "If the idols had been called by His name, they would have been worthwhile." Behold, then, they have been called by His name and they are not worthwhile anyhow. And when were they called by His name? In the days of Enosh the son of Seth. It is said: *"Then began men to call upon the name of the Lord"* *(Gen. 4:26).* At that time the ocean rose and flooded a third of the world. God said to them, "You have done something new by calling yourselves 'gods.' I also will do something new and will call Myself 'the Lord.'" And thus it says: *"That calls for the waters of the sea, and pours them out upon the face of the earth; the Lord is His name"* *(Amos 5:8).*

R. Eliezer says, *"Other Gods*—For every day they make for themselves new gods. How so? If one has an idol of gold and then needs the gold, he makes the idol of silver. If he has one of silver and then needs the silver, he makes the idol of copper. If he has an idol of copper and needs the copper, he makes it of iron. And so also with one of tin and so also with one of lead, as it is said: *'New gods that came newly up'* *(Deut. 32:17)."*

R. Isaac says, "If the name of every idol were to be specifically mentioned, all skins (parchments) in the world would not suffice."

R. Hananiah b. Antigonos says, "Come and consider the expression chosen by the Torah: *'To Molek'* 'to a ruler' *(Lev. 18:21)*—that is, anything at all which you declare as ruling over you, even if it be a chip of wood or a piece of potsherd."

Rabbi says, *Other Gods*—Gods that are later than he who was last in the order of creation. And who is it that was the last of the things created? The one who calls them "gods."

Before Me. Why is this said? In order not to give Israel an excuse for saying: Only those who came out from Egypt were commanded not to worship idols. Therefore, it is said: *"Before Me,"* as much as to say: Just as I am living and enduring for ever and for all eternity, so also you and your son and your son's son to the end of generation shall not worship idols.

Sifra

Translated by Jacob Neusner in *A History of the Mishnaic Law of Purities. VI. Negaim. Sifra* (Leiden: E. J. Brill, 1975), 6:31–44.

PARASHAT NEGAIM PARASHAH II AND
PEREQ 2, TO LEVITICUS 13:4–8.

[A] *"A white spot" (Lev. 13:4: "But if the spot is white in the skin of his body and appears no deeper than the skin" . . .)*—
[B] I know only the white spot.
[C] How do we know that we should include the swelling [that it too is white (Hillel)]?
[D] Scripture says below, *"A white swelling" (Lev. 13:9: "And if there is a white swelling in the skin . . .").*
[E] And how do we know that we should include the other shades?
[F] Scripture says, *"And if a bright spot."*　　　　　　　　　NII:1

[G] Might one say that just as it is third in Scripture [1. swelling, 2. eruption, 3. spot], so it should be third in the shades [of white] [that is, it need not be so white as the others]?
[H] Scripture says, *"White" (Lev. 13:4), "white" (Lev. 13:9).*
[I] It is white, and there is no brighter than it.
[J] And how white must it be?
[K] Like snow, as it is said, *"And lo, Miriam was leprous like snow" (Num. 12:10).*　　　　　　　　　NII.2

[L] Might one say that on account of every shade of snow they should be unclean, but [if they are as white as] all other shades [of white, except for the range of snow], they should be clean?
[M] Scripture says, *"It is a tetter" (Lev. 13:38).*
[N] [That which is as dull as] a tetter is clean. From it [a tetter] and brighter, it is unclean.　　　　　　　　　NII.3

[O] On this basis have they said:
[P] **The shades of plagues are two which are four.**
　　A bright spot is as bright as snow. Secondary to it is [white] as the plaster of the Temple.
　　The rising is as white as the skin of an egg.
　　Secondary to it is a shade of white like wool, the words of R. Meir.

140

And sages say, The rising is [white] as wool, and secondary to it is [white] as the skin of an egg [= M. Neg. 1:1].   NII.4

[Q] The variegation of the snow is like mixed wine.

The variegation of the lime is like blood mixed in water, the words of R. Ishmael.

R. Aqiba says, The reddishness which is in this and in that is like wine mixed in water.

But that of snow is bright, and that of plaster is duller than it [= M. Neg. 1:2].   NII:5

[R] R. Hanina Prefect of the Priests says, The shades of plagues are sixteen.

R. Dosa b. Harkinas says, Thirty-six.

Aqavya b. Mehallel: Seventy-two [= M. Neg. 1:4A–C].

[S] Said R. Yose, R. Joshua the son of R. Aqiba asked R. Aqiba, saying to him, Why have they said, The shades of plagues are two which are four?

He said to him, If not, what should they say?

He said to him, Let them say, From the white of the skin of an egg and brighter is unclean, and they join together with one another.

[T] Said R. Yose, R. Joshua the son of R. Aqiba asked R. Aqiba, saying to him, Why have they said, The shades of plagues are two which are four?

He said to him, If not, what should they say?

He said to him, Let them say, From the shade of white like the skin of the egg and brighter is unclean.

He said to him, To teach you that they join together with one another.

He said to him, Let them say, Anything which is as white as the skin of an egg or brighter is unclean, and they [the colors] join together with one another.

He said to him, It teaches that if one is not an expert in them and in their names, he should not examine plagues [T. Neg. 1:1].   NII:6

[A] *And its hair [has not turned white] (Lev. 13:4)*—

[B] Not the hair of its quick flesh.

[C] How so?

[D] A bright spot the size of a split bean, and in it is quick flesh the size of a lentil—

and white hair is in the midst of the quick flesh—

the quick flesh went away—it is unclean because of the white hair.

The white hair went away—it is unclean because of the quick flesh.

R. Simeon declares clean, because the bright spot did not turn it [the hair white] [M. Neg. 4:6].

[E] He [Hillel: *They*] said to him, And has it not already been said, *And*

141

hair in the plague has turned white (Lev. 13:4)?
[F] This [quick flesh] is a plague in any event. NII:7

[G] *And its hair has not turned white (Lev. 13:4).*
[H] And not hair or part of it.
[I] How so?
[J] A bright spot—
  it [and] its quick flesh are the size of a split bean—
  and white hair is in the midst of the bright spot—
  the quick flesh went away—
  it is unclean because of the white hair.
  The white hair went away—
  it is unclean because of the quick flesh.
  R. Simeon declares clean, because the bright spot the size of a split bean did not turn it [white].
  And they agree [better: He (Simeon) agrees] that if there is in the place of white hair an area the size of a split bean, it is clean [= M. Neg. 4:6]. NII:8

[K] *And its hair has not turned white, and he will shut up (Lev. 13:4).*
[L] Lo, if there is in it black hair, it does not diminish it.
[M] The disciples asked R. Yose, A bright spot and in it is black hair: do we take account of the possibility that its place has diminished the bright spot to a size less than a split bean?
  He said to them, A bright spot, and [supply: in it is] white hair—do we take account of the possibility that its place has diminished the bright spot to less than a split bean?
  They said to him, No. If you have said so concerning white hair, which is a sign of uncleanness [itself], will you say so concerning black hair, which is not a sign of uncleanness?
  He said to them, Lo, if there are in it ten white hairs, in any event are more than two of them tokens of uncleanness? Do we take account of the possibility that the excess has diminished the place of the bright spot to less than a split bean?
  They said to him, No. If you have said so concerning white hair, which is a kind of uncleanness, will you say so concerning black hair, which in any event is not a variety of uncleanness?
  He said to them, Also black hair turns and becomes a kind of uncleanness [T. Neg. 2:3 = M. Neg. 4:4].
[N] But it says, *And its hair has not turned white, and he shuts up*—lo, if there is in it black hair, it does not diminish [the area of the spot].
[O] *And the priest shall shut up the diseased spot seven days (Lev. 13:5)*—first [this is the first of two quarantines]. NII:9

[A] *[And the priest shall examine him] on the seventh [day] (Lev. 13:5)—*
[B] Might one say, Whether by day or by night?
[C] Scripture says, *On [the seventh] day (Lev. 13:5),* and not by night.
                                                                    N2*:1

[D] Might one say, In any light of the day they should be suitable [for examination]?
[E] Scripture says, *In accord with whatever the priest shall see (Lev. 13:12).*
[F] And just as [we speak of] a priest, excluding the one the light of whose eyes has darkened, so [we speak of] the day, excluding [a day] which has grown dark [lit: the light of whose eyes has darkened].   N2*:2

[G] On this basis have they said:
[H] **They do not examine the plagues at dawn or at sunset, and not inside the house, and not on a cloudy day, because the dim appears bright, and not at noon, because the bright appears dim.**
[I] **When do they examine [plagues]? At three, four, five, seven, eight, and nine, the words of R. Meir.**
   R. Judah says, At four, five, six, eight, and nine [M. Neg. 2:2].
[J] R. Yose says, At four, five, nine, ten.
[K] But he said, I see the words of Rabbi.   N2*:3

[A] *[And the disease has not spread], and lo, the plague mark has stood in his eyes (Lev. 13:5)—*
[B] For **if it grew bright and then grew dim, grew dim and grew bright,** it is as if it did not grow dim.
[C] *And it did not spread (Lev. 13:5).*
[D] For **if it contracted and spread, or spread and contracted,** it is as if it did not spread.
[E] *And he will shut him up for seven days a second time (Lev. 13:5).*
[F] This teaches that the seventh day goes to his credit both for the preceding week and for the following week.
[G] *And the priest will shut him up for seven days a second time (Lev. 13:5).*
[H] The priest who saw him on the first inspection examines him on the second.
[I] **But if he died, another priest examines him.**   N2*:4

[A] *And lo, it [the plague] grew dim (Lev. 13:6).*
[B] Might one say this applies [only] if it grew dimmer [absolutely] than the four shades?
[C] Scripture says, *And the plague (Lev. 13:6).*

143

[D] If it is the diseased spot, might one say, in accord with its colors?

[E] Scripture says, *And lo, it grew dim.*

[F] How so?

[G] *It grew dim (Lev. 13:6)*—dimmer within its color-range [relatively], not dimmer than the four shades.   N2*:5

[I] *And lo, it grew dim (Lev. 13:6)*—

[J] For if it grew bright and then grew dim, it is as if it did not grow bright.

[K] *The diseased spot (Lev. 13:6)*—

[L] for if it grew dim and grew bright, it is as if it did not grow dim.

                                                                         N2*:6

[M] *It did not spread (Lev. 13:6)*—

[N] For if it contracted and spread, it is as if it did not contract.

[O] *The plague (Lev. 13:6)*—

[P] For if it spread and contracted, it is as if it did not spread.   N2*:7

[A] If [these things] are said with reference to the first week [Lev. 13:5], why have they been said with reference to the second week [Lev. 13:6]?

[B] But a garment which remains [unchanged] in the first week is shut up, and in the second week it is burned [as unclean].

[C] But a man who remains unchanged in the first week is shut up, and in the second, is declared clear [and not unclean].

[D] [Therefore] one has to refer [explicitly to the law pertaining to] the end of the first week, and one has to refer [explicitly to the law pertaining to] the end of the second week.   N2*:8

[A] *And the priest shall declare him clean; [it is only] an eruption (Lev. 13:6)*—

[B] Even though its color did not change.

[C] Or perhaps should we say [that the point is], Even though it went away and came back?

Scripture says, *It (Lev. 13:6).*

[D] What should one do for it?

R. Judah says, Let it be examined afresh.

And sages declare clean.   N2*:9

[A] *And he will wash his clothing (Lev. 13:6).*

[B] *And he will wash his clothing:* so that he does not render unclean through lying and sitting, and so that he does not render unclean through entry.

[C] *And he is clean (Lev. 13:6)*—[free] from tearing [the clothing] and from disheveling [his hair] (Lev. 13:45), and from shaving, and from birds.

[D] *And he will wash his clothing (Lev. 13:6)—*

[E] Might one say, Lo, it has [totally] disappeared [and not further going to be unclean at all]?

Scripture says, *It will spread . . . it is unclean (Lev. 13:8)* [even after clearance].   N2*:10

[A] I know only that [spreading] which conforms to the color [of the primary sign].

[B] That which does not conform [to the primary sign] in color [but exhibits a different, still unclean, shade]—how do we know [that this counts as spreading]?

[C] Scripture says [not only], *It will spread* [but also] *And if spreading it will spread (Lev. 13:7).*   N2*:11

[A] **One certified him unclean because of white hair, the white hair went away, and the black [sic] hair came back, and so with quick flesh and with spreading, in the beginning, at the end of the first week, at the end of the second week, after the clearance, lo, it is as it was.**

[B] **One certified him unclean through quick flesh, the quick flesh went away, and the quick flesh returned, and so with white hair and spreading, in the first instance, at the end of the first week, at the end of the second week, after the clearance, lo, it is as it was [= M. Neg. 5:2].**

[C] Scripture says, *It will spread—And if spreading it will spread (Lev. 13:7).*   N2*:12

[A] Might one say that the spreading should render unclean at the very first inspection [if others have noticed the spreading (Hillel)]?

[B] Scripture says, *[But if the eruption spreads] after he has shown himself to the priest for his cleansing (Lev. 13:7).*

[C] Might one say if the priest saw it, that it is spreading, and [if] it goes away [during the inspection (Hillel)], he should [nonetheless] be subject to it?

[D] Scripture says, *For his cleansing (Lev. 13:7).*

[E] He is only subject to it [for quarantine] from the time that he sees it—from uncleanness to cleanness.

[F] *And he will appear a second time to the priest (Lev. 13:7).*

[G] The priest who sees him in the first inspection sees him in the second.

[H] But if he died, another priest sees him.   N2*:13

[A] *And the priest will examine, and behold, the eruption has spread on the flesh (Lev. 13:8)—*

145

[B] Lo, this comes to teach concerning the spreading that it renders unclean only in the four [basic] colors. And in them [those four colors] are the shades in which [both] the primary sign renders unclean, and the spreading [therefrom] renders unclean.   N2*:14

[C] But is it not logical? The primary sign renders unclean, and the spreading renders unclean.
[D] Just as the primary sign renders unclean only in one of the four specified shades, so the spreading should render unclean only in one of the four specified shades.   N2*:15

[E] Or take this route:
White hair is a token of uncleanness and spreading is a token of uncleanness. Just as white hair renders unclean in any shade of white [not only in one of the four specified shades], so spreading should render unclean in any shade of white [not only in the four specified ones].   N2*:16

[F] Let us see to which it is similar:
[G] They should reason about something which renders unclean in all plagues from something which renders unclean in all plagues. But let not white hair prove the matter, for it does not render unclean in all plagues [but only in bright spots].
[H] Or take this route:
[I] They should compare something which is a token of uncleanness [spreading] with something which is a token of uncleanness [white hair], but let not the primary sign prove matters, for it is not [by itself] a token of uncleanness.
[J] Scripture says, *And the priest shall declare it unclean. It is a leprous disease (Lev. 13:8).*
[K] Lo, this comes to teach concerning spreading, that it renders unclean only in one of the four specified shades.
[L] *It (Lev. 13:8: It is leprosy).*
[M] Excluding that which spread to the tetter [which is not unclean].
                                    N2*:17

Sifre Numbers

Translated by Paul P. Levertoff in *Midrash Sifre on Numbers* (London: A. Golub, 1926), 3–9,

SIFRE NUM. 2–4 TO NUM. 5:5–9

§2.

And the Lord spake unto Moses. If any man or woman commit any sins of men in breaking faith with the Lord, and that person incur guilt [e.g., by any wrongs referred to in Lev. 5:21, such as the denial of the receipt of a deposit or of the finding of lost goods], then they shall confess their sins which they have done: and he shall return back that which he had wrongfully in his possession in full, and add unto it the fifth part thereof and give it unto him against whom he has trespassed. But if the man [be dead and] have no kinsman to whom the property wrongfully held may be restored, the property wrongfully held which becomes the Lord's shall be the priest's, over and above the ram of propitiation with which he [the priest] makes propitiation for him [i.e., the man who had confessed his error].

What is the special purpose of this section? Because, although a law is provided (Lev. 5:20) concerning a person confessing to the wrongful possession of property, yet, nowhere in Scripture do we hear anything about [what is to be done in the case of] a person wrongfully possessing the property of a proselyte; therefore this passage supplements the above mentioned one by making provision that he, who wrongfully possesses the property of a proselyte and has sworn [to the contrary], [the proselyte] having died, must pay the principal value of the property, together with the addition of a fifth part to the priest, and bring a guilt offering "to the altar."

This is a general principle: every scriptural doublet contains some particular point to be emphasized and is not a mere repetition.

R. Josiah says: "Why does it say here, 'a man or a woman'? In order to show the equality of woman with man in all cases where a sin-offering is required and in all laws concerning indemnity for injuries and damages. For otherwise we might deduce from (Ex. 21:33) 'If a man shall open a pit, [etc.]' that in cases like these woman is not included."

R. Jonathan says: "It is not necessary [to deduce the equality of woman with man in connection with the Exodus section from the word 'woman' in our passage], for it says in another place, 'the *owner* of the pit shall pay.' Also: 'the *person* that kindled the fire shall make restitution.' In that case, why does it say here, 'or woman'? The words apply only to this particular case."

Any sins of man. What do these words imply? That all sins against man are also sins against God. For otherwise we might infer (from the passage in Lev. 5:20–26, where particular sins against man are connected with faithlessness to the Lord), that it does not apply to *all* sins.

In breaking faith. These words always mean *treachery* (lying), cf. 1 Chron. 5:25; 1 Chron. 10:13; 2 Chron. 26:18; Josh. 7:1; Num. 5:12.

And that person [lit. soul] incur guilt. Why this phrase? Because otherwise we might conclude from the expression "man or woman" that it excludes those of doubtful or double sex.

That person. All are included: men, women, and proselytes. Perchance also minors? There is an *a fortiori* argument [that they are excluded]: If they are exempt [from punishment] in cases of idolatry, how much more so in lighter cases!

And that soul incur guilt. Why this expression? In order to teach us that he who puts fire to a neighbor's stock of grain on the Day of Atonement, while the court of justice cannot make him pay for the damage, yet *his soul incurs guilt*, i.e., he is punished directly by God.

Then they shall confess. From the verse [Lev. 5:5] *"And he should confess that he sinned,"* we only gather that a *sin-offering* is accompanied by *confession.* Whence do we know that also a guilt-offering [must be accompanied by confession]? Because it says here, "And that soul be *guilty,* then they shall confess."

R. Nathan says: "This is a principle: all those who are about to die must confess their sins."

§3.

And they should confess their sins which they have done. That is, in cases like these only the person himself must bring a guilt-offering and confess, but not his son. [For instance,] if one says to another: "Give me back the deposit which I left with your father," [and that one replies]: "You have not left any deposit,"—"I adjure you!"—and that one says: "Amen," and then he remembered [that the claimant was right], are we to suppose that he is obliged [to bring a guilt-offering]? [No.] For it says here: "They shall confess their sin which *they* have done."

§4.

To the priest. That is, to one of the priests who are attached to the division of duty in the Temple. You say so, but perchance it may be given to any priest (whether on duty or not)? But it says, "Except the hart of the atonement by which *atonement* will be wrought for him," which can only refer to those priests who bring forth *atonement* at the time being, namely, those attached to the particular division at that time.

If he defrauded a priest (and then confessed, etc.) can the latter claim (the money)? We might deduce it by a logical inference [that he could]: if he can claim what belongs to other people, should he have no right to claim what originally belonged to him?

R. Nathan used to express it differently: "If a thing to which I have no right is put into my hands, once there no one dare take it away from me, the more so must it be with a thing which belonged to me by right before it actually came into my hand, that when I do get it, no one should be able to claim and take it from me!" The sages said to him: "It is right in a case in which no others have a part, but here the other (priests) also have a part in it, and therefore it must be taken out of his hand and divided among all the priests belonging to the division."

Beside the hart of the atonement by which atonement is wrought. Whence do we know that when a person has defrauded a proselyte and sworn [that he did not and then remembered that he did] and has gone to bring the money and the guilt-offering, but died in the meantime, that the heirs are not obliged [to bring the offering]? Because it says here, "By which atonement is wrought for *him.*"

Thus R. Aqiba used to teach before he went to Ziffirin. But when he returned from there, he said, "Even if he had already given the money to the priests belonging to the division and then died [before bringing the sacrifice], the heirs are not obliged [to bring the offering], for it says, 'Except the hart of the atonement *by which atonement is wrought for him,*' which words suggest [that a guilt-offering is only to be brought for a person] who is in need of atonement, but not for a dead person for whom his own soul has already wrought atonement."

Sifre Deuteronomy

PISKA 32.

Translated by Robert Hammer. Previously unpublished.

"You shall love the Lord your God." Perform [God's will] out of love. Scripture makes a distinction between one who performs out of love and one who performs out of fear; he who performs out of love receives a doubled and redoubled reward. As it says, *"You must fear the Lord your God and serve Him" (Deut. 10:20):* a person may [serve someone] because he is afraid of him, but when that person needs him, he abandons him and goes his own way, but you should perform because of love. Only in regard to God do we find love combined with fear and fear combined with love.

Another interpretation: *You shall love the Lord your God.* Make Him beloved to humanity, as did Abraham our father in the matter referred to in the verse *"And the souls he made in Haran" (Gen. 12:5).* Is it not true that if one were to convene everyone in the world in order to create one gnat and infuse it with a soul, they could not do so? Therefore this verse must indicate that Abraham converted people, bringing them under the wings of the Shekhinah.

With all your heart: With both your inclinations, the inclination to good and the inclination to evil.

Another interpretation: *With all your heart.* With all the heart that is within you; your heart should not be divided in regard to God.

And with all your soul. Even if he takes away your soul. Similarly it says, *"For your sake we were killed all day long. We are regarded as sheep for the slaughter" (Ps. 44:23).* R. Simeon ben Menasya says, How can a man be slain daily? Rather [it means that] the Holy One, blessed is He, credits the righteous as if they were slain daily.

149

Simeon ben Azzai says, *With all your soul*—love Him until the last drop of life is wrung out.

R. Eliezer says, If it states *with all your soul*, why does it say *with all your might?* And if it states *with all your might*, why does it say *with all your soul?* There are those whose body is more precious to them than their wealth. *With all your soul* is directed to them. There are those whose wealth is more precious to them than their body. *With all your might* is directed to them.

R. Aqiba says, Since it states *with all your soul*, we would certainly infer *with all your might* which is of lesser import. Why then is *with all your might* stated? Because *might* implies whatever measure He metes out to you, whether it be of good or of punishment. Similarly David says, *"How can I repay the Lord for all His benefits toward me? I will lift the cup of salvation and call upon the name of the Lord"* (Ps. 116:12–13). *"I found trouble and sorrow. Then I called upon the name of the Lord"* (Ps. 116:3–4). Similarly Job says, *"The Lord gave and the Lord has taken away. Blessed be the name of the Lord"* (Job 1:21)—both for the measure of good and for the measure of punishment. What did his wife say to him? *"Do you still retain your integrity? Curse God and die!"* (Job 2:9). What did he say in reply? *"You speak as one of the impious women. Shall we accept the good from God but not the evil?"* (Job 2:10). "The people of the generation of the flood were vile during good times, yet when punishment came upon them they accepted it whether they liked it or not. This is a matter of reasoning from the minor to the major: if one who is vile during good times is well behaved during punishment, should not we, who are well behaved during good times, be well behaved also during punishment?" That is what he meant when he said to her, *"You speak like one of the impious women!"*

Furthermore, a man should rejoice more in chastisement than in times of prosperity. For if a man is prosperous all his life, no sin of his can be forgiven. What brings him forgiveness of sin? Suffering. R. Eliezer ben Jacob said, Scripture says, *"The Lord reproves him who He loves, as a father the son in whom he delights"* (Prov. 3:12). What causes a son to be delighted in by his father? Suffering. R. Meir says, Scripture says, *"Know in your heart that the Lord your God chastises you just as a man chastises his son"* (Deut. 8:5). You and your heart know the deeds that you have done, and you know that whatever sufferings I have brought upon you do not outweigh all your deeds.

R. Yose ben R. Judah says, Precious are chastisements, for the name of the Omnipresent One rests upon one who suffers them, as it says, *"The Lord your God chastises you"* (ibid). R. Nathan ben R. Joseph says, Just as a covenant is made concerning the land, so is a covenant made concerning chastisement, as it says, *"The Lord your God chastises you"* (ibid), and further on, *"For the Lord your God brings you to a good land"* (Deut. 8:7).

R. Simeon ben Yohai says, Precious are chastisements, for three excellent gifts coveted by all the nations of the world were given to Israel solely through suffering, and they are: Torah, the Land of Israel and the world to come. Where do we learn this concerning Torah? *"To know wisdom and chastisement"* (Prov. 1:2) and *"Happy is the man you chastise and whom you instruct in Torah"* (Ps. 94:12). Where do we learn this concerning the Land of Israel? *"The Lord your God disciplines you . . . for the Lord your God brings you to a good land"* (Deut. 8:5, 7). Where concerning the world to come? *"The commandment is a flame and the Torah is a light, and reproofs of instruction are the way of life"* (Prov. 6:23). What is the way that leads a man to the world to come? Chastisements. R. Nehemiah says, Precious are chastisements, for just as sacrifices bring appeasement, so do chastisements bring appeasement. Concerning sacrifices it states, *" . . . that it may be acceptable in his behalf, in expiation for him"* (Lev. 1:4), while concerning chastisements it states, *" . . . while they atone for their iniquity"* (Lev. 26:43). Indeed suffering appeases even more than sacrifices, for sacrifices involve wealth, but suffering involves one's body, as it says, *"Skin for skin, all a man has he will give for his life"* (Job 2:4)

Once R. Eliezer was ill, and R. Tarfon, R. Joshua, R. Eleazar ben Azariah and R. Aqiba came to visit him. R. Tarfon said to him, "My master, you are more precious to Israel than the orb of the sun, for the orb of the sun gives light in this world, while you have enlightened both this world and the world to come!" R. Joshua said to him, "My master, you are more precious to Israel than the gift of rain, for rain gives life in this world, and you give it in this world and in the world to come!" R. Eleazar ben Azaria said to him, "My master, you are more precious to Israel than father and mother, for father and mother bring one into this world, while you brought us to this world and to the world to come!" R. Aqiba said to him, "My master, precious are chastisements. . . ." R. Eliezer said to his disciples, "Prop me up." When R. Eliezer had seated himself, he said to Aqiba, "Speak, Aqiba." Aqiba went on: "It is stated, *'Menasseh was twelve years old when he began to reign, and he reigned fifty-five years in Jerusalem'* (2 Chron. 33:1), and it says, *'These also are the proverbs of Solomon, which the men of Hezekiah king of Judah copied out'* (Prov. 25:1). Could one imagine that Hezekiah taught Torah to all Israel but did not teach it to Menasseh, his son? Rather all his instructions and all his work were of no avail. Only chastisement availed, as it says, *'And the Lord spoke to Menasseh and to his people but they would not hearken. So the Lord brought upon them the captains of the host of the king of Asshur, who took Menasseh with hooks and bound him with fetters and carried him to Babylon. And when he was in affliction, he besought the Lord his God and humbled himself greatly before the God of his fathers, and prayed to him, and He received his entreaty and heard his supplication and brought him back to Jerusalem, into his kingdom' (2 Chron. 33:10–13).* Hence precious are chastisements!"

R. Meir says, Behold it says, *You shall love the Lord your God with all your heart.* Love Him with all your heart, as did Abraham your father, of whom it is written, *"But you Israel, My servant, Jacob whom I have chosen, seed of Abraham My beloved" (Isa. 41:8). And with all your soul,* as did Isaac who bound himself upon the altar, as it is written, *"And Abraham picked up the knife to slay his son" (Gen. 22:10). With all your might.* Thank him as did Jacob, as it says, *"I am unworthy of all the kindness that you have so steadfastly shown your servant: with my staff alone I crossed this Jordan and now I have become two camps" (Gen. 32:11).*

PISKA 105.

Translated by Martin S. Jaffee, in *Mishnah's Theology of Tithing. A study of Tractate Maaserot* (Chico, Calif.: Scholars Press for Brown Judaic Studies, 1981), 31–32, 38–39, 60–61.

You shall tithe all the yield of your seed, which comes forth from the field year by year (Deut. 14:22).

This teaches that people may not set aside tithe from produce grown in a given year in behalf of produce grown in another year. [The tithe of the crop of a given year must be separated from produce grown in that year.]

I know that that is the case only with reference to second tithe, to which Scripture makes explicit reference [in the cited verse]. How do I know that the same rule encompasses all other forms of tithing?

Scripture states, *You shall tithe* [encompassing all forms of agricultural offerings].

How do I know that in the case of the tithe owing from beasts people do not separate tithe [from a herd] among beasts born in a given year in behalf of beasts born in a different year?

Scripture states, *You shall tithe all the yield of your seed, which comes forth from the field year by year (Deut. 14:22).*

R. Simeon b. Judah says in the name of R. Simeon, "How do we know concerning tithe of beasts, that that tithe is subject to the positive commandment that [one must] tithe [his herd]? [That is to say, how do we know that it is a matter of obligation, not option?] Scripture states, *You shall tithe . . . (Deut. 14:22)* [as a matter of obligation].

Is it possible that something which grows from the earth, such as woad or madder, is subject [to the law of tithes]? Scripture says: *You shall tithe (Deut. 14:22)* and *You shall eat (Deut. 14:23).*

Is it possible that even honey and milk [are subject to the law of tithes]? Scripture says: *which comes forth from the field year by year.*

Conclude from this [that Scripture prescribes tithing only for] something which comes from the domain of the field "which comes from the field and is eaten."

Since it is said: *And before the Lord your God, in the place he will choose, to make his name dwell there, you shall eat the tithe of your grain, of your wine and of your oil . . . (Deut. 14:23),* is it possible that one obligates nothing but grain, wine and oil [to the laws of tithes]?

On what basis [do I know] to include other types of fruit? Scripture says: *(All) the yield of your seed (Deut. 14:22).*

This must be stated,

for if it were not so I should say: Just as grain is distinctive in that one places it in storage and it is normally eaten as it is, so too I need include only similar items.

What, then, do I include? Rice and millet and panicum and sesame.

On what basis do I include other types of pulse?

Scripture says: *You shall tithe (all the yield of your seed).*

Shall I include pulse which is normally eaten as it is, yet not include lupine and mustard seed which are not normally eaten as they are? Scripture says: *You shall tithe (all . . . that comes forth from the field) (Deut. 14:22).*

Is it possible [that they are subject to the law] even though they have not taken root? Scripture says *and you shall eat.*

On what basis [do I know] to include green vegetables among produce subject to the laws of tithes? Scripture says: *all the tithe of the land (Lev. 27:30).*

Of the seed of the land (Lev. 27:30)—to include garlic, pepperwort and field rocket.

Should I include turnip, radish and garden seeds which are not eaten? Scripture says: *of the seed of the land,* but not all the seed of the land.

Of the fruit of the trees (Lev. 27:30)—to include the fruits of trees.

Should I include sycamore pods, carobs [from the area of] Salmonah and carobs [from the area of] Gedurah which are not eaten? Scripture says: *of the fruit of the trees,* but not all the fruit of the trees.

On what basis [do I know] that a man tithes what he eats? Scripture says: *You shall tithe (Deut. 14:22).*

Is it possible [to tithe produce] even though its processing is not completed in the field?

Scripture says: *as the corn of the threshing floor (Num. 18:27)*—lo, it [i.e., the threshing floor] is in the field.

And as the fullness of the wine press (Num. 18:27)—[he is not required to tithe] until it [i.e., the wine] is in the wine press [but he is *permitted* to tithe beforehand],

Is it possible that a man make a snack in the field [after processing is complete]? Scripture says: *You shall tithe (Deut. 14:22).*

On what basis do I know that he must tithe what he sows? Scripture says: *what comes forth from the field (Deut. 14:22).*

How do I know that he must tithe what he stores away (but does not eat)?

Scripture says, *The yield of your seed.*

They said: They destroyed the stalls of the sons of Hanan three years before [the fall of] the Land of Israel [to the Romans] because they [i.e., the stall owners] would remove their produce from the scope of the tithing laws.

For they would interpret [Scripture] to mean [the following]: *You shall tithe . . . and you shall eat (Deut. 14:22)*—[that is, the one who eats shall tithe] but not the merchant.

The yield of your seed (Deut. 14:22)—[that is, the farmer shall tithe,] but not the buyer.

COMPOSITIONS BASED ON BOTH CLOSE READING OF
VERSES OF SCRIPTURE AND SPECULATIVE
DISCOURSE ON SCRIPTURAL THEMES

Genesis Rabbah

Translated by H. Freedman, in *Midrash Rabbah,* ed. H. Freedman and Maurice Simon (London: The Soncino Press, 1939). Genesis. 1:249–256.

GENESIS RABBAH CHAPTER 32 (TO GEN. 7:1).

[I.A] *And the Lord said unto Noah: Come thou and all thy house into the ark [etc.] (Gen. 7:1).* It is written, *You destroy them that speak falsehood [etc.] (Ps. 5:7):* this refers to Doeg and Ahitophel; *"Them that speak falsehood":* them and their speech. R. Phinehas´ said: Them and their company. *The man of blood and deceit (ibid):* the one permitted incest and bloodshed, and the other permitted incest and bloodshed. The one [Ahitophel] permitted incest and bloodshed, [when he counselled Absalom], *Go in unto your father's concubines (2 Sam. 16:21).* The other [Doeg] permitted incest: [Where do we find this?] Said R. Nahman b. Samuel b. Nahman: He annulled his [David's] citizen rights and declared him an outlaw and as one dead, so that his blood was permitted and his wife was permitted. *The Lord abhors (Ps. loc. cit.):* this means that they will neither be resurrected nor judged. *But as for me (ibid. 8):* as they have acted so have I acted; yet what is the difference between me and them? Only that You have shown me love and said to me, *The Lord also has put away your sin: you shall not die (2 Sam. 12:13).*

[B] [Another interpretation:] It refers to the generation of the Flood: "*You destroy them that speak falsehood*": them and their speech. "*The man of blood,*" as it is written, *The murderer rises with the light [etc.] (Job 24:14);* "*And deceit,*" as it is written, *For the earth is filled with violence (Gen. 6:13).* "*The Lord abhors*": they [the generation of the Flood] will neither be resurrected nor judged. "*But as for me*" [Noah]: as they have acted so have I acted, yet what is the difference between me and them? Only that You have shown love to me and said to me: *Come you and all your house into the ark.*

[II] *For the Lord is righteous, He loves righteousness; the upright shall behold His face (Ps. 11:7).* R. Tanhuma in R. Judah's name and R. Menahem in R. Eleazar's name said: No man loves his fellow-craftsman. A Sage, however, loves his compeer, e.g., R. Hiyya loves his colleagues and R. Hoshaya his. The Holy One, blessed be He, also loves His fellow-craftsman: hence, *For the Lord is righteous, He loves righteousness. The upright shall behold His face* applies to Noah, as it is written, *And the Lord said unto Noah: Come you . . . for you have I seen righteous before me.*

[III.A] *The Lord tries the righteous; but the wicked and him that loves violence His soul hates (Ps. 11:5).* R. Jonathan said: A potter does not test defective vessels, because he cannot give them a single blow without breaking them. Similarly the Holy One, blessed be He, does not test the wicked but only the righteous: thus, "*The Lord tries the righteous.*" R. Yose b. R. Hanina said: When a flax worker knows that his flax is of good quality, the more he beats it the more it improves and the more it glistens; but if it is of inferior quality, he cannot give it one knock without its splitting. Similarly, the Lord does not test the wicked but only the righteous, as it says, "*The Lord tries the righteous.*" R. Eleazar said: When a man possesses two cows, one strong and the other feeble, upon which does he put the yoke? Surely upon the strong one. Similarly, the Lord tests none but the righteous: hence, "*The Lord tries the righteous.*" Another interpretation: "*The Lord tries the righteous*" applies to Noah: hence, *And the Lord said unto Noah: Come you and all your house into the ark; for you have I seen righteous [etc.].*

[B] *For you have I seen righteous [etc.].* R. Eleazar b. Azariah said: We find that a portion of a man's merits may be declared in his presence, but all of them only in his absence. For thus it says in reference to Noah, *For you have I seen righteous,* whereas in his absence it says, *A man righteous and whole-hearted (Gen. 6:9).* R. Eliezer b. R. Yose the Galilean said: We find that we utter but a portion of the praise of Him at whose word the world came into being, for it is said, *Say unto God: How tremendous is Your work!* *(Ps. 66:3)*, and it says, *O give thanks unto the Lord, for He is good (Ps. 118:1)*.

[IV.A] *Of every clean beast you shall take with you . . . and of the beasts that are not clean [etc.] (Gen. 7:2)*. R. Judan in R. Yohanan's name, R. Berekiah in R. Leazar's name, and R. Jacob in R. Joshua's name said: We find that the Holy One, blessed be He, employed a circumlocution of three words in order to avoid uttering an unclean [indelicate] expression: It is not written, 'And of the unclean beasts," but *". . . that are not clean."* R. Judan said: Even when [Scripture] comes to enumerate the signs of unclean animals, it commences first with the signs of cleanness [which they possess]: it is not written, "The camel, because he parts not the hoof," but, *Because he chews the cud but parts not the hoof (Lev. 11:4); The rock-badger, because he chews the cud but parts not the hoof (Lev. 11:5); The hare, because she chews the cud but parts not the hoof (Lev. 11:6); The swine, because he parts the hoof, and is cloven-footed, but chews not the cud (Lev. 11:7)*.

[B] *Of the fowl also of the air, seven each*—E.V. *"Seven and Seven" (Gen. 7:3)*. If you say that it means seven of each kind, one of them would lack a mate; hence it means seven males and seven females; "not that I need them" [said God], "but *to keep seed alive upon the face of all the earth."*

[V.A] *For yet seven days [etc.] (Gen. 7:4)*. R. Simeon b. Yohai said: They have transgressed the Torah which was given after forty days, therefore *"I will cause it to rain . . . forty days and forty nights."* R. Yohanan said: They corrupted the features which take shape after forty days, therefore *"I will cause it to rain . . . forty days and forty nights."*

[B] *And every living substance [Yekum] that I have made will I blot out*. R. Berekiah said: That means, whatever exists (kayomaya) upon it. R. Abin said: The one who arose against him [his brother]. R. Levi said in the name of Resh Lakish: He [God] kept him [Cain] in suspense until the Flood came and swept him away: hence it is written, *And He blotted out every one that had arisen (Gen. 7:23)*.

[C] *And Noah did according unto all [etc.] (Gen. 7:5)*. The present verse refers to the taking in of the animals, beasts, and birds.

[VI.A] *And Noah was six hundred years old [etc.] (Gen. 7:6)*. R. Judah said: The year of the Flood is not counted in the number [of Noah's years]. Said R. Nehemiah to him: It is counted in the chronological reckoning.

[B] *And Noah went in, and his sons, [etc.] . . . because of the waters of the flood (Gen. 7:7)*. R. Yohanan said: He lacked faith: had not the water reached his ankles he would not have entered the Ark.

[VII.A] *And it came to pass after the seven days (Gen. 7:10)*. This teaches that the Holy One, blessed be He, gave them a respite during the seven days' mourning for the righteous Methusaleh, so that they might repent, yet they did not. Another interpretation: *And it came to pass after the seven days:* R. Joshuab. Levi said: Seven days the Holy One, blessed be He, mourned for His world before bringing the Flood, the proof being the text, *And it grieved Him (Gen.6:6),* while elsewhere we read, *The king is grieving for his son (2 Sam. 19:3).*

[B] *On the same day were all the fountains of the great deep broken up [etc.] (Gen. 7:11).* R. Yose b. Durmaskith said: They sinned through the eyeball, which is like water, therefore the Holy One, blessed be He, punished them by water. R. Levi said: They abused their fountains, therefore the Lord reversed the natural order: the natural order is for rain to descend and the deep to come up, but here, *Deep calls unto deep (Ps. 42:8).*

[VIII.A] *In the selfsame day entered Noah (Gen. 7:13).* R. Yohanan said: Had Noah entered the Ark at night his whole generation would have said, "We did not know what he was doing, but had we known we would not have permitted him to enter." Hence he entered *"In the selfsame day"* [with the challenge], "Let him who objects speak out!"

[B] *They, and every beast after its kind [etc.] (Gen. 7:14).* They were the principals and all others were secondary.

[C] *Every bird of every wing.* R. Eleazar said: R. Yose interpreted this to his colleagues: This excludes those which were moulting or maimed as unfit for the sacrifices of the Noachides.

[D] *And they that went in, went in male and female of all flesh (Gen. 7:16).* Said he to him: "Am I a hunter!" "Does that matter to you," He retorted; it is not written, "And they that were brought," but, *And they that went in*—of their own accord. R. Yohanan quoted: *Seek out of the book of the Lord, and read (Is. 34:16):* if they came of their own accord in order to be shut up twelve months in the Ark, how much the more [will they come] to gorge on the flesh of tyrants! Hence it is written, *And thou, son of man, thus says the Lord God: Speak to the birds of every sort, and to every beast of the field: Assemble yourselves, and come; gather yourselves on every side to My feast that I do prepare for you, even a great feast, upon the mountains of Israel, that you may eat flesh and drink blood. The flesh of the mighty shall you eat, and the blood of the princes of the earth shall you drink [etc.] (Ezek. 39:17f.).*

[E] *And the Lord shut him in.* R. Levi said: This may be compared to a king who decreed a general execution in a country, but took his friend, immured him in prison, and set his seal upon him. Even so, *And the Lord shut him in.*

[IX.A] *And the waters increased, and bore up the ark [etc.] (Gen. 17).* R

Phinehas said in R. Levi's name: Noah's ark thus sank in the water like a ship standing in harbour.

[B] *And the waters prevailed . . . and the ark went upon the face of the waters (Gen. 7:18).* R. Phinehas said in R. Levi's name: The ark thus floated upon the water as upon two planks [covering a distance] as from Tiberias to Susitha.

[X] *And the waters prevailed . . . and all the high mountains were covered (Gen. 7:19).* R. Jonathan was going up to worship in Jerusalem, when he passed the Palatinus and was seen by a Samaritan, who asked him, "Whither are you going?" "To worship in Jerusalem," replied he. "Would it not be better to pray at this holy mountain than at that dunghill?" he jeered. "Wherein is it blessed?" inquired he. "Because it was not submerged by the Flood." Now R. Jonathan momentarily forgot the teaching [on the subject], but his ass-driver said to him, "Rabbi, with your permission I will answer him," "Do," said he. "If it is of the high mountain," he answered, "then it is written, 'And all the high mountains were covered.' While if it is of the low ones, Scripture ignored it." R. Jonathan immediately descended from his ass and made him [the driver] ride three miles and applied three verses to him: (i) *There shall not be male or female barren among you, or among your cattle (Deut. 7:14)*—i.e., even among your cattle drivers; (ii) *Rakkathek [E.V. "thy temples"] is like a pomegranate split open (Song 4:3):* even the emptiest (*rekanim*) among you are as full of answers as a pomegranate [is of seeds]; and thus it is written, (iii) *No weapon that is formed against you shall prosper; and every tongue that shall rise against you in judgment you shall condemn (Is. 54:17).*

[XI.A] *Fifteen cubits upward did the waters prevail (Gen. 7:20).* R. Judah said: Fifteen cubits over the mountains and fifteen cubits over the plains. R. Nehemiah said: Fifteen cubits over the mountains, but over the plains, any height.

[B] *And all the flesh perished . . . all in whose nostrils was the breath of (nishmath) the spirit of (ruah) life [etc.] (Gen. 7:21f.)* R. Samuel the son-in-law of R. Hanina the colleague of the Rabbis said: Here the *neshamah* is made identical with *ruah*, whereas in an earlier passage the *neshamah* is identified with *nefesh*. How do we know that we should apply the teaching of each passage to the other? Because "life" is written in both places, proving that they are analogous.

[C] *Whatsoever was in the dry land, died.* This excludes fish. But some maintain that they too were included among those who were to be gathered into [the ark], but they fled to the Ocean [the Mediterranean].

[D] *And he blotted out every living substance . . . and Noah only (Ak) was left (Gen. 7:23): Ak* is a diminishing particle: he too coughed blood on account of the cold.

Leviticus Rabbah

Translated by J. Israelstam in H. Freedman and M. Simon, eds., *Midrash Rabbah*. Leviticus. Chapters I–XIX translated by J. Israelstam. Chapters XX–XXXVII translated by Judah J. Slotki (London: The Soncino Press, 1939), 4:188–198.

LEVITICUS RABBAH CHAPTER 15
(TO LEV. 13:2FF.)

[I] *When a man shall have in the skin of his flesh a rising, or a scab, or a bright spot, and it becomes in the skin of his flesh the plague of leprosy [etc.] (Lev. 13:2)*. This is [alluded to in] what is written, *He appoints a weight for the wind, and metes out the waters by measure (Job 28:25)*. R. Huna said: In three instances did a wind go forth of unmeasured force, which was capable of destroying the world, namely, one in the days of Job, another in the days of Jonah, and another in the days of Elijah; in the days of Job, as it is said, *And behold, a great wind came from across the wilderness [etc.] (Job 1:19)*; in the days of Jonah, as it is said, *But the Lord hurled a great wind into the sea [etc.] (Jon. 1:4)*; in the days of Elijah, as it is said, *And He said: Go forth and stand upon the mount before the Lord. And, behold, the Lord passed by, and a great and strong wind rent the mountains, and broke in pieces the rocks [etc.] (1 Kings 19:11)*. R. Judah b. R. Shalom said: The one [i.e., the wind] in the case of Job was the same as in the case of Jonah, and as in that of Elijah. The wind in the case of Job was intended for that house only, the one in the case of Jonah for that ship only, the one in the case of Elijah for that occasion only. The greatest of them all was the one in the case of Elijah. This is indicated by what is written, "*And He said . . . a great and strong wind rent the mountains, and broke in pieces the rocks.*" R. Tanhum b. R. Hiyya said, and some say it in the name of the Rabbis: the King-Messiah will not come until all the souls which it was originally the divine intention to create shall have come to an end, namely, those spoken of in the book of Adam, the first man, of which it is said, *This is the book of the generation of Adam (Gen. 5:1)*. R. Joshua b. Hananiah said: When a wind issues forth, the Holy One, blessed be He, breaks it through the mountains and weakens it by means of the hills and says to it: "Take care not to harm My creatures," as it is said, *For the wind that is from Me becomes faint, and souls which I have made (Is. 57:16)*, [render the latter part of the verse,] "For the sake of the souls which I have made."

"*And metes out the waters by measure.*" R. Judan b. R. Simeon said: Even the waters which come down from above are given by measure. This is [indicated by] what is written, *For he reduces (gara) the drops of water*

which distill as rain from His vapor (Job 36:27), and it is written, *And a reduction shall be made (gara) from your valuation (Lev. 27:18).*

[II] Another exposition: *"He makes a weight for the spirit [etc.]."* R. Aha
said: Even the Holy Spirit resting on the prophets does so by weight, one
prophet speaking one book of prophecy and another speaking two books.
R. Simon said: Two things [i.e., verses] did Beeri speak as a prophet, and
because they were not sufficient to form a book they were included in the
Book of Isaiah, namely, *And when they shall say unto you: Seek unto the
ghosts and the familiar spirits [etc.],* and its companion verse—*"And He
metes out the waters by measure."* R. Judah b. R. Samuel said: This means:
Even the words of the Torah which were given from above were given by
measure, namely Scripture, Mishnah, Talmud, "Halachah," and "Haggadah." One man becomes versed in Scripture, another in Mishnah, another
in Talmud, another in "Haggadah," yet another in all of them.

Another exposition: *"He appoints a weight for the wind."* Often people
say: "So-and-so has an unusually long breath, So-and-so's breath is short,
one who has a catarrhal breath."—*"And he metes out the water by measure."* Man is evenly balanced, half of him is water, and the other half is
blood. When he is deserving the water does not exceed the blood, nor does
the blood exceed the water; but when he sins, it sometimes happens that
the water gains over the blood and he then becomes a sufferer from dropsy;
at other times the blood gains over the water and he then becomes leprous.
This is [indicated by] what is written, *Adam* [i.e., *A man,*] read as if *O
dam,* "Or [if it be] blood [that exceeds].

[III] Another exposition on *When a man shall have in the skin of his flesh
[etc.].* This is alluded to in what is written, *Who has cleft a hollow for the
waterflood [shetef] (Job 38:25).* R. Berekiah said: There are places where
they call hair by the term *shitfa.* There is a story about a man who sat and
delivered a homily: There is no single hair for which the Holy One, blessed
be He, did not create its own follicle, so that one should not draw away
sustenance from the other. Said his wife to him: "And now you wish to go
forth to seek your livelihood? Stay and your Creator will sustain you." He
listened to her and stayed, and his Creator sustained him. *Or [cleft] a way
for the lightning of the thunder (ibid.).* Even for the thunder that issues
out of the firmament did the Holy One, blessed be He, make a path all for
itself. And why all that?—So that it should not go forth and destroy the
world. R. Abin said: [The tests mentioned by Scripture] may be compared
to the case of a vegetable garden into which a spring flows. As long as the
spring flows into it the vegetables in it are dark, if the spring ceases, the
vegetables in it fade. Even so, if a man proves worthy, *But if . . . and black
hair be grown therein; the scall is healed, he is clean (Lev. 13:37),* but if
not, *And the hair in the plague be turned white . . . it is the plague of lep-*

rosy, and the priest shall . . . pronounce him unclean (Lev. 13:3). It is therefore written, *Adam* [to be read as if] *O dam.*

[IV] Another exposition on *When a man shall have in the skin of his flesh a rising [etc.].* This is alluded to in what is written, *Judgments are prepared for the scorners, and stripes for the back of fools (Prov. 19:29).* Punishments are prepared for the scoffers. Usually when a man rides an ass, if it is recalcitrant he beats it, and if it plays pranks with him he beats it [but not otherwise]. In this instance, however, *"For the scorners judgments are prepared"*—*"And stripes,"* etc. This may be compared to the case of a lady of rank who, on entering the king's palace, saw whips hanging [around], and was terrified; but the king said to her: "Be not afraid; these are meant for the male and female slaves, but you are here to eat and drink and make merry." So, too, when Israel heard the section of Scripture dealing with leprous affections, they became afraid. Said Moses to them: "These are meant for the wicked nations, but you are intended to eat, drink and be joyful," as it is said, *Many are the sufferings of the wicked; but he that trusts in the Lord, mercy encompasses him about (Ps. 32:10).*

Rabbi and R. Ishmael b. Jose were engaged on the study of the Scroll of Lamentations on the eve of the [Fast of the] Ninth of Ab which fell on a Sabbath, when it was growing dark, from *Minhah*-time onwards, and omitted one alphabetical chapter, saying: We shall complete it to-morrow. When Rabbi left he suffered injury to his little finger, and applied to himself that passage, viz., *"Many are the sufferings of the wicked."* [Said R. Hiyya to him: "For *our* sins has this happened to you, as it is written, *The breath of our nostrils, the anointed of the Lord, was caught for their corrupt deeds (Lam. 4:20]."* R. Ishmael b. R. Jose said to him: "Even had we not been engaged on this passage, I would have said so; now that we have been engaged thereon, there is so much the more reason to say so." When he [i.e., Rabbi] reached home, he put on it [i.e., his finger] a dry sponge and wrapped reed-grass round it, outside thereof [i.e., of the sponge]. Said R. Ishmael b. R. Jose: From him we then learnt three things, viz., (a) a sponge does not heal, it only protects the wound, (b) it is permitted to tie round it reed-grass which is in the house, since it is designedly kept in readiness [for such purposes], and (c) it is not permitted to read the Hagiographa [on a Sabbath] except from *Minhah*-time onwards, but one may recite them by heart and deliver expositions on them, and if it is required for some purpose to examine [a passage of the Hagiographa], one may take up [a copy] and examine it. Samuel said: A small piece of potsherd and a small piece of reed-grass [it is permitted to handle in the house]. R. Judan taught in the name of R. Samuel: It is permitted to handle the stopper of a cask and broken pieces thereof on the Sabbath [within the house], but if one has thrown them on the dustheap it is forbidden to handle them.

R. Eleazar and R. Tanhum of Bozrah said in the name of R. Jeremiah: Even a wicked man who has repented is accepted by the Holy One, blessed be He, as it is said, *"Many are the sufferings of the Wicked, but he* [who was wicked] *that* [now] *trusts in the Lord, mercy encompasses him about."*

[V] What is written prior to the present subject?—*If a woman produce offspring, bearing a male child, she shall be unclean seven days (Lev. 12:1).* What is written after this?—*When a man shall have in the skin of his flesh a rising [etc.].* What has one subject to do with the other [that they should be juxtaposed]?—Said R. Tanhum b. Hanilai: This may be compared to a she-ass which was sick and was cauterized, and her foetus emerged with a cauterization mark. What caused it to come out with a cauterization mark?—The fact that its mother was cauterized. Likewise, who causes a new-born child to be leprous?—Its mother, who did not observe her period of separation.

R. Abin said: This may be compared to a vegetable garden into which a well empties; as long as the well empties into it, it will grow lichen. Likewise if a man comes in unto his wife during the period of her separation, he produces leprous children. R. Abin applied to this the verse, *The fathers have eaten sour grapes, and the children's teeth are set on edge (Jer. 31:29);* and these [i.e., the children] apply to their parents the following verse, *Our fathers have sinned, and are not; and we have borne their sins (Lam. 5:7).*

[VI] R. Abin said in the name of R. Yohanah: It is written, *And if she be not able to bring a lamb, [etc.] (Lev. 12:8).* What is written immediately after this?—*When a man shall have in the skin of his flesh a rising [etc.].* What has one subject to do with the other [that they should be juxtaposed]?—The Holy One, blessed be He, said: "I told you: Bring a sacrifice after [the] birth [of a child], but you did not do so. As you live, I shall oblige you to go to the priest"; as it is said [of a leper], *He shall be brought unto Aaron the priest (ibid.).*

R. Yohanan said: Why was the passage relating to *hallah* juxtaposed with one relating to idolatry?—To inform you that if one fulfills the precept of *hallah* it is as if he abolished idolatry; but if one neglects the precept of *hallah* it is as if he maintains idolatry. R. Eleazar said: It is written, *For* [one comes to grief] *through a harlot even through a loaf of bread (Prov. 6:26).* What causes him to come to grief through a harlot? The fact that he has eaten of her loaf which was not tithed.

R. Simeon b. Laqish said: It is written, *And every man's hallowed things shall be his: whatsoever any man gives the priest, it shall be his (Num. 5:10).* Immediately thereafter it is written, *If any man's wife go aside, and act unfaithfully against him . . . then shall the man bring his wife to the priest (Num. 5:12–15).* What has one subject to do with the other [that they should be juxtaposed]?—The Holy One, blessed be He, said: "I said to you: Bring your gift to the priest. You did not do so. As you live, I will oblige you to bring your wife to the priest," as it is said, *Then shall the man bring his wife to the priest.*"

[VII] R. Levi said: Blessed actions bless those that are responsible for them, but cursed actions curse those that are responsible for them. It is written, *A perfect and just weight—you shall have [etc.] (Deut. 25:15).* This means: If you act thus, you will have something to take and something to give, something to buy and something to sell. Cursed actions curse those responsible for them, as it is written, *You shall not have—[if there be] in your bag diverse weights, a great and a small. You shall not have—[if there be] in your house diverse measures, a great and a small (Deut. 25:13f.).* [This means:] If you do such things, you will not have anything to take or give, to buy or sell. The Holy One, blessed be He, said: "I said to you: You may not make one measure great and another small: Now if you have made, as you live, you will not make sufficient profit even with [using] a small measure [for purposes of selling]." Similar thereto is [the implication of the verse], *You shall not make with Me—gods of silver, or gods of gold, you shall not make unto you (Ex. 20:20),* but if you do, then, by your life, you will not be able to afford to have even gods of wood or stone.

[VIII] How [much of a person's body] is [to be visible at] an examination for leprosy?—In the case of a man, as [much as is visible] when one digs, and as when one plucks olives; as when one digs, for [the examination of] the privy parts, and as when one plucks olives, for [the examination of] the arm-pit. In the case of a woman, as [much as is visible] when she is preparing bread, and as when she is suckling her child; [as when she is preparing bread, for the examination of the privy parts, and as when she is suckling her child] for the examination under the breasts, and as when weaving at an upright loom for [an examination] of the arm-pit of the right hand. R. Judah said: Also as when spinning flax for [an examination of the arm-pit] of the left hand. Moreover, precisely the extent to which one need be visible [when examined] for leprosy, need one be visible for the process of [purification from leprosy by the bringing of a sacrifice and] shaving. We have learnt in the Mishnah: One is entitled to examine for [and pronounce on] any leprosy except his own leprosy. R. Meir said: Not even for the leprosy of one's relatives. Who then examined the leprosy of Miriam? If you should say it was Moses who examined, why, a non-priest may not examine for leprosy. If you should say it was Aaron who examined her, why, a relative may not examine for leprosy. [The answer is:] The Holy One, blessed be He, said: "I am a priest, I shut her up and I shall declare her clean." This is indicated by what is written, *And the Lord said: . . . let her be shut up without the camp seven days, and after that she shall be brought in again . . . and the people journeyed not till Miriam was brought in again*

(Num. 12:14f.). Since it is the case that the people [halted and journed] with the "Shechinah," it follows that the "Shechinah" waited for her [i.e., Miriam].

R. Levi said in the name of R. Hama b. R. Hanina: Moses was much grieved on account of this matter, saying: "Is it in accordance with the dignity of my brother Aaron that he should have to examine for leprosy?" Said the Holy One, blessed be He, to him: "Does he not [by way of recompense] have the benefit of the twenty-four gifts [which are the prescribed perquisites] of the priesthood?" The proverb says: "He who eats of the palm's heart will be beaten with the stick of the dried up palm."

[IX] *A rising (seeth)* alludes to Babel, since it is said, *You shall take up this parable against the king of Babylon, and say: How have the oppressor ceased! The exactress of gold ("madhebah") ceased! (Isa. 14:4).* R. Abba b. Kahana said: "*Madhebah*" means a kingdom which says "*Medod, habe*" [i.e., "measure out and bring," sc. tribute]. R. Samuel b. Nahman said: ["*Madhebah*" means] a kingdom which causes to flame up the face of anyone who comes to it. The Rabbis say: [Babylon is called "*Madhebah*"] because *Its head was of gold—(dehab) (Dan. 2:32),* [and it is further said,] *You* [Nebuchadnezzar, king of Babylon,] *are the head of gold (Dan. 2:38).*

A scab (sappahath) alludes to Media which reared Haman who inflamed *(shaf)* the people [of Media] like a snake, of which it is said, *Upon your belly shall you go (Gen. 3:14).*

A bright spot [bahereth] alludes to Greece [i.e., Syria] who made herself conspicuous by her decrees against Israel, saying to them: "Write on the horn of an ox that you have no share in the God of Israel." *The plague of leprosy* alludes to Edom [i.e., Rome], because it[s power] is derived from the strength of [the blessing of] the old man [viz. Isaac]; *And it become in the skin of his flesh the plague of leprosy.* In this world the priest examines for leprosy; but in the World to Come—says the Holy One, blessed be He—"I will render you clean." Thus it is written, *And I will sprinkle clean water upon you, and you shall be clean [Ezek. 36:25).*

COMPOSITIONS BASED ON SPECULATIVE DISCOURSE ON SCRIPTURAL THEMES

Lamentations Rabbah

Translated by A. Cohen in *Midrash Rabbah,* ed. by H. Freedman and Maurice Simon. *Lamentations* (London: The Soncino Press, 1939), 7:6–9, 105–113.

LAMENTATIONS RABBAH PROEMS 3–5.

[III] R. Abba b. Kahana opened his discourse with the text, *I saw not in the assembly of them that make merry, nor rejoiced (Jer. 15:17).* The Community of Israel spoke before the Holy One, blessed be He: "Sovereign of the Universe, never did I enter the theatres and circuses of the heathen peoples and make merry and rejoice." *I sat alone because of your hand* (*ibid.*): Pharaoh's hand attacked me, but I sat not alone. Sennacherib's hand attacked me, but I sat not alone. Since, however, Your hand attacked me, I sat alone. *"How sits solitary" (Lam. 1:1).*

[IV] R. Abbahu opened his discourse with the text, *But they like men have transgressed the covenant (Hos. 6:7).* This alludes to the first man, of whom the Holy One, blessed be He, said, "I brought him into the Garden of Eden and imposed a command upon him, but he transgressed it; so I punished him by driving him out and sending him forth, and lamented over him, *Ekah.*" "I brought him into the Garden of Eden," as it is said, *And the Lord God took the man, and put him into the Garden of Eden (Gen. 2:15).* "I imposed a command upon him," as it is said, *And the Lord God commanded the man, saying (Gen. 2:16).* "But he transgressed My command," as it is said, *Have you eaten of the tree, whereof I commanded you that you should not eat? (Gen. 3:11).* "So I punished him by driving him out," as it is said, *So He drove out the man (Gen. 3:24),* and "by sending him forth," as it is said, *Therefore the Lord God sent him forth (Gen. 3:23),* and "lamented over him, *Ekah,*" as it is said, *Where are you?—[ayyekah] (Gen. 3:9),* this being written *ekah.*

Similarly with his descendants. I brought them into the land of Israel, as it is said, *And I brought you into a land of fruitful fields (Jer. 2:7).* I gave them commandments, as it is said, *Command the children of Israel (Lev. 24:2).* They transgressed My ordinances, as it is said, *Yea, all Israel have transgressed Thy law (Dan. 9:11).* So I punished them by driving them out, as it is said, *I will drive them out of My house (Hos. 9:15),* and by sending them forth, as it is said, *Cast them out of My sight and let them go forth (Jer. 15:1);* and I lamented over them, *"How sits solitary."*

[V] R. Abbahu, in the name of R. Yose b. Hanina, opened his discourse with the text, *Therefore thus says the Lord God: Woe to the bloody city (Ezek. 24:6):* alas for the city in the midst of which they shed blood. *"To the pot whose filth is therein":* in which the dregs remain. *"And whose filth is not gone out of it":* whose dregs have not departed from it. *"Bring it out piece by piece":* they went into exile in sections.

In what order were they exiled? R. Eleazar says: "The tribes of Reuben and Gad went into exile first. R. Samuel b. Nahman says: The tribes of Zebulun and Naphtali went into exile first; and so it is written, *As at the first time He made light the land of Zebulun and the land of Naphtali (Is. 8:23).* How, then, does R. Eleazar interpret the verse quoted by R. Samuel b. Nahman? As the tribes of Reuben and Gad went into exile, so did the tribes of Zebulun and Naphtali go into exile. *"But the latter has dealt a more serious blow [hikbid]":* R. Abba b. Kahana said: [The meaning is,] He swept them as with a broom (*makbid*): and so it is written, *I will sweep it with the broom of destruction (Is. 14:23). No lot is fallen upon it (Ezek. 24:6)*: R. Nahman said in the name of R. Aha: What means "*no lot is fallen upon it*"? The Holy One, blessed be He, said, "At the time when I caused lots to be cast for the heathen nations of the world to be exiled, they did not go into captivity; so why were *you* exiled? *Because her blood is in the midst of her (Ezek. 24:7).*" To what purpose is all this? *That it might cause fury to come up (Ezek. 24:8).*

R. Judan asked R. Aha, "Where did the Israelites slay Zechariah, in the Court of Israel or the Court of Women?" He replied, "In neither of these, but it was in the Court of the Priests. Nor did they treat his blood as was done with the blood of a ram or hind; for in connection with the blood of these animals it is written, *He shall pour out the blood thereof and cover it with dust (Lev. 17:13)*, but of this incident it is written, *For her blood is in the midst of her, she set it upon the bare rock; she poured it not upon the ground, to cover it with dust (Ezek. 24:7).*"

Another interpretation of "*Therefore thus says the Lord God, Woe to the bloody city (Ezek. 24:9)*": alas for the city in the midst of which they shed blood. "*I also will make the pile great (Ezek. 24:9)*": I will multiply punishments. "*Heaping on the wood (Ezek. 24:10)*": these are the enemy's legions. "*Kindling the fire*": these are the kings. "*That the flesh be consumed*": this refers to the Community. "*And preparing the mixture*": R. Joshua and R. Nehemiah in the name of R. Aha said: Inasmuch as all Israel kept saying, "Nebuchadnezzar has gathered to himself all the wealth of the world, will he need ours?" the Holy One, blessed be He, retorted: "By your lives, I will make your wealth as desirable to him as the spices which are used at a banquet." "*That the bones also may be burned*": you find that at the time when the Israelites went into exile, their bodies steamed like a spiced dish. "*Then will I set it empty upon the coals thereof (Ezek. 24:11)*": R. Eleazar said: Had the text said, "broken," there would never have been a remedy for them; but since it says, "empty," [there is hope of a remedy, because] an empty vessel may eventually be filled. To what purpose is all this? "*That it may be hot, and the bottom thereof may burn, and that the impurity of it may be molten in it, that the filth of it may be consumed.*" Since they sinned, they were exiled; and since they were exiled, Jeremiah began to lament over them, "*How sits solitary.*"

LAMENTATIONS RABBAH TO LAM. 1:5–9

[32] *For the Lord has afflicted her for the multitude of her transgressions.* Perhaps He acted so without reason; therefore it is stated, *For the multitude of her transgressions.*

Her young children are gone into captivity before the adversary. R. Judah said: Come and see how beloved are children by the Holy One, blessed be He. The Sanhedrin was exiled, but the *Shechinah* did not go into exile with him. The priestly watches were exiled, but the *Shechinah* did not go into exile with them. When, however, the children were exiled, the *Shechinah* went into exile with them. That is what is written, *Her young children are gone into captivity before the enemy.* This is immediately followed by *[And gone is from the daughter of Zion her splendor]*.

[33] *And gone is from the daughter of Zion all her splendor (Lam. 1:6).* The scriptural text reads *min bath.* R. Aha said: We possess one excellent portion, viz. the Holy One, blessed be He, of whom it is written, *O Lord, the portion of [menath] mine inheritance and of my cup (Ps. 16:5). All her splendor:* this alludes to the Holy One, blessed be He; as it is said, *Thou art clothed with glory and splendor (Ps. 104:1).* Another interpretation of *All her splendor:* this alludes to the Sanhedrin; as it is written, *Strength and splendor are her clothing (Prov. 31:25).* Another interpretation of *All her splendor:* this alludes to the disciples of the sages; as it is written, *You shall rise up before the hoary head, and honor the face of the old man (Lev. 19:32).* Another interpretation of *All her splendor:* this alludes to the priestly watches; as it is written, *And praise in the splendor of holiness (2 Chron. 20:21).* Another interpretation of *All her splendor:* this alludes to the children. R. Judah said: Come and see how beloved are children by the Holy One, blessed be He. The Sanhedrin were exiled but the *Shechinah* did not go into exile with them. The priestly watches were exiled but the *Shechinah* did not go into exile with them. When, however, the children were exiled, the *Shechinah* went into exile with them. For is it not written, *Her young children are gone into captivity before the adversary,* which is immediately followed by *And gone is from the daughter of Zion all her splendor?*

Her princes are become like harts that find no pasture. R. Judah said: When they are tender-hearted they are likened to lambs; as it is said, *Then shall the lambs feed as in their pasture (Is. 5:17);* but when they are hard-hearted they are likened to harts, as it is said *Her princes are become like harts.* R. Simon said in the name of R. Simeon b. Abba and R. Simeon b. Laqish said in the name of R. Joshua: As harts turn their faces one beneath the other in the time of intense heat, so the eminent men of Israel would see a transgression committed but turn their faces away from it. The Holy One, blessed be He, said, "A time will come when I will do the same to you."

And they are gone without strength before the pursuer. R. Azariah said in the name of R. Judah b. R. Simon: When Israel perform the will of the Omnipresent they add strength to the heavenly power; as it is said, *To God*

167

we render strength (Ps. 60:14). When, however, Israel does not perform the will of the Omnipresent, they weaken, if it is possible to say so, the great power of Him Who is above; as it is written, *You weakened the Rock that begot you (Deut. 32:18)*. R. Judah b. R. Simon said in the name of R. Levi b. R. Tarfon: When Israel perform the will of the Omnipresent they add strength to the heavenly power; as it is stated, *And now, I pray thee, let the power of the Lord be great (Num. 14:17)*. When, however, Israel do not perform the will of the Omnipresent they weaken, if it is possible to say so, the great power of Him Who is above, and they too *are gone without strength before the pursuer*.

R. Huna, R. Aha, and R. Simon said in the name of R. Simeon b. Laqish, and the Rabbis said it in the name of R. Hanina: A man would say to his fellow in Jerusalem, "Teach me a page of Scripture," but he would reply, "I have not the strength." [He would say,] "Teach me a chapter of Mishnah," but he would reply, "I have not the strength." The Holy One, blessed be He, said to them, "A time will come when I will act so with you." *And they are gone without strength before the pursuer:* R. Aha said: Just as Israel was sent into exile by a "pursuer," written *plene*, so will they be rescued by a "redeemer," written *plene*, as it says, *And a redeemer will come to Zion (Is. 59:20)*, where the word is written *plene*.

[34] *Jerusalem remembers in the days of her affliction and her anguish [merudehah] (Lam. 1:7)*. In the days of her affliction she remembered the revolts *(meradin)* in which she rebelled against the Holy One, blessed be He. *All her treasures that she had:* these are the words of the Torah, as it is stated, *More to be desired are they than gold, yea, than much fine gold (Ps. 19:11)*.

Now that her people fall by the hand of the adversary. The Babylonian Rabbis say: When the ox falls many are the slaughterers; while the Palestinian Rabbis say: When the ox falls men sharpen their knives.

And none does help her. The Babylonian Rabbis say: When the bride is ill-treated, she recalls the seven days of her marriage feast; while the Palestinian Rabbis say: When the son goes barefoot he recalls the comfort of his father's house.

The adversaries have seen her, they have mocked at her desolation [mishbattehah]: i.e., at her sabbaths, as it is stated, *Remember the sabbath day, to keep it holy (Ex. 20:8)*. Another interpretation of *mishbattehah:* at her sabbatical years, as it is stated, *But in the seventh year shall be a sabbath of solemn rest for the land (Lev. 25:4)*. Another interpretation of *mishbattehah:* this alludes to R. Yohanan b. Zakkai who ceased to be in Jerusalem.

[35] *Jerusalem have grievously sinned (Lam. 1:8)*. Do the heathen nations, then, not sin? But although they sin, it has no sequel in punishment.

Israel, however, sinned and were punished. *There she is become as one un-clean [le-nidah]:* i.e., she was doomed to vagabondage.

All that honored her despise her, because they have seen her nakedness. She herself also sighs, and turns backward; backward from the priesthood, *backward* from kingship.

[36] *Her filthiness was in her skirts (Lam. 1:9).* R. Berekiah said in the name of R. Abba b. Kahana: All the priests who officiated in the days of Zedekiah were uncircumcised. That is what is stated, *In that you have brought in aliens, uncircumcised in heart and uncircumcised in flesh, to be in My sanctuary (Ezek. 44:7).* Another interpretation of *her filthiness was in her skirts:* in her nether limbs, as it is stated, *Upon the skirts of the robe (Ex. 28:34).* Another interpretation of *her filthiness was in her skirts:* As we have learnt: There was a place below Jerusalem with the name Topheth. R. Judah said: [It was so called] because of the seduction *(tophteh)* to idolatry which was there. R. Yose said: [The Targum translates it] "the valley of Bar Hinnon." A hollow image was set up there within the innermost of seven chambers, holding a copper plate in its hand upon which a fire-pan was placed. When a person brought an offering of flour one chamber was opened for him; when he brought one of doves and pigeons, two chambers were opened for him; of a lamb, three were opened for him; of a ram, four were opened for him; of a calf, five were opened for him; of an ox, six were opened for him; but when a person brought an offering of his child the seven were opened for him. They placed the child on the copper plate, kindled the fire-pan beneath him, and sang before the image, "May the sacrifice be pleasant and sweet to thee!" Why did they do this? So that the parents should not hear the groans of their children and retract.

A heathen priest went to a certain man and said to him, "[I have come to you] because the image has declared to me that of all the children you have you are unwilling to sacrifice one." He replied, "Are they, then, under my control? One works with gold, another with silver, a third with sheep, and a fourth with the herds. But wait! You have seen that I have a young child at school. When he arrives home I will give him to you." The Holy One, blessed be He, said to him, "Wretch! Of all the sons you have there is none you are willing to sacrifice for idol-worship except this child who is conse-crated to My name!" R. Judan b. R. Simon said in the name of R. Levi b. Parta: It may be likened to a lady whose lover said to her, "Prepare some hot food for me." So she took the king's portrait and used it as fuel to pre-pare hot food for him. The king said to her, "Of all the wood that is in this house you could not use any to prepare hot food for your lover except my image!" In like manner the Holy One, blessed be He, said to the wicked man: "Of all the sons you have there is none you are willing to sacrifice for idol-worship except the child who is consecrated to My name!" That is what is stated, *Moreover you took your sons and your daughters, whom you had borne to me, and these you sacrificed to them to be devoured (Ezek. 16:20)*. Nevertheless, *Therefore is she come down wonderfully:* she is come down into sore trials.

Esther Rabbah I

Translated by Maurice Simon in *Midrash Rabbah*, ed. H. Freedman and Maurice Simon (London: The Soncino Press, 1939), 9:5–9, 18–32.

PROEMS 4–8

[4] Samuel opened with the text: *And yet for all that, when they are in the land of their enemies, I did [E.V. "will"] not reject them, neither did I abhor them, to destroy them utterly, to break My covenant with them; for I am the Lord their God (Lev. 26:44)*. "*I did not reject them,*" in Babylon; "*Neither did I abhor them*"—in Media. "*To destroy them utterly*"—when subject to Greece. "*To break My covenant with them,*"—when subject to the kingdom of wickedness. "*For I am the Lord their God*"—in the Messianic era. R. Hiyya taught: "*I did not reject them*"—in the days of Vespasian; "*Neither did I abhor them*"—in the days of Trajan. "*To destroy them utterly*"—in the days of Haman. "*To break my covenant with them*"—in the days of the Romans. "*For I am the Lord their God*"—in the days of Gog and Magog.

[5] R. Judah b. R. Simon opened with the text: *As if a man did flee from a lion [etc.] (Amos 5:19)*. R. Huna and R. Hama in the name of R. Hanina said: "*As if a man did flee from a lion*"—this refers to Babylon, which is designated by the words, *The first was like a lion (Dan. 7:4). And a bear met him (Amos, loc. cit.)*, this refers to Media, designated in the words, *And behold another beast, a second, like to a bear (Dan. 7:5)*. (R. Yohanan said: The word "*ledob*" (a bear) is written defectively. This accords with the opinion of R. Yohanan given in his dictum, *Therefore a lion out of the forest slays them (Jer. 5:6)*: this refers to Babylon. *A wolf of the desert spoils them (ibid.)*, this refers to Media. *A leopard watches over their cities*—this refers to Greece. *Everyone that goes thence is torn in pieces*—this refers to Edom.) *And he went into the house (Amos, loc. cit.)*—this refers to Greece, in the era of which the Temple was still standing. *And a serpent bit him*—this refers to Edom, of which it says, *The sound thereof shall go like the serpent's (Jer. 46:22)*. Similarly it says, *Open to me, my sister (Song 5:2)*: this refers to [Israel under] Babylon. *My love (ibid.)*—this refers to Media. *My dove*—this refers to Greece. *My undefiled*—this refers to Edom. "*Dove*" refers to Greece because throughout the days of the Grecian domination the Temple stood and Israel used to offer pigeons and doves on the altar.

R. Phinehas and R. Levi in the name of R. Hama b. Hanina explain as follows: It is written, *In my distress I called upon the Lord (Ps. 18:7)*—in Babylon. *And cried to my God*—in Media. *Out of His temple He heard my voice*—in Greece. For R. Huna said on his own account: *"My dove"* refers to the kingdom of Greece, because throughout the Grecian domination the Temple was standing and Israel used to offer pigeons and doves on the altar. Hence, *"Out of His temple He heard my voice."* *And my cry came before Him unto His ears*—this refers to Edom. Another explanation: *"As if a man did flee from a lion"*—this refers to Nebuchadnezzar. *"And a bear met him"*—this refers to Belshazzar. *And went into the house and leaned his hand on the wall, and a serpent bit him (Amos, loc. cit.)*—this refers to Haman, who hissed at the people like a serpent; for so it is written, *Rehum the commander and Shimshai the scribe*—the latter being the son of Haman—*wrote a letter . . . to Artaxerxes the king in this sort (Ezra 4:8).* What was written in it? *Be it known now to the king . . . they will not pay "minda," "belo," or "halak" (ib. 13).* *"Minda"* is the land tax, *"belo"* is the poll-tax. *"Halak"* is forced labor. *The "apsom" of the kings will be damaged.* R. Huna and R. Phinehas explain: Even the things with which royalty entertains itself *(mithpateh),* such as theatres and circuses, this city injures. When he heard this, he sent and stopped the building of the Temple, and when they saw this they began to cry, Woe! this being the meaning of *Wayyehi (there was woe) in the days of Ahasuerus.*

[6] R. Isaac opened with the text, *When the righteous are increased the people rejoice; but when the wicked beareth rule, the people sigh (Prov. 29:2).* When the righteous attain greatness, there is joy and gladness in the world, there is *wah! wah!* in the world. Thus it says, *Now king (weha-melek) David (1 Kings 1:1)*—as if to say, *wah!* that David is become king. *Now king [weha-melek] Solomon (ib. 11:1)*—as if to say, *wah!* that Solomon is king. *Then king [weha-melek] Asa (ib. 15:22)*—as if to say, *wah!* that Asa is king. These cases refer to kings of Israel. How do we know the same of Gentile kings? Because it says, *Also Cyrus the king—[weha-melek] (Ezra 1:7)*—*wah!* that Cyrus is king. When, however, the wicked attain to greatness, there is woe *(way)* and groaning and fierce anger in the world. Thus it says, *And Ahab, the son of Omri reigned—[wayyimlok] (1 Kings 16:29)*—as if to say, woe *(way)* that Ahab son of Omri is become king! Again, And Hosea son of Elah reigned—woe that Hosea son of Elah is become king. *And Zedekiah the son of Josiah reigned [vayyimlok] as king (Jer. 37:1)*—woe that Zedekiah son of Josiah is become king. We find the same with Gentile kings, as it is written, *And it came to pass [wayyehi] in the days of Ahasuerus*—woe that Ahasuerus is become king!

[7] R. Levi opened with the text, *But if you will not drive out the inhabitants of the land from before you, then shall those that you let remain of*

them be as thorns in your eyes, and as pricks in your sides (Num. 33:55).
This may be applied to Saul, at the time when Samuel said to him, *Now go
and smite Amelek (1 Sam. 15:3).* He said to him on his return: You went
forth virtuous and have brought back a sinner and spared him, as it says,
But Saul and the people spared Agag (ib. 9). Lo, a scion shall spring from
him who shall inflict on you hardships like thorns in your eyes and pricks in
your sides. Who will this be? Haman, who decreed to destroy, to slay, and
to cause to perish. When they all saw this, they began crying, Woe!
Wayyehi (there was woe) in the days of Ahasuerus.

[8] R. Hanina b. Adda opened with the text, *The words of a wise man's
mouth are gracious (Eccl. 10:12).* This refers to Cyrus, of whom we read,
*Thus says Cyrus king of Persia: All the kingdoms of the earth have the
Lord, the God of heaven, given me; and He has charged me to build Him a
house in Jerusalem which is in Judah (Ezra 1:2).* But *the lips of a fool will
swallow up himself (Eccl., loc. cit.)* because he went on, *The God who is in
Jerusalem (Ezra 1:3). The beginning of the words of his mouth is foolishness (Eccl. 10:13).* Wherein lay the foolishness? In his saying, *Whosoever
there is among you of all His people, his God be with him (Ezra, loc. cit.)
And the end of his talk is grievous madness (Eccl., loc. cit.)*—because he
decreed that whoever had crossed the Euphrates might remain across, but
he who had not yet crossed should no longer do so. Another explanation of
"The beginning of the words [etc.]": This refers to Ahasuerus, of whom we
read, *And in the reign of Ahasuerus in the beginning of his reign wrote
they an accusation [etc.] (Ezra 4:6). "And the end of his talk [etc.]"*: because he rose and put a stop to the building of the Temple. When they all
saw this, they began to cry, Woe! *Wayyehi (there was woe) in the days of
Ahasuerus!*

ESTHER RABBAH 1:1–16

[1] *Now it came to pass in the days of Ahasuerus (Esther 1:1).* R. Joshua
b. Karhah said: [He was called Ahasuerus] because he made the face of Israel black *(hishhir)* like the sides of a pot. R. Berekiah said: Because he
made the head of Israel ache *(hikhish rosh)* with fasting and affliction. R.
Levi said: Because he made them drink gall *(hihkah rosh)* and wormwood.
R. Judah said: Because he sought to uproot Israel from the foundation. R.
Tahalifa b. Bar Hanah said: Because he was the brother of the head *(ahiw
shel rosh)*, the brother of Nebuchadnezzar. How could he be his brother?
Was not one a Chaldean and the other a Median? The fact is that one
stopped the building of the Temple and the other destroyed the Temple;
therefore Scripture put them on the same level; and so we read, *Even one
that is slack in his work is brother to him that is a destroyer (Prov. 18:9).
"Even one that is slack in his work"*—this is Ahasuerus who stopped the

172

building of the Temple. *"Is brother to him that is a destroyer"*—this is Nebuchadnezzar who destroyed the Temple.

This is [hu] Ahasuerus. R. Judah and R. Nehemiah explained differently. One said: Ahasuerus who put his wife to death on account of his friend, *This is [the same] Ahasuerus* who put his friend to death on account of his wife. R. Nehemiah said: Ahasuerus who stopped the building of the Temple, *This is [the same] Ahasuerus* who ordered that it should be built. But did he order this? Was it not Cyrus who ordered this, as it is written, *In the first year of Cyrus the king, Cyrus the king made a decree concerning the house of God . . . let the house be built [etc.] (Ezra 6:3)?* But the fact is that at that time all his counsellors came before him [Darius] and said: "Your father decreed that it should not be built, and will you order it to be built? Can a king annul another king's decree?" He said to them: "Bring me the copies of the State archives." Forthwith they brought them to him; thus it is written, *Then there was found at Ahmetha, in the palace . . . a roll (ib. 2).* What was written therein? *Make ye now a decree to cause these men to cease (ib. 4:21).* He said to them: "Is it written, for ever? It says only, *Until a decree shall be made by me (ib.).* Who can say that if my father had been alive he would not have built it?" Hence the Scripture mentions him along with the prophets, as it says, *And the elders of the Jews built and prospered, through the prophesying of Haggai [etc.] (ib. 6:14).*

[2] The word *hu* (he was) is found five times in a bad and five times in a good sense. The five times in a bad sense are: *He [Nimrod] was [hu] a mighty hunter before the Lord (Gen. 10:9); This is [hu] Esau the father of the Edomites (ib. 36:43); These are [hu] that Dathan and Abiram (Num. 26:9); This same [hu] king Ahaz (2 Chron. 28:22);* and *This is [hu] Ahasuerus.* Five times in a good sense, namely, *Abram—the same [hu] is Abraham (1 Chron. 1:27); These are that [hu] Moses and Aaron (Ex. 6:27), and These are that [hu] Aaron and Moses (ib. 26); And David was [hu] the youngest (1 Sam. 17:14); Has not the same [hu] Hezekiah (2 Chron. 32:12); This [hu] Ezra went up from Babylon (Ezra 7:6).* R. Berekiah said in the name of the Rabbis of Babylon; We have one better than all of them, namely, *He is [hu] the Lord our God; His judgments are in all the earth (Ps. 105:7),* implying that the Attribute of Mercy is everlasting.

[3] *Ahasuerus.* R. Levi and the Rabbis differed on this. R. Levi said: Ahasuerus is the same as Artaxerxes; and why was he called Ahasuerus? Because no one could mention him without feeling a headache (*hosesh et rosho*). The Rabbis said: Artaxerxes was the same as Ahasuerus; and why was he called Artaxerxes? Because he used to fall into a passion and then be sorry (*martiah vehash*). *Ahasuerus: this is Ahasuerus.* R. Isaac and the Rabbis explained differently. R. Isaac said: [He was the] *Ahasuerus* in whose days all trouble came, as it says, *There was great mourning among the Jews*

173

(*Esther 4:3*). *This is Ahasuerus:* in whose days all blessings came, as it says, *The Jews had gladness and joy, a feast and a good day* (*ib.* 8:17). The Rabbis say: *Ahasuerus*, before Esther went in unto him; *This is Ahasuerus;* after Esther went in unto him he did not have intercourse with women in the period of their separation.

[4] *Who reigned:* but up to now he had not reigned. *From Hodu even up to Cush.* Is it not merely a short distance from Hodu to Cush? What it means is that as he reigned from Hodu to Cush, so he reigned over a hundred and twenty-seven provinces. Similarly we find: *For he had dominion over all the region on this side the River, from Tiphsah even unto Gaza* (*1 Kings 5:4*). Now is it not only a short distance from Tiphsah to Gaza? What it means, however, is that as he ruled from Tiphsah to Gaza, so he ruled over the whole world. Similarly we find, *From the Temple up to Jerusalem, kings shall bring presents unto Thee* (*Ps.* 68:30). Is it not only a short distance from the Temple to Jerusalem? What it means, however, is that just as the offerings extend from the Temple to Jerusalem, so there will be a procession of messengers with gifts for the Messiah, as it is written, *Yea, all kings shall prostrate themselves before him* (*ib.* 72:11). R. Cohen the brother of R. Hiyya b. Abba said: As the Divine Presence stretches from the Temple to Jerusalem, so will the Divine Presence one day fill the world from end to end, as it is written, *And let the whole earth be filled with His glory, Amen, and Amen* (*ib.* 19).

[5] *A hundred and seven and twenty.* R. Eleazer said in the name of R. Hanina: Are there not two hundred and fifty-two governorships in the world? Now David ruled over all of them, as it is written, *And the fame of David went out into all lands* (*1 Chron.* 14:17). Solomon also ruled over all of them, as it says, *And Solomon ruled over all the kingdoms, [etc.]* (*1 Kings 5:1*). Aha also ruled over all of them, as it is written, *As the Lord your God lives, there is no nation or kingdom, whither my Lord has not sent to seek you . . . and imposed an oath on the kingdom [etc.]* (*ib.* 18:10). Now can one impose an oath where he is not suzerain? Another proof is from this verse: *Then he numbered the young men of the princes of the provinces, and they were two hundred and thirty-two* (*ib.* 20:15). Where were the rest? R. Levi and the Rabbis gave different answers. R. Levi said: They perished of famine in the days of Elijah; the Rabbis said that Benhadad came and took them, as it says, *And Ben-hadad the king of Aram gathered all his host together; and there were thirty and two kings with him, and horses and chariots; and he went up and besieged Samaria, and fought against it* (*ib.* 1). We only require twenty and you say thirty-two! There were some provinces which were rebellious, and he took a couple of men and kept them as hostages in his power. (R. Berekiah and the Rabbis [explained the verse, *He has caused the arrows of His quiver to enter into*

my reins (Lam. 3:13)]. R. Berekiah said: This means that they took prisoners (*bene ukaifi*) and hostages (*bene amorai*). The Rabbis said: The prisoners were called *bene ukaifi* because they were curbed with manacles (*arkuf*). The hostages are called *bene amorai* because they are exchanges (*temuroth*) for their fathers; and so it says, *The hostages [bene hataaruboth] also (2 Kings 14:14)*, so called because they were substitutes (*meuraboth*) for their fathers.) Nebuchadnezzar ruled over all countries, as it says, *And wheresoever the children of men, the beasts of the field, and the fowls of the heaven dwell, has He given them unto your hand (Dan. 2:38)*. Cyrus ruled over all of them, as it is written, *Thus said Cyrus . . . All the kingdoms of the earth has the Lord . . . given me (Ezra 1:2)*. Darius ruled over all of them, as it says, *Then king Darius wrote unto all the peoples (Dan. 6:26)*. Ahasuerus ruled over half of them. Why only over half? R. Huna gave different explanations in the names of R. Aha and the Rabbis. R. Huna said in the name of R. Aha: God said to him: "You have halved My kingdom, in saying, *He is the God who is in Jerusalem (Ezra 1:3)*. As you live, I will halve your kingdom." The Rabbis say: God said to him: "You halved the size of My house, saying, *The height thereof threescore cubits (ib. 6:3)*; as you live, I will halve your kingdom." Then let it say in the text, "a hundred and twenty-six provinces." Why does it say, *A hundred and twenty-seven?* In truth God said to him: "You added one ascent to My house, saying, *Whosoever there is among you of all His people . . . let him go up (ib. 1:3)*. I too will grant you an ascent, an addition from Myself"; and so God gave him an additional province over the half, as it says, *A hundred and twenty-seven provinces*.

[6] R. Levi said in the name of R. Samuel b. Nahman: It is written, *And the hair of His head like pure wool (Dan. 7:9)*, indicating that no creature has the least claim upon Him. R. Judan said in the name of R. Aibu: It is written, *I have trodden the winepress alone, and of the peoples there was no man with Me (Is. 63:3)*. Does God require the assistance of the nations that He says, "*And of the peoples there was no man with Me*"? What the Holy One, blessed be He, really said was this: "When I shall examine the records of the nations and they shall be found to have no merit before Me, then *I shall tread them in My anger, and trample them in My fury*." R. Phinehas and R. Hilkiah in the name of R. Simon said: It is written, *And it shall come to pass in that day, that I will seek to destroy all the nations [etc.] (Zech. 12:9)*. "*I will seek!*" Who can prevent Him? In fact what God meant was this: When I shall examine the records of the nations and they will not be found to have any merit before Me, then "*I will seek to destroy all the nations*." R. Simon said in the name of R. Yohanan: It is written, *Vengeance is Mine, and recompense, against the time when their foot shall slip (Deut. 32:35)*. Is it any sign of might to say, "When the enemies of Is-

rael become feeble I shall punish them?" What God really said was this: "When they shall cease performing their usual good deeds and shall not be able to point to any merit before Me, then, 'Vengeance is Mine, and recompense.' " R. Berekiah in the name of R. Levi and R. Huna in the name of R. Levi and R. Judan in the name of R. Levi all expounded in the same way the verse, Your hand shall be equal to all your enemies; your right hand shall overtake those that hate you (Ps. 21:9). This means: May Your right hand be ready to punish Your enemies; may the Attribute of Justice be at hand for them; may [Your right hand] disclose how few good deeds they have performed. Therefore it is said, "May Your right hand find those that hate You."

[7] Another explanation of A hundred and seven and twenty provinces: R. Judah and R. Nehemiah joined issue. R. Judah said: He subdued seven which were as formidable as twenty and twenty which were as formidable as a hundred. R. Nehemiah said: He took troops from seven and conquered twenty and then he took troops from twenty and conquered a hundred. How did he conquer them? R. Judah and R. Nehemiah gave different answers. R. Judah said: They lay in the shape of a semi-circle, so that when those on the circumference were conquered, the rest were conquered ipso facto. (R. Phinehas said: The [inhabited] world is circular in shape. R. Abun said: Like the surface of a kab measure.) R. Nehemiah said: They were like a watercourse; if you conquer those on the outside, those within are conquered automatically.

[8] As. R. Aqiba was once sitting and expounding, the disciples became drowsy. In order to rouse them he said: How did Esther merit to reign over a hundred and twenty-seven provinces? Because thus said God: "Let Esther the descendant of Sarah who lived a hundred and twenty-seven years come and reign over a hundred and twenty-seven provinces."

[9] R. Levi said: Wherever you find the word "field" (sadeh) in Scripture, it implies a city; wherever you find "city" (ir) it implies a metropolis; wherever you find metropolis (medinah) it implies a province. Whence do we know that "field" implies "city"? Because it says, Go to Anathoth, to your own fields (1 Kings 2:26). Whence do we know that "city" implies metropolis? Because it says, Go through the midst of the city, through the midst of Jerusalem (Ezek. 9:4). Whence do we know that metropolis implies a province? Because it says, A hundred and seven and twenty provinces [medinah].

[10] That in those days (Esther 1:2). This was one of the occasions on which the ministering angels lodged complaints before the Holy One, blessed be He, saying: "Sovereign of the Universe, the Sanctuary is destroyed and this wretch sits and makes carousal!" God answered them: "Set 'days' against 'days'"; for so it is written, In those [days] saw I in Judah

some treading winepresses on the sabbath [etc.] (Neh. 13:15). R. Helbo
said, A time of wailing and woe were those days. R. Bibi said: The word
"hahem" (those) implies, *hah* (woe) for those days, as we read, *Wail ye:
Woe worth [hah] the day! (Ezek. 30:1)*. R. Isaac said: Let there be lament
(*nihyah*) for those days, as we read, *And lament [nihyah] with a doleful
lamentation (Mich. 2:4)*.

[11] *When the king . . . sat*. R. Isaac said: The other nations have no permanent seat. They cited in objection the verse, *When the king Ahasuerus
sat*. He replied: It is not written here *be-shebeth* [lit. "in sitting"], but *"ke-
shebeth"* [lit. "as sitting"], as if to say, a seat which was yet no seat. But the
seat of Israel is a real seat, as it says, *While Israel dwelt [be-shebeth] in
Heshbon (Judg. 11:26)*.

[12] *On the throne of his kingdom*. R. Cohen said in the name of R.
Azariah: The word *malkutho* (his kingdom) is written defectively: he
wanted to sit on the throne of Solomon, but was not permitted. They said
to him: "No king who is not ruler of the world can sit on it." He thereupon
made himself a throne of his own like it. Hence it says, *On the throne of
his kingdom*, the word *malkutho* being written defectively. What then was
[the greatness of] that throne, of which it says, *Moreover the king [Solo-
mon] made a great throne of ivory (2 Chron. 9:17)*? For R. Aha observed:
Surely it is written, *Now Ahab had seventy sons in Samaria (2 Kings 10:1)*
and R. Hoshaia said that as he had seventy sons in Samaria so he had seventy in Jezreel, and each had two palaces, one for winter and one for sum-
mer, as it says, *And I will smite the winter-house with the summer-house
(Amos 3:15)*, while R. Judah b. R. Simon says that each had four, as it says,
And the houses of ivory shall perish (ib.)—the Rabbis say that each had
six, as it says, *And the great houses shall have an end (ib.)*—and here it
[merely] says, *"A great throne of ivory"*? R. Hoshaia Rabbah explained that
it was made like the Chariot of Him at whose word the world came into being, the Holy One, blessed be He; and so it says, *There were six steps to
the throne (2 Chron. 9:18)*—six corresponding to the six firmaments. But
are there not seven? R. Abun said: The one in which the King abides is
specially reserved. There were six corresponding to the six earths, viz.
eretz, adamah, arka, ge, ziah, neshiah. There is also *tebel*, but [this is not
counted because it is written, *And He will judge the world [tebel] in righteousness (Ps. 9:9)*. There were six corresponding to the six orders of the
Mishnah—*Zeraim, Moed, Nashim, Nezikin, Kodeshim* and *Tohoroth*.
There were six corresponding to the six days of Creation. There were six
corresponding to the six matriarchs—Sarah, Rebekah, Rachel, Leah,
Bilhah and Zilpah. R. Huna said: There were six corresponding to the six
precepts which the king was specially admonished to keep, as it is written,
(i) *He shall not multiply wives to himself*, (ii) *he shall not multiply horses to*

177

himself, (iii) *neither shall he greatly multiply to himself silver and gold (Deut. 17:16f.);* and further, (iv) *You shall not wrest judgment;* (v) *You shall not respect persons;* (vi) *neither shall you take a gift (ib. 16:19).* As he ascended the first step the herald proclaimed, addressing him, *"He shall not multiply wives to himself."* At the second he proclaimed, *"He shall not multiply horses to himself."* At the third he proclaimed, *"Neither shall he multiply to himself silver and gold."* At the fourth, *"You shall not wrest judgment";* at the fifth, *"You shall not respect persons";* at the sixth, *"You shall not take a gift."* Similarly it says, *And arms on either side by the place of the seat (2 Chron., loc. cit.).* As he went to take his seat, the herald said to him: "Know before whom you sit—before Him at whose word the world came into being." It is related that when Solomon died, Shishak, king of Egypt, came up and took it from them. R. Samuel b. Nahman said: Shishak is the same as Pharaoh. And why was he called Shishak? Because he came impelled by greed *(shekikuth)* against Israel, saying, "I am taking it in lieu of my daughter's marriage settlement." He made war with Zerah the Ethiopian, who took it from him. Then Asa made war with Zerah the Ethiopian and he conquered him and took it from him. It has been taught: Asa and all the kings of Judah sat upon it, and when Nebuchadnezzar came up and sacked Jerusalem he carried it off to Babylon. From Babylon it was taken to Media and from Media to Greece, and from Greece to Edom. R. Eleazer b. R. Yose said: I have seen its fragments in Rome. Nebuchadnezzar sat on it; Cyrus sat on it; Ahasuerus wanted to sit on it, but was not permitted. They said to him: "No one who is not ruler over the whole world can sit on it." He accordingly made one for himself which he paid for; hence it is written, *On the throne of his kingdom,* the word *malkutho (kingdom)* being written defectively. *And the top of the throne was round behind (1 Kings 10:19):* R. Aha said: like an arm-chair with a footstool. *And there were arms on either side (ib.).* As he ascended the first step, a lion stretched out an arm to him; at the second, an eagle stretched out an arm. *By the place of the seat (ib.):* so they received him. By the seat itself there was a golden sceptre behind, at the top of which was a dove with a golden crown in its mouth, so that the king should be seated on the throne with the golden crown just barely resting on his head.

[13] R. Aibu said: It is written, *For the kingdom is the Lord's; and He is the ruler over the nations (Ps. 22:29),* and yet you say here [that Ahasuerus sat] *On the throne of his kingdom?* The truth is that formerly sovereignty was vested in Israel, but when they sinned it was taken from them and given to the other nations, as it says, *And I will give the land over into the hand of evil men (Ezek. 30:12),* which R. Isaac explained to mean, "Into the hand of evil stewards." But tomorrow when Israel repent God will take it from the idolaters and restore it to them. When will this be? *When saviors shall come up on Mount Zion (Obad. 1:21).*

178

[14] *Which was in Shushan the castle.* R. Phinehas said in the name of R. Hananel: Said the Holy One, blessed be He, to him: "Cyrus [in mentioning the Temple] mentioned also its city and its country, since he said, *[To build him a house] in Jerusalem, which is in Judah (Ezra 1:2);* I also will mention [along with your throne] the name of your capital"; and so it says, *Which was in Shushan the castle.*

[15] *In the third year of his reign, he made a feast (Esther 1:3).* R. Judah and R. Nehemiah gave different explanations. R. Judah said: It means, in the third year of the making of the throne. When he finished making the throne, *He made a feast unto all his princes and his servants.* R. Nehemiah said: In the third year after he stopped the building of the Temple. When three years had passed after he stopped the building of the Temple, *He made a feast unto all his princes and his servants.* R. Samuel b. Imi said: There were four good points in Ahasuerus. He allowed three years to elapse before he assumed the crown or ascended the throne, he waited four years before he found a suitable wife, and he did nothing without taking counsel. R. Phinehas said: Moreover, if anyone did him a good turn, he recorded it in writing; and so it says, *And it was found written that Mordecai had told [etc.] (Esther 6:2).*

[16] *He made a feast unto all his princes and his servants.* Antoninus gave a repast to Rabbi. Said Rabbi to him: "Cannot you afford a really bright lamp?" He said to him: "Why should I trouble about these?" He replied: "Perhaps they will put thick oil into the lamps [for us also] and spoil the repast." "What makes you think so?" he asked. He said: "I learn it from Ahasuerus, of whom we read, *He made a feast unto all his princes and his servants.*"

Pesikta deRab Kahana

Translated by William G. Braude and Israel J. Kapstein, *Pesikta deRab Kahana. R. Kahana's Compilation of Discourses for Sabbaths and Festal Days* (Philadelphia: Jewish Publication Society of America, 1975), 140–152.

PISKA 7 (7:1–9).

And it came to pass at midnight, that the Lord smote all the first-born in the land of Egypt (Ex. 12:29).

[1] R. Tanhum of Jaffa, in the name of R. Nunya of Caesarea, began his discourse by citing the verse *When I pondered how I might apprehend this, it proved too difficult for me (Ps. 73:16).* By these words David meant that no creature could be so knowing as to apprehend the exact instant of midnight—only the Holy One could. For the likes of me, said David, it is too difficult. And so because no creature can be so knowing as to apprehend the exact instant of midnight—only the Holy One can—therefore

179

Scripture says, *And it came to pass [precisely] at midnight that* the Lord *smote*.

[2] R. Aha began his discourse by citing the verse, *I am the Lord, that is My name; and My glory I do not give to a delayed one, neither My renown to things hewn out (Is. 42:8). I am the Lord, that is My name (ibid.)* means, according to R. Aha, that the Holy One said: I am the Lord, that is My name, the name which Adam called Me; that is My name, the name I have consented to be called by; that is My name which I have consented to be called by when I am with the ministering angels. *And My glory I do not give to a delayed one (ibid.)* means, according to R. Menahema citing R. Abin, that God did not give [any kind of independent power] to the demons, [whose creation was delayed to the end of the sixth day of creation].

But R. Nehemiah, citing R. Mani, [read the end of the verse in Isaiah *And my glory I do not give to another,* and] understood by it that God was saying: No other being in the world is able to distinguish between the seed of a first birth and the seed which is not that of a first birth—only the Holy One can so distinguish. For my part, said Moses, making a distinction of this kind is utterly beyond me. And because, by the same token, no other being can be so knowing as to apprehend the exact instant of midnight—only the Holy One can—therefore Scripture says, *and it came to pass [precisely] at midnight, that the Lord smote all the first-born.*

[3] *It is He that confirms the word of His servant, and performs the counsel of His messengers, each of whom says of Jerusalem: "She shall be inhabited"; and of the cities of Judah: "They shall be rebuilt, and I will raise up the waste places thereof" (Isa. 44:26).* R. Berechiah said in the name of R. Levi: Since we know of an instance in which God confirmed the word of a servant of His, is it not certain that He will [confirm the word] and *perform the counsel of His [many] messengers, each of whom says of Jerusalem: "She shall be inhabited"; and of the cities of Judah: "They shall be rebuilt"?* The instance [R. Berechiah had in mind] was God's confirmation of the word of His angelic servant who appeared from on high to Jacob our father and said to him: *"What is your name?" And he replied "Jacob." And he said: "Your name shall be called no more Jacob, but Israel" (Gen. 32:28–29).* Whereupon the Holy One from on high appeared to Jacob our father and confirmed the word of the angelic servant: *God said to Jacob, "Your name shall not be called any more Jacob, but Israel shall be your name" (Gen. 35:10).* Hence all the more certain is it that Jerusalem will be rebuilt, for all prophetic messengers predict that it will be rebuilt, [and God will confirm their words].

Another comment: In the phrase *confirms the word of His servant (Is. 44:26),* the word of Moses, [he whom God called] "My servant Moses" (Num. 12:7), is meant; and in the words *performs the counsel of His messengers,* Moses is again referred to, [for it is said of him that the Lord]

180

"sent a messenger and brought us forth out of Egypt" (Num. 20:16). Thus the Holy One said to Moses: Go tell them, tell Israel, *I will go through the land of Egypt in that night (Ex. 12:12)*. And Moses went, but specified an exact time, saying to Israel: *Thus says the Lord: At the time of midnight will I go out into the midst of Egypt (Ex. 11:4)*. Whereupon the Holy One said to Himself: I declared My trust in Moses long ago when I said of Him: *He is trusted in all My house (Num. 12:7)*. Shall My servant Moses be made out to be a liar? Since Moses said *At the time of midnight*, I will act *at midnight (Ex. 12:29)*. Hence *And it came to pass [precisely] at midnight (ibid.)*.

[4] *At midnight I will rise to give thanks unto Thee because of Thy judgments, of Thy mercy (Ps. 119:62)*. In regard to this verse, R. Phinehas said in the name of R. Eleazar bar R. Menahem: What did David use to do? He used to take a psaltery and a harp, put them at the head of his couch, and rising at midnight would play upon them. Thereupon the studious in Israel, upon hearing the sound of David's playing, used to say: "If David, the king, occupies himself [at midnight] with Torah, so much the more should we." And so it turned out that all in Israel occupied themselves with Torah.

R. Levi said: A window to the north side was left open above David's couch, and over against the window was hung the harp. When the north wind came up at midnight it blew through the strings, and the harp then played of itself. Hence the text *when [the instrument] played (2 Kings 3:15)*. Note that the text does not say "when the minstrel played," but *when the instrument played*, meaning that the harp played of itself. Thereat all in Israel, upon hearing David's voice [accompanying the harp], used to say: If David, the king, so occupies himself, all the more should we. And so it turned out that all in Israel occupied themselves with Torah.

It was of this rising at midnight that David sang: *Awake, my glory; awake, psaltery and harp; I will awake the dawn (Ps. 57:9)*, as if to say: Let my glory—the glory of a king—awake for the sake of my Maker's glory, for my glory is nothing at all before my Maker's glory. *I will awake the dawn:* that is, "I will awake the dawn, the dawn shall not awake me." For his inclination to evil, inciting David, would say to him: "David! It is the imperious way of kings to let the dawn awake them. Yet you declare *I will awake the dawn*. It is the imperious way of kings to sleep three hours into the day. Yet you say humbly *At midnight I will rise to thank Thee because of the judgments, because of Thy mercy (Ps. 119:62)*." What did David mean by *because of the judgments, because of Thy mercy?* He meant: Because of the judgments Thou brought upon the wicked Pharaoh and because of the mercy Thou showed to my grandmother Sarah, as is said, *And the Lord plagued Pharaoh . . . with great plagues because of Sarai, Abram's wife (Gen. 12:17)*.

Or, by *because of the judgments, because of Thy mercy*, David meant:

Because of the judgments which Thou brought upon certain nations of the earth, [such as the Ammonites and the Moabites]; and because of the mercy which Thou showed to my grandfather [Boaz] and to my grandmother [Ruth]. Had Boaz, [giving in to his sexual desire], permitted himself to slip into her as she lay at his feet, whence would I have had my origin? Instead Thou did put a blessing into his heart so that, [restraining his sexual desire], he said: *May you be blessed by the Lord, my daughter (Ruth 3:10).*

Or, by *because of the judgments [etc.] (Ps. 119:62),* David meant: Because of the judgments which Thou brought upon the Egyptians in Egypt; and because of the mercy Thou showed our fathers in Egypt at a time when they had not the merit of obedience to Thy various commandments, obedience whereby they might have won redemption; for at that time they were obedient to only two of Thy commands, those concerned with the blood of Passover and the blood of circumcision. Of His mercy then, it is written, *When I passed by you, and saw you wallowing in your blood, I said to you: In your bloods, live (Ezek. 16:6)*—through your bloods, that is, through the blood of the Passover lamb and the blood of circumcision.

[5] [*And it came to pass in the (precise) middle of the night (etc.) (Ex. 12:29).*] R. Simeon ben Yohai taught: Moses did not know the exact duration of an *"et, of a rega,* or a *zeman* in the night. Therefore he said *about midnight (Ex. 11:4).* But the Holy One knows the exact duration of an *et,* of a *rega,* or of a *zeman* in the night. Therefore with hairbreadth precision He could smite the first-born at the very middle of the night.

Another comment on an event which took place on the same midnight many years before, when *The night was divided* (for Abraham and his servants while they were pursuing the marauding kings) *(Gen. 14:15).* How did the division of that night come about? R. Benjamin bar Japheth said in the name of R. Yohanan: It just happened that way. But the Rabbis said: Its Creator divided it, for in the light of the verse *And it came to pass at the time of [God's] dividing of the night (Ex. 12:29),* the verse in Genesis is to be read not, "*The night was divided,*" etc., but *He divided the night* [for Abraham and his servants], etc. *(Gen. 14:15).* According to R. Tanhuma, the Holy One said: Your father Abraham went forth to war at midnight; I, with his sons, will likewise go forth to war at midnight. And according to the Rabbis, the Holy One said: Your father went forth with Me from nightfall until midnight; and I will go forth with his sons from midnight until dawn.

[In seeking to reconcile the statement that *At midnight . . . the Lord smote all the first-born in the land of Egypt (Ex. 12:29)* with the contradictory statement, *On the day that I smote all the first-born in the land of Egypt (Num. 3:13),*] R. Yohanan construed the latter verse as asserting that it was the princely counterpart of Egypt in heaven—[symbolic of Egypt's pride in her power as a nation]—who was smitten in the daytime [as distinguished from the Egyptians on earth who were smitten at night]. And the proof? The verse, *At Tehaphnehes also the day shall withdraw itself, when I shall break there the yokes of Egypt, and the pride of her power shall cease in her [etc.] (Ezek. 30:18).* In further proof [that *on the day* refers to the smiting of Egypt's pride in her power as a nation], R. Yohanan cited another verse [which likewise says of the time-to-come], *In that day there shall be five cities in the land of Egypt that speak the language of Canaan, and swear to the Lord of hosts; one shall be the city of Heres (Is. 19:18)*—[a name which signifies either the "city of sherds" or "city of the sun"]. (By what names are the five cities known now? R. Hilkiah said in the name of R. Simon: No is Alexandria; Noph is Memphis; Tehaphnehes is Hupianas; the "city of sherds" is Ostracena; and the "city of the sun" is Heliopolis.)

R. Yohanan ben Zakkai explained away the apparent contradiction, saying: We find in Scripture that the day and the night together are spoken of as a day, as is said, *And there was evening and there was morning, one day (Gen. 1:5).*

R. Joshua bar R. Nehemiah resolved the apparent contradiction on the basis of the following verse: *Even the darkness is not too dark for Thee; the night shines as the day; the darkness is even as the light (Ps. 139:12).* The verse intimates that God is saying: The darkness, which is the same as light to Me, is night only so far as its use to mortals is concerned.

Another comment: In one place in Scripture it is written, *And it came to pass at midnight that the Lord smote all the first-born in the land of Egypt (Ex. 12:29);* but elsewhere Scripture says, *On the day that I smote all the first-born in the land of Egypt (Num. 8:17),* a verse which leads one to suppose that the first-born of Egypt died during the daytime. How are the two verses to be reconciled? As follows: At nightfall the first-born were smitten with a death-stroke, so that they were in convulsions throughout the night and died on the following day. And the proof? Scripture does not say, "We are all dead men," but *We are all dying men (Ex. 12:33),* that is, dying hour by hour.

As for the repetition of the verse, *On the day that I smote all the first-born in the land of Egypt (Num. 8:17),* in the verse, *On the day that I smote all the first-born in the land of Egypt I hallowed unto Me all the first-born in Israel (Num. 3:13),* you may say that God meant: On the day that the first-born of Egypt died, that was the day on which I hallowed unto Me all the first-born [of Israel] to minister as My priests.

[6/9] *The Lord smote all the first-born in the land of Egypt (Ex. 12:29)* —"the first-born" signifying every kind of first-born: a man's first-born or a woman's first-born, whether the first-born was a male or the first-born was a female. How so? If one man had cohabited with ten women and each of

183

them had had a son by him, then all of the sons were considered the women's first-born; or if ten men had cohabited with one woman and she had had a son by each of the men, then all of the sons were considered the men's first-born.

Now suppose that in a household there was no first-born, belonging either to a man or a woman, how would then the verse *There was not a house where there was not one dead (Ex. 12:30)* be justified? R. Abba bar Aha explained: The one who had charge of the household was smitten, such a one as is referred to in the verse *Shimri the one in charge—for though he was not the first-born, yet his father put him in charge (1 Chron. 26:10).*

[Not only was the one in charge smitten.] It is taught in the name of R. Nathan: There was a custom in an Egyptian household that when a first-born died, a statue of him was wrought for the house he had lived in. Hence, on the day the Lord smote the first-born, this statue, too, was smashed, broken up into fragments, and scattered. And for the father of the dead first-born, the statue's destruction was as grievous as though he had buried his first-born that very day.

R. Yudan went further, saying: Since the Egyptians buried their dead inside their houses, [on the day the first-born were smitten], dogs, entering through sewer pipes, dragged from among the dead the bodies of the first-born and sported grotesquely with them. For the fathers of the dead first-born, the dogs' sport was as grievous as though they had buried their first-born that very day.

At midnight . . . the Lord smote all the first-born . . . from the first-born of Pharaoh that was to sit on his throne (Ex. 12:29). From this verse it is assumed that Pharaoh himself was a first-born.

All the first-born gathered around their fathers and pleaded with them: "Now that Moses has said *All the first born in the land of Egypt shall die (Ex. 11:5)* and all that he had predicted heretofore concerning the Egyptian people has befallen them, we must bestir ourselves and get these Hebrews out of our midst, else the Egyptian people will die." The fathers replied: "Each one of us has ten sons: let one of them die, just so that the Hebrews be not permitted to get out." The first-born then said: "There is but one way to settle the matter: let us go to Pharaoh, himself a first-born, who may take pity upon himself and let these Hebrews get out of our midst.'"

They went to Pharaoh and said to him: "Since Moses has said *All the first-born . . . shall die* and since all that he had predicted heretofore concerning the Egyptian people has befallen them, rise up and let these Hebrews get out of our midst, else the Egyptian people will die."

But Pharaoh said [to his servants]: "Get going and beat these poltroons until they are humpbacked"; and to the first-born he said: "I have sworn: 'My life or the lives of the Hebrews!' And you dare speak thus!"

At once the first-born went out and slew sixty myriads of their fathers. Of this it is written, *To Him that smote Egypt with their first-born (Ps. 136:10)*. Scripture does not say here, "To Him that smote the first-born of Egypt," but says, *To him that smote Egypt with their first-born*, which is to say, it was the first-born of Egypt that slew sixty myriads of their fathers.

R. Abun said in the name of R. Judah ben Pazzi: Bithiah the daughter of Pharaoh was a first-born. By what merit did she escape death? Through the merit of Moses' prayer for her. Of her it is written, "She perceived that [Moses], who was called a goodly child, was a shield, and that therefore her lamp—her soul—had not gone out by night" (*Prov. 31:18*). Since the word for "night" is spelled here not, as is customary, *laylah*, but *layil*, the verse is to be read in the light of another verse where *layil* is also exceptionally used. This other verse, *It was a night (layil) of watching unto the Lord (Ex. 12:42)*, refers to the night when the first-born of Egypt were smitten. [Hence it is assumed that on this night Bithiah's lamp did not go out—that is, her life was spared.]

Even unto the first-born of the maidservant that is behind the mill (Ex. 11:5). R. Huna and R. Aha [taught] in the name of R. Eleazar ben R. Yose the Galilean: Smitten even were the first-born of Egyptian maidservants, who, bent over mills in forced labor, used to say, "We are glad to remain in slavery so long as Israel remains in slavery, [particularly so long as Israel's well-born women remain in slavery]." The Egyptian maidservants were alluding to women such as Serah daughter of Asher, who, upon coming down into Egypt, was enslaved and compelled to bend over a mill in forced labor. So said R. Judah ben Pazzi citing a traditional Agadah transmitted from generation to generation.

And all the first-born of cattle (Ex. 11:5). Men sinned, to be sure; but how can cattle be said to have sinned? Since the Egyptians worshiped the ram, however, [the first-born of their cattle were smitten] in order that the Egyptians should be unable to say: It is our deity who has brought this punishment upon us. Our deity is strong and can stand up for himself, as is shown by the fact that this punishment did not come upon such animals as represent him.

Songs Rabbah

Translated by Maurice Simon in *Midrash Rabbah*, ed. H. Freedman and Maurice Simon (London: The Soncino Press, 1939), 9:91–94.

SONG OF SONGS RABBAH 2:1–2.

Song 2:1. [1] *I am a rose (habazeleth) of Sharon*. Said the Community of Israel: I am the one, and beloved (*habibah*) am I. I am she whom the Holy One, blessed be He, loved more than the seventy nations. *A rose of Sharon*: so called because I made Him a shade (*zel*) by the hand of Bezalel, as it is written, *And Bezalel made the ark (Ex. 37:1)*. *Of Sharon*: so called because I chanted to him a song (*shirah*) together with Moses, as it is written, *Then sang Moses and the children of Israel (ib. 15:1)*. Another explanation: *I am the rose of Sharon:* I am the one, and beloved am I. I am she who was hidden (*habuyah*) in the shadow (*bezel*) of Egypt, and in a brief space the Holy One, blessed be He, brought me to Raamses, and I blossomed forth in good deeds like a rose, and I chanted before Him the song, as it says, *You shall have a song as in the night when a feast is hallowed (Is. 30:29)*. Another explanation: *I am a rose of Sharon.* I am the one and beloved am I. I am she who was hidden in the shadow of the sea, and in a brief space I blossomed forth with good deeds before Him like a rose, and I pointed to Him with the finger (opposite to me), as it says, *This is my God, and I will glorify Him (Ex. 15:2)*. Another explanation: *I am a rose of Sharon.* I am the one, and beloved am I. I am she that was hidden in the shadow of Mount Sinai, and in a brief space I blossomed forth in good deeds before Him like a lily with hand and heart, and I said before Him, *All that the Lord has said will we do, and obey (Ex. 24:7)*. Another explanation: *I am a rose of Sharon.* I am the one and beloved am I. I am she that was hidden and thrust away in the shadow of the ruling powers. Tomorrow when God will deliver me from the shadow of the ruling powers I will blossom like a rose and chant before Him a new song, as it says, *Sing unto the Lord a new song; for He has done marvelous things; His right hand, and His holy arm, have wrought salvation for him (Ps. 98:1)*.

[2] R. Berekiah said: this verse is spoken by the wilderness. Said the wilderness: "I am the wilderness, and beloved am I, for all the good things of the world are hidden in me, as it says, *I will plant in the wilderness the cedar, the acacia tree (Is. 41:19);* God has placed them in me for safe keeping, and when God requires them from me, I shall return to Him His deposit unimpaired. I also shall blossom with good deeds, and chant a song before Him, as it says, *The wilderness and parched land shall be glad (ib. 35:1).*" In the name of the Rabbis it was said: This verse is said by the land [of Israel]. It says: "I am it, and I am beloved, since all the dead are hidden in me, as it says, *Thy dead shall live, my dead bodies shall arise (ib. 26:19)*. When God shall require them from me I shall return them to Him, and I shall blossom forth with good deeds like a rose, and chant a song before Him, as it says, *From the uttermost parts of the earth have we heard songs (ib. 24:16).*"

[3] R. Judan and R. Eliezer each gave an exposition [of "rose" and "lily"]. R. Judan said: Is not *habazeleth* the same as *shoshanah?* The fact is, however, that while it is still small it is called *habazeleth,* but when it becomes full-sized it is called *shoshanah.* And why is it called *habazeleth?* Because it is hidden in its own shadow (*habuyah bezillah*). R. Eliezer said: The righteous are compared by Scripture to the most excellent of plants and the most excellent species of that plant. To the most excellent of

plants—namely, the lily; and the most excellent species of that plant —namely, the lily of the valleys. Not to the lily of the mountains, which soon withers, but to the lily of the valleys, which goes on blooming. The wicked are compared to the vilest of things, and the vilest kind of that thing. They are compared to the vilest of things, namely, chaff, and not to the chaff of the valley, which has some moisture in it, but [as it is written], *And they shall be chased as the chaff of the* mountains *before the wind (Is. 17:13).*

R. Abba b. Kahana said: The Community of Israel said before the Holy One, blessed be He: "I am she, and beloved am I. For I am plunged into the depth of sorrow, but when the Holy One, blessed be He, shall rescue me from my sorrows, I shall blossom forth into good deeds before Him like a lily, and utter song"; and so it is written, *Lord, in trouble have they sought Thee (Is. 26:6).* R. Aha said: The Community of Israel said: "When you look piercingly at me, I blossom forth with good deeds like a lily and utter song; as it says, *A song of ascents; out of the depths have I called Thee, O Lord (Ps. 130:1).*" The Rabbis said: It is the Community of Israel that says this verse. Said the community of Israel: "I am she and beloved am I. For I am plunged into the depths of Gehinnom, but when the Holy One, blessed be He, shall deliver me from its depths, as it says, *He brought me up also out of the tumultuous pit (ib. 60:3),* I shall blossom forth in good deeds and utter song before Him, as it says, *And He has put a new song in my mouth (ib. 4).*" This dictum of the Rabbis agrees with the following of R. Eleazar the Modiite: In the time to come the guardian angels of the nations will come to accuse Israel before the Almighty, and they will say: "Sovereign of the Universe, these worshipped idols and these worshipped idols; these were guilty of immorality and these were guilty of immorality; these shed blood and these shed blood. Why then do these go down to Gehinnom while these do not go down?" Then God will answer them saying: "If that is so, let all the peoples go down with their gods to Gehinnom," and so it is written, *For let all the peoples walk each one in the name of its god (Mic. 4:5).* Said R. Reuben: Were it not written in the Scripture, it would be impossible to say such a thing: so to speak, *For by fire will the Lord be judged (Is. 66:16):* it does not say *shofet* (judges), but *nishpat* (is judged). And David said the same thing in the holy spirit: *Yea, though I walk through the valley of the shadow of death, I will fear no evil, for Thou art with me (Ps. 23:4).* Another explanation: *"Thy rod" (ib.).* This refers to chastisements. *"And thy staff":* by this is meant the Torah. *"They comfort me":* shall I say, without chastisements? Not so, since it says, *Only.* Shall I say, in this world? Not so, since it says, *Only goodness and mercy shall follow me all the days of my life, and I shall dwell in the house of the Lord for ever (ib. 6).*

Song 2:2. [1] *As a lily among thorns.* R. Isaac applied this verse to

Rebekah, as it says, *And Isaac was forty years old when he took Rebekah, the daughter of Bethuel the Aramean, of Paddan-aram, the sister of Laban the Aramean, to be his wife (Gen. 25:20)*. If the verse wishes to inform us that she was from Paddan-aram, why state that she was the sister of Laban the Aramean? It is to tell us that her father was a trickster *(ramai)*, her brother was a trickster, and all the men of her place were tricksters, and this virtuous one came forth from the midst of them. What does she resemble? *A lily among thorns*. R. Phinehas said in the name of R. Simon: It is written, *And Isaac sent away Jacob, and he went to Paddan-aram unto Laban, son of Bethuel the Aramean*, implying that they were all tricksters.

[2] R. Eliezer applied the verse to the redemption from Egypt. Just as a lily when it is situated between thorns is difficult to pluck, so the deliverance of Israel was a difficult matter for the Holy One, blessed be He, and so it says, *Or has God assayed to go and take Him a nation from the midst of another nation (Deut. 4:34)*. R. Joshua said in the name of R. Hanan: jiqt does not say here, "A nation from the midst of a people," or "a people from the midst of a nation," but "*a nation from the midst of a nation*," since both were equally uncircumcised, both equally wore front curls, both equally wore garments of mixed kinds. That being so, the Attribute of Justice did not allow that Israel should ever be delivered. R. Samuel b. Nahman said: Had not God bound Himself with an oath, Israel would never have been redeemed, for so it says, *Wherefore say to the children of Israel, I am the Lord, and I will bring you out from under the burdens of the Egyptians (Ex. 6:6)*. The word "*wherefore*" *(laken)* signifies an oath, as it says, *Therefore [laken] I have sworn unto the house of Eli (1 Sam. 3:14)*. R. Berekiah said: It says, *Thou hast with a [strong] arm redeemed Thy people (Ps. 77:16)*, as if to say, with main force. R. Judan said: The words "*to go to take him a nation*" to "*great terrors*" *(Deut. 4:34)* contain seventy-two letters. Should it be objected that there are seventy-five, take out the second "*goy*" (nation) which is not counted. R. Abin said: He redeemed them with His name, the full name of the Holy One, blessed be He, containing seventy-two letters.

[3] R. Azariah said in the name of R. Judah who had it from R. Simon: A king once had an orchard in which they went and planted a row of fig-trees and a row of vines and a row of apples and a row of pomegranates, and then he handed it over to a keeper and went away. After a time the king came and inspected the orchard to see how it was getting on, and he found it full of thorns and briars. So he brought wood-cutters to cut it down. Seeing in it a beautiful rose, he took and smelt it and was appeased, and said: "For the sake of this rose the orchard shall be spared." So the world was created only for the sake of Israel. After twenty-six generations the Holy One, blessed be He, inspected His garden to see how it was getting on, and he found it one mass of water. The generation of Enosh was wiped out with

water; the generation of the dispersion was punished with water. So He brought wood-cutters to cut it down, as it says, *The Lord sat enthroned at the Flood (Ps. 29:10)*, but He saw a beautiful rose, namely Israel, and He took and smelt it, at the time when Israel received the Ten Commandments, and He was appeased, at the time when Israel said, *We will do and obey*. Said the Holy One, blessed be He: For the sake of this rose let the garden be spared; for the sake of the Torah and those who study it let the world be spared.

[4] R. Hanan of Sepphoris applied the verse to the performance of acts of piety. It often happens that ten men go to a house of mourning and not one of them is able to open his mouth to say the mourners' blessing, until one comes and opens his mouth and says the mourners' blessing. What does he resemble? *A rose among thorns*. Again, it often happens that ten men go to a wedding feast and not one of them can open his mouth to say the bridegroom's blessing, until one comes who can open his mouth and say the bridegroom's blessing. What does he resemble? *A rose among thorns*. It often happens that ten men go into a synagogue and not one of them can say the blessings before the *shema* or pass before the Ark, till one of them says the blessings before the *shema* and passes before the Ark. What does he resemble? *A rose among thorns*. R. Eleazar went to a certain place where they said to him, "Say the blessings before the *shema*." He said to them: "I don't know them." They said, "Pass before the Ark," [He said: I cannot.] They thereupon said: "Is this R. Eleazar? Is this the man of whom they make such a fuss? What is he called Rabbi for?" He felt deeply mortified and went to R. Aqiba, his teacher. He said to him: "Why do you look so pale?" He told him what had happened. He then said to him: "Would you, Sir, be willing to teach me?" He consented and taught him. After a time he went again to the same place. They invited him to say the blessing before the *shema*, and he did so; to pass before the Ark, and he did so. They thereupon said: "R. Eleazar had become tongue-free *(ithhasam)*, and they called him R. Eleazar Hisma. R. Jonah used to teach his disciples the bridegrooms' blessing and the mourners' blessing, so that they might be ready for any call upon them.

[5] R. Huna applied the verse to the [oppression of the] secular powers. Just as a rose, if situated between thorns, when the north wind blows is bent towards the south and pricked by the thorns, and nevertheless its heart is still turned upwards, so with Israel, although taxes in kind and other tributes are exacted from them, nevertheless their hearts are fixed upon their Father in heaven, as it says, *My eyes are ever toward the Lord (Ps. 25:15)*. R. Aibo applied the verse to the deliverance of tomorrow. When the lily is between thorns it is difficult for the owner to pluck, so what does he do? He brings fire and burns all round and then plucks it. So *The Lord has commanded concerning Jacob, that they that are round*

about him should be his adversaries (Lam. 1:17), like Halamish to Gava, Jericho to Noadan, Susisan to Tiberias, Kastera to Haifa, Lydda to Ono, and so it is written, *This is Jerusalem! I have set her in the midst of the nations (Ezek. 5:5)*. Tomorrow when the end shall come, what will the Holy One, blessed be He, do? He will bring fire and burn all round her, and so it is written, *And the peoples shall be as the burnings of lime (Is. 33:12)*. What is written in that connection? *The Lord alone shall lead him (Deut. 32:12)*.

[6] R. Abun said: This lily when the sun beats upon it withers, but when the dew falls it revives. So Israel, so long as the shadow of Esau is in the ascendant, seem to be withered in this world, but when the shadow of Esau shall pass away Israel shall blossom forth, as it says, *I will be as the dew unto Israel; he shall blossom as the lily (Hos. 14:6)*. Just as the lily expires only with its scent, so Israel expire only with religious acts and good deeds. Just as the whole purpose of the lily is to give scent, so the righteous are created only for the deliverance of Israel. Just as the lily is set on the table of kings at the beginning and at the end of the meal, so Israel are found in this world and are found in the next world. Just as the lily is conspicuous among plants, so Israel are conspicuous among the nations, as it says, *All that see them shall acknowledge them (Is. 61:9)*. Just as the lily is kept for Sabbaths and festivals, so Israel are kept for the deliverance of tomorrow. R. Berekiah said: The Holy One, blessed be He, said to Moses: "Go and say to Israel: 'My children, when you were in Egypt you were like a lily among thorns. Now that you are entering into the land of Canaan, be also like a lily among thorns; take good heed that you follow the ways neither of the one nor of the other'"; and so it says, *After the doings of the land of Egypt, wherein you dwelt, shall you not do; and after the doings of the land of Canaan, whither I bring you, shall you not do (Lev. 18:3)*.

Ruth Rabbah

Translated by L. Rabinowitz, in *Midrash Rabbah*, ed. H. Freedman and Maurice Simon (London: The Soncino Press, 1939), 8:1–5, 16–22.

RUTH RABBAH PROEMS 1–2.

[I] *And it came to pass, in the days that the judges judged (Ruth 1:1)*. R. Yohanan introduced his exposition with the verse, *Hear, O my people, and I will speak; O Israel, and I will testify against you (Ps. 50:7)*. R. Yohanan said: Evidence is given only in the hearing [of the defendant]. R. Judan b. R. Simon said: In the past, Israel had a name like all the nations, [for instance] *And Sabta, and Raamah, and Sabteca (Gen. 10:7)*; henceforth they are called solely *"My people,"* thus: *"Hear, O my people, and I will speak"*: Whence have you merited to be called *"My people"*? From the time of *"and I will speak,"* from that which you uttered before Me at Sinai and said, *All that the Lord has spoken will we do, and hearken (Ex. 24:7).*

R. Yohanan said *"Hear, O My people,"* to that [which was said] in the past; *"and I will speak"* in the future; *"Hear, O My people"* in this world; *"and I will speak"* in the World to Come, in order that I may have a retort to the princes of the nations of the world, who are destined to act as their prosecutors before Me, and say, "Lord of the Universe, they have served idols and we have served idols; they have been guilty of immorality and we have been guilty of immorality; they have shed blood and we have shed blood. Why do they go into the Garden of Eden while we descend to Gehenna? In that moment the defender of Israel keeps silence. That is the meaning of the verse, *And at that time shall Michael stand up (Dan. 12:1).* Do they then as a rule sit in Heaven? Did not R. Hanina say, there is no sitting in Heaven, as it is written, *I came near unto one of [kaamaya] (ib. 7:16),* the meaning of this word *"kaamaya"* being *that stood by,* as it is written, *Above him stood the seraphim (Is. 6:2),* and it is also written, *And all the host of heaven standing on His right hand and on His left (2 Chron. 18:18)?* And yet the verse says, *"shall [Michael] stand up"!* What then is the meaning here of *"stand up"?* "Stand silent," as it is said, *And shall I wait because they speak not, because they stand still, and answer no more? (Job 32:16).* And the Holy One, blessed be He, says to him: "Do you stand silent and have no defense to offer for My people? By your life, I will speak righteousness and save My people!" With what righteousness? R. Eleazar and R. Yohanan:—one says: The righteousness which you wrought for My word in that you accepted My Torah, for had you not accepted My Torah, I should have caused the world to revert to void and desolation. For R. Huna said in the name of R. Aha: *When the earth and all the inhabitants thereof are dissolved (Ps. 75:4)* means that the world would long have gone into dissolution had not Israel stood before Mount Sinai. Who then set the world firmly upon its foundation? *I myself establish the pillars of it (ib.).* By the merit of *"I":* I have established its pillars for ever. The other Rabbi says: By the righteousness which you wrought unto yourselves in that you accepted my Torah; for were it not for this, I should have caused you to disappear from the nations.

God, your God, am I. R. Yohanan said: It means, Let it suffice you that I am your patron. Resh Laqish says: It means even although I am your patron, what does patronage help in the day of judgment?

R. Simeon b. Yohai taught: I am God to all the inhabitants of the world, but I have associated My name only with my people Israel. I am not called the God of the nations, only the God of Israel. *"God, your God, am I."* R. Judan interpreted this verse to apply to Moses. The Holy One, blessed be He, said, "Even although I called you a god to Pharaoh, *I am your God,* I am over you." R. Abba b. Judan interpreted the verse to apply to Israel.

Even although I called you godlike beings, as it is said, *"I said: You are godlike beings (Ps. 82:6)*, yet *"I am your God"*: know nevertheless that I am over you. The Rabbis interpreted the verse to refer to the judges. Even although I called you gods, as it is said, *You shall not revile judges (Ex. 22:27)*, know that I am over you. And He spoke to Israel again and said: "I have imparted of my glory to the judges and called them gods, and they condemn them. Woe unto the generation that judges its judges!"

[II] *And it came to pass, in the days that the judges judged: Slothfulness casts into a deep sleep (Prov. 19:15)*. [Israel was cast into a deep sleep] in that they were negligent in paying the appropriate honors to Joshua after his death. That is the meaning of the verse, *And they buried him in the border of his inheritance . . . on the north of the mountain of Gaash (Josh. 24:30)*. R. Berekiah said: We have examined the whole of Scripture and we have not found mention of a place called Gaash. What then is the meaning of *"the mountain of Gaash"?* That Israel were too much preoccupied *(nith-gaashu)* to pay proper honor to Joshua after his death. The land of Israel was divided up at that time, and they became unduly absorbed in the division. Israel were all occupied with their tasks. One was occupied with his field, the other with his vineyard, yet another with his olive trees, and a fourth with quarrying stones, thus exemplifying the words, *And the idle soul shall suffer hunger (Prov., loc. cit.)*. They therefore neglected to show honor to Joshua after his death, and the Holy One, blessed be He, sought to bring an earthquake upon the inhabitants of the world, as it is said, *Then the earth did shake [wa-tigash] and quake (Ps. 18:8)*. *"And the idle soul shall suffer hunger."* In that there were among them those who deceived God by idolatry; he therefore starved them of the Holy Spirit, as it is written, *And the word of the Lord was precious in those days (1 Sam. 3:1)*.

Another interpretation of *"Slothfulness casts into a deep sleep"* is that Israel were neglectful in doing repentance during the days of Elijah, and "a deep sleep was cast," i.e., prophecy increased. Increased? But the verse says *"casts."* It is as one says, "the market for fruit has fallen." R. Simon says: It is as if a man were to say to his fellow, "Here is the bag, and here the money, and here the measure. Arise and eat." For R. Derusa said: Sixty myriads of prophets arose in Israel during the days of Elijah. R. Jacob said: One hundred and twenty myriads. R. Yohanan said: Between Gabbath and Antipatris there were sixty myriads of townships and none were more corrupt than Jericho and Bethel, Jericho because Joshua cursed it, and Bethel because the Golden Calf of Jeroboam was set up there, and yet it is written, *And the sons of the prophets who were at Bethel came forth to Elisha (2 Kings 2:3)*. The verse says *"prophets,"* which signifies a minimum of two. For what reasons were not their prophecies made public? Because they had no *permanent* value for [future] generations. Deduce from this that a prophecy of which there is no need for [future] generations is not published. But in the time to come the Holy One, blessed be He, will come and bring them with Him and their prophecies will be published. That is the meaning of, *And the Lord my God shall come, and all the holy ones with Thee (Zech. 14:5).*

"And the idle soul shall suffer hunger." They deceived God in that some of them worshipped idols, and others worshipped the Holy One, blessed be He. That is the meaning of what Elijah said to them, *How long halt you between two opinions (1 Kings 18:21). "Shall suffer hunger,"* in that the Lord brought a famine in the days of Elijah, as it is said, *As the Lord of hosts lives, before whom I stand [etc.] (ib. 15).* Another interpretation of *"slothfulness casts into a deep sleep,"* is that, because Israel was neglectful in doing repentance in the days of the Judges, they were cast into a deep sleep. *"And the idle soul shall suffer hunger';* because they sought to deceive the Holy One, blessed be He, some serving idols and others serving God, the Holy One, blessed be He, caused them to suffer hunger in the famine of t he days of the Judges.

RUTH RABBAH 1:1–5.

[1] *And it came to pass, in the days of the judging of the judges.* Woe unto that generation which judges its judges, and woe unto the generation whose judges are in need of being judged! As it is said, *And yet they hearkened not unto their judges (Judg. 2:17).* Who were [the judges referred to]? Rab said: They were Barak and Deborah; R. Joshua b. Levi said: They were Shamgar and Ehud; R. Huna said: They were Deborah, Barak, and Jael. The word *"judge"* implies one, *"judges"* implies two, *"the judges"* three.

[2] Rabbi [Judah Ha-nasi] asked R. Bezalel: What is the meaning of the verse, *For their mother has played the harlot (Hos. 2:7)?* Is it conceivable that our matriarch Sarah was a harlot? He answered: God forbid! But [the meaning is], when are the words of the Torah despised by the common people? When those who are versed in the Torah themselves despise it. R. Jacob b. Abdimi came and made an exposition of it. When are the words of the Torah regarded as harlots by the ignorant? When its own possessors despise it. R. Yohanan deduced it from the following verse: *The poor man's wisdom is despised (Eccl. 9:16).* Was then the wisdom of R. Aqiba, who was a poor man, despised? What then is the meaning of *"a poor man"?* One who is despised on account of his own words. For instance, a sage sits and expounds, *You shall not wrest judgment (Deut. 16:19),* and yet he wrests judgment; *You shall not respect persons (ib.),* and yet he is a respecter of persons. *Neither shall you take a gift,* and he accepts bribes; *You shall not afflict any widow, or fatherless child (Ex. 22:21),* and he does afflict them. Samson followed the desire of his eyes, as it is said, *Get her for me; for she pleases me well (Judg. 14:3).* Gideon worshipped idols, as it is said, *And*

Gideon made an ephod thereof (ib. 8:27). There is no greater *"poor man"* than this. Woe unto the judge who respects persons in judgment! R. Hiyya taught: *You shall do no unrighteousness in judgment (Lev. 19:15).* This teaches that the judge who perverts justice is called by five names, unrighteous, hated, repulsive, accursed, and an abomination. And the Holy One, blessed be He, also calls him five [names], viz., evil, despiser, a breaker of the covenant, an incenser, and a rebel against God. And he is the cause of five evils to the world, in that he pollutes the land, profanes the name of God, causes the *Shechinah* to depart, makes Israel fall by the sword, and is the cause of their exile from their land. Woe unto the generation which is corrupt in this respect!

R. Hiyya taught: *You shall do no unrighteousness in judgment (ib. 35),* that is, in law. But if it refers to law, this has already been mentioned. If so, why is it stated: *in judgment, in meteyard (ib.)?* To teach that a man who measures is called a judge, and if he falsifies [his measures], he is called by these five names and is the cause of these five evils. Woe unto the generation which has false measures; for R. Banya said in the name of R. Huna: If you have seen a generation whose measures are false, the government comes and launches an attack against that generation. Whence do we know? [Since it is written,] *A false balance is an abomination to the Lord,* which is followed by, *When presumption comes, then comes shame (Prov. 11:1f.).*

R. Berekiah said in the name of R. Abba: It is written, *Shall I be pure with wicked balances (Mic. 6:11)?* Is it possible for a generation whose measures are false to be meritorious? No! [For the verse continues] *And with a bag of deceitful weights.*

R. Levi said: Moses also hinted at this fact to Israel in the Torah. [It is written,] *You shall not have in your bag diverse weights . . . you shall not have in your house diverse measures (Deut. 25:13f.).* But if you do, the result will be that the government will come and attack you, as it is written, *For all that do such things, even all that do unrighteously, are an abomination unto the Lord your God,* and there immediately follows, *Remember what Amalek did unto you by the way as you came forth out of Egypt (ib. 16f.).*

[3] Rabba said: Blessings bless those who deserve them, and curses curse those who deserve them. Blessings bless those who deserve them, since it is written, *A perfect and just weight there shall be;* and if you have acted so, *there shall be to you [i.e., you shall have];* curses curse those who deserve them, as it is written, *You shall not have in your bag diverse weights.* But if you have acted so, the Holy One, blessed be He, says: "You have sought to make both large and small. By your life! That wicked man will not manage to have even small," as it is written, "You *shall not have in your bag."* Similarly [with the verse] *You shall not make with Me—gods of*

silver, or gods of gold (Ex. 20:20). The Holy One, blessed be He, said: "You have sought to make with Me gods of silver and gods of gold. By your life! That wicked man will not even manage to have gods of wood," as it goes on, *You shall not make [aught] unto you!*

[4] *That there was a famine in the land*. Ten famines have come upon the world. One in the days of Adam, one in the days of Lamech, one in the days of Abraham, one in the days of Isaac, one in the days of Jacob, one in the days of Elijah, one in the days of Elisha, one in the days of David, one in the days when the judges judged, and one which is destined still to come upon the world.

One in the days of Adam, as it is said, *Cursed is the ground for your sake (Gen. 3:17);* one in the days of Lamech, as it is said, *From the ground which the Lord has cursed (ib. 5:29);* one in the days of Abraham, as it is said, *And there was a famine in the land; and Abram went down into Egypt (ib. 12:10);* one in the days of Isaac, as it is said, *And there was a famine in the land beside the first famine (ib. 26:1);* one in the days of Jacob, as it is said, *For these two years have the famine been in the land (ib. 45:6);* one in the days of Elijah, as it is said, *There shall not be dew nor rain these years (1 Kings 17:1);* one in the days of Elisha, as it is said, *And there was a great famine in Samaria (2 Kings 6:25);* one in the days of David, as it is said, *And there was a famine in the days of David three years (2 Sam. 21:1);* one in the days of the judges, as it is said, *There was a famine in the land;* and one which is destined to come to the world, as it is said, *That I will send a famine in the land, not a famine of bread, nor a thirst for water, but of hearing the words of the Lord (Amos 8:11)*.

R. Huna said in the name of Samuel: The real famine ought to have come in the days of Saul, and not in the days of David, but since Saul was but the stump of a sycamore-tree and would have been unable to withstand it, the Holy One, blessed be He, deferred it and brought it in the time of David who, since he was a scion of an olive-tree, was able to withstand it. As the proverb expresses it, "Shela has sinned, but John must pay." So all these [famines] did not come upon feeble people, but upon strong ones, who could withstand them. R. Hiyya Rabbah said in the name of R. Simeon b. Eleazar: It is as if a dealer in glassware has in his hand a basket of cut glass, and, wanting to hang the basket up, he brings a peg and hammers it into the wall, upon which he suspends the basket; so all these famines came, not upon [spiritually] enfeebled men, but upon mighty men. R. Berekiah applied to them the verse, *He gives power to the faint (Is. 40:29)*. R. Berekiah said in the name of R. Helbo: Two [famines] came in the days of Adam. R. Huna said in the name of R. Aha: One in the days of Abraham, and one in the days of Lamech.

The famine which came in the days of Elijah was a famine of dearth, a year of produce followed by a year of no produce, but the famine which

195

came in the days of Elisha was a famine due to war, as it is said, *Until an ass's head was sold for fourscore pieces of silver (2 Kings 6:25)*.

Of the famine which came in the days when the judges judged, however, R. Huna said in the name of R. Dosa that instead of the normal produce of forty-two *seahs*, there were only forty-one. But we have learnt: A man should not leave Palestine unless two *seahs* [of wheat] cost a shekel? And Rabban Simeon b. Gamaliel said: When is this? When even then it is difficult to obtain, but if it is possible to obtain even one *seah* for a shekel, a Jew should not leave Palestine? But it has been taught: In time of pestilence and in time of war, gather in your feet, and in time of famine, spread out your feet. Why then was Elimelech punished? Because he struck despair into the hearts of Israel. He was like a prominent man who dwelt in a certain country, and the people of that country depended upon him and said that if a dearth should come he could supply the whole country with food for ten years. When a dearth came, however, his maidservant went out and stood in the marketplace with her basket in her hand. And the people of the country said, "This is the man upon whom we depended that if a dearth should come he would supply our wants for ten years, and here his maidservant stands in the marketplace with her basket in her hand!" So with Elimelech! He was one of the notables of his place and one of the leaders of his generation. But when the famine came he said, "Now all Israel will come knocking at my door [for help], each one with his basket." He therefore arose and fled from them. This is the meaning of the verse, *And a certain man of Bethlehem in Judah went.*

[5] *And a certain man . . . went*—like a mere stump! See now how the Holy One, blessed be He, favors the entry into Eretz Israel over the departure therefrom! In the former case it is written, *Their horses . . . their mules . . . their camels [etc.] (Ezra 2:66)*, but in this case it is written, *And a certain man went*—like a mere stump. The reason is that in the latter case, since they were leaving the country for another land, Scripture makes no mention of their property, [but states simply], *And a certain man went*—as though empty-handed.

To sojourn in the fields of Moab (Ruth 1:1). R. Levi said: Whenever the word "field" occurs, it refers to the city; the word "city" refers to the province. Where "province" occurs, it refers to the whole administrative district. The word "field" refers to the city, [as it is said,] *Go to Anathoth, to your own fields (1 Kings 2:26)*. "City" means "province," [as in the verse,] *Go through the midst of the city, through the midst of Jerusalem (Ezek. 9:4)*. "Province" means administrative district, [as in the verse,] *Over a hundred and seven and twenty provinces (Esther 1:1)*.

He and his wife and his two sons. He was the prime mover, and his wife secondary to him, and his two sons secondary to both of them.

Bibliography on Midrash

LEE HAAS

This bibliography consists of books and articles on the subject of *midrash*. The purpose of this endeavor is to assist scholars by assembling in a single list references to *midrash* scattered throughout the bibliographic literature. My bibliography consists of two major parts. First, I have listed works concerning the nature and character of *midrash* in general. Secondly, I have listed separately references to the following books of *midrash*: Genesis Rabbah, Leviticus Rabbah, Pesiqta de Rab Kahana, Pesiqta Rabbati, Mekhilta de Rabbi Ishmael, Mekhilta de Rabbi Simeon ben Yohai, Sifra, Sifre and Sifre Zuta. In compiling this bibliography, I have consulted the catalogues of major Judaica collections, periodical indexes, bibliographies in books about *midrash*, and indexes to festschriften. Languages of the bibliographical items include English, French, German, Italian and Hebrew. For titles of Hebrew books and articles, I have used the standard system of transliteration. Titles of Hebrew journals are written according to common library spelling.

PART I   GENERAL WORKS

Abrahams, I., "The Midrash and Its Poetry." In *Understanding the Talmud*, edited by A. Corré. New York, 1975.

Albeck, Chanoch, *Mavo la-Talmudim*. Tel Aviv, 1969.

———, *Untersuchungen über die halakischen Midraschim*. Berlin, 1927.

Altmann, Alexander, "Mdrs 'lygwry 'l py drk "hqblh hpnymyt" 'l br'st rbh 24." In *Essays Presented to Chief Rabbi Israel Brodie on the Occasion of his Seventieth Birthday*, edited by Hirsch Jakob Zimmels. London, 1967.

Aptowitzer, V., "Untersuchungen zur gaonäischen Literatur." *HUC Annual* 8–9 (1931–32): 373–442.

Arzt, Max, "Prqym mmdrs thlym kt"y." In *Alexander Marx Jubilee Volume on the Occasion of his Seventieth Birthday*. New York, 1950.

Auerbach, A., "Hpdgwg bsprwt hmdrsym." *Shebilei HaHinukh* 30 (1970): 37–45.

Bacher, Wilhelm, *Die Agada der babylonischen Amoräer*. Strassburg, 1878.

————, *Die Agada der palästinischen Amoräer*. Strassburg, 1892.

————, *Die Agada der Tannaiten*. Strassburg, 1890.

————, *Die exegitische Terminologie der jüdischen Traditions-literatur*. Leipzig, 1899–1905.

————, *Die Proömien der alten jüdischen Homilie*. Leipzig, 1913.

Baeck, Leo, "Haggadah and Christian Doctrine." *HUC Annual* 23 (1950–51 Part One): 549–60.

————, "Zwei Beispiele midraschischer Predigt." *Monatsschrift für Geschichte und Wissenschaft des Judenthums* 69 (1925): 258–71.

Ben Amos, D., *Narrative Forms of the Haggadah: Structural Analysis*. Bloomington, Ind., 1967.

————, "'ywn swrny wmbny b'gdwt htlmwd whmdrs." *Papers of the Sixth World Congress of Jewish Studies* 2 (1977): 357–59.

Berliner, Abraham, *Beiträge zur Geographie und Ethnographie Babyloniens im Talmud und Midrasch*. Berlin, 1884.

Bettan, I., *Studies in Jewish Preaching*. Cincinnati, 1939.

Bin Gorion, Micha Joseph, *Der Born Judas*. Berlin, 1934.

————,*Die Sagen der Juden*, 5 vols. Frankfurt a.M., 1914–27.

Bischoff, Oswald Erich, *Babylonisch-Astrales im Weltbilde des Thalmud und Midrasch*. Leipzig, 1907.

Bloch, Philipp, "Studien zur Aggadah." *Monatsschrift für Geschichte und Wissenschaft des Judenthums* 34 (1885–86).

Bloch, Renée, "Écriture et tradition dans le judaisme: Apercus sur l'origine du midrash." *Cahiers sioniens* 8 (1954): 1–34.

————, "Methodological Note for the Study of Rabbinic Literature." In *Approaches to Ancient Judaism: Theory and Practice*, edited by William Scott Green. Missoula, Mont., 1978.

————, "Midrash." In *Approaches to Ancient Judaism: Theory and Practice*, edited by William Scott Green. Missoula, Mont., 1978.

Bohl, F.M., Th. deLiagre, "Wortspiele im Alttestament." *Journal of the Palestine Oriental Society* 6 (1926): 196–216.

Bonfil, R., "Saggio di analisi strutturale in Haggada." In *Miscellanea di Studi in Memoria di D. Disegni*. Torino, 1969.

Bonsirven, Joseph, *Exégèse Rabbinique et Exégèse Paulinienne*. Paris, 1939.

————, "Genres littéraires dans la littérature juive post-biblique." *Biblica* 35 (1954): 328–45.

Bowker, J., *The Targums and Rabbinic Literature*. London, 1969.

Braude, William G., "Maimonides' Attitude to Midrash." In *Studies in Jewish Bibliography, History and Literature in Honour of I. E. Kiev*. New York, 1971.

————, *The Midrash on Psalms*. Yale Judaica Series, no. 13. New Haven, 1959.

————, "'Open thou mine eyes' [to Midrash]." In *Understanding the Talmud*, edited by A. Corré. New York, 1975.

Brown, Ronald, "Midrashim as Oral Traditions." *HUC Annual* 47 (1976): 181–89.

Buchanan, G. W., "Midrashim prétannaites; a propos de Prov. I–IX." *Revue Biblique* 72 (1965): 227–39.

Camps, Dom G. M., "Midras sobre la Historia de los Plagues." In *Miscellanea biblica B. Ubach*, edited by Romualdo Maria Diaz Carbonell. Monteserrat, 1953.

Chajes-Preisstiftung, H. P., *Yḥs h'gdh lhlkh*. Vienna, 1929.

Chernus, Ira, "'A wall of fire round about': The Development of a Theme in Rabbinic Midrash." *Journal of Jewish Studies* 30 (1979): 68–84.

Cohen, A., "Gemara and Midrash." In *Understanding the Talmud*, edited by A. Corré. New York, 1975.

Daube, David, "Rabbinic methods of interpretation and Hellenistic rhetoric." *HUC Annual* 22 (1949): 239–64.

Davies, W. D., "Reflection on the Spirit in the Mekilta: A Suggestion." *Jewish and Pauline Studies* (Philadelphia: Fortress Press, 1983).

Dienemann, Max, *Midraschim der klage und des zuspruchs*. Berlin, 1935.

Drury, J., "Midrash and gospel." *Theology* 77 (1974): 291–96.

Ehrmann, Daniel, *Aus Palästina und Babylon*. Vienna, 1882.

Eisenstein, J. D., *Bibliotheca Midraschica: A Library of 200 Minor Midrashim*. New York, 1915.

Feldman, Asher, *The Parables and Similes of the Rabbis, Agricultural and Pastoral*. Cambridge, Eng., 1924.

Finkel, Asher, "Midrash and the Synoptic Gospels: An Introductory abstract." *Society of Biblical Literature Seminar Papers* 11 (1977): 251–56.

Finkel, Joshua, "The Alexandrian Tradition and the Midrash ha-ne'elam." In *The Leo Jung Jubilee Volume*, edited by Menachem Mendel Kasher. New York, 1962.

Finkelstein, Eliezer Aryah, "Tyqwny gyrs'wt bspry (dwgm'wt'ḥdwt)." *Tarbiz* 3 (1933): 198–204.

Finkelstein, Louis, *Maimonides and the Tannaitic Midrashim*. Philadelphia, 1935.

———, "The Oldest Midrash: Pre-Rabbinic Ideals and Teachings in the Passover Haggadah." *Harvard Theological Review* 31 (1938): 291–317.

———, "Sources of the Tannaitic Midrashim." *Jewish Quarterly Review* 31 (1940–41): 211–43.

———, "Studies in the Tannaitic Midrashim." *Proceedings of the American Academy of Jewish Research* 6 (1934–35): 189–228.

———, "Hsp't byt sm'y 'l spry dbrym." In *Spr 'sp*, edited by Umberto Cassuto et al. Jerusalem, 1952–53.

———, "Mdrs hlkwt whgdwt." In *Spr ywbl lyṣḥq b 'r bml't lw sb'ym snh*, edited by Salo Baron et al. Jerusalem, 1960.

———, "Tqwny grsh btwrt khnym." In *Qwbṣ md'y lzkr msh swr*, edited by Louis Ginzberg et al. New York, 1944.

Fischel, Henry A., *Rabbinic Literature and Greco-Roman Philosophy*. Leiden, 1973.

Frankel, Israel, *Peshat (plain exegesis) in Talmudic and Midrashic Literature*. Toronto, 1956.

Gertner, M., "Midrashim in the New Testament." In *Studies in Honour of G. R. Driver*, edited by Godfrey R. Driver. Manchester, 1962.

Ginzberg, Louis, *Legends of the Jews*. Philadelphia, 1910–46.

———, *Qṭ' mdrs lhgdh mn hgnyzh sbmṣrym*. New York, 1928.

Glatzer, Nahum, *Gespräche der Weisen*. Berlin, 1935.

Goetschel, R., "Le midrash de la seconde Pâque." *Revue des Sciences Religieuses* 47 (1973): 162–68.

Goldberg, Arnold, "Entwurf einer formanalytischen Methode für die Exegese der rabbinischen Traditions-literatur." *Frankfurter Judaistische Beiträge* 5 (1977): 1–41.

———, *Untersuchungen über die Vorstellung von der Schekhinah ın der frühen rabbinischen Literatur—Talmud und Midrasch*. Berlin, 1969.

———, "Hmwnḥ 'gwph' bmdrs wyqr' rbh." *Leshonenu* 38 (1972): 163–69.

Goldin, J., "Of Change and Adaptation in Judaism." *History of Religions* 4 (1965): 269–94.

Gottlieb, Wolf, *From Days of Old: Stories and Sayings from Talmud and Midrash*. London, 1948.

Grözinger, K. E., "Midraschisch erweiterte Priestersegen in Qumran." *Frankfurter Judaistische Beiträge* 2 (1974): 39–52.

Grünhut, Lazar, *Spr hlqwṭym*. Jerusalem, 1898.

Halevny, D., "Hbnym ywsbym hskynh 'wmdt [br'syt rbh 48]. In *Hgwt 'bryt b'mryqh*. Tel Aviv, 1972.

Heinemann, Isaak, *Altjüdische Allegoristik*. Breslau, 1936.

———, *Darké Ha'aggadah*. Jerusalem, 1950.

Heinemann, Joseph, "Anti-Samaritan Polemics in the Aggadah." *Proceedings of the Sixth World Congress of Jewish Studies* 6 (1977): 57–69.

———, *Derasot beṣibbur bitequpat hattalmud*. Jerusalem, 1971.

———, "The Proem in the Aggadic Midrashim: A Form-Critical Study." *Scripta Hierosolymitana* 22 (1971): 100–122.

———, "Profile of a Midrash: The Art of Composition in Leviticus Rabba." *Journal of the American Academy of Religion* 39 (1971): 141–50.

———, *'aggadot wetoldotehen*. Jerusalem, 1974.

———, "'mwr'y 'rṣ yśr'l k'mny hdrsh nytwḥ sl sty ptyḥt'wt." *Ha-Sifrut* 25 (1977): 69–79.

———, "Hptyḥwt bmdrsy h'gdh—mqwrn wtpqydn." In *Papers of the Fourth World Congress of Jewish Studies* 2 (1965): 43–44.

Herford, Robert Travers, *Christianity in Talmud and Midrash*. London, 1903.

Herr, Moshe David, "Midrash." *Encyclopaedia Judaica*.

———, "Midrashei Halakhah." *Encyclopaedia Judaica*.

Hershkovitz, Yehudah, "'rṣ yśr'l bmdrs h'gdh." In *Yavneh Me'asef I*, edited by Samuel Klein. Jerusalem, 1939.

Heschel, Abraham Joshua, "'ywnym bmdrs." In *Spr ywbl lkbwd hrb dr̈ 'brhm wwyys*, edited by Abraham Weiss. New York, 1964.

Hoffmann, David, *Zur Enleitung in die halachischen Midraschim*. Berlin, 1887.

Horovitz, Saul, "Midrash." *Jewish Encyclopedia*.

Hruby, K., "Exégèse rabbinique et exégèse patristique." *Revue des Sciences Religieuses* 47 (1973): 341–72.

Jacobs, Irving, "Elements of Near-Eastern Mythology in Rabbinic Aggadah." *Journal of Jewish Studies* 28 (1977): 1–11.

Kadushin, M., *The Rabbinic Mind*. New York, 1965.

Kagan, Z., "Divergent Tendencies and their Literary Moulding in the Aggadah." *Scripta Hierosolymitana* 22 (1971): 151–70.

Karff, S. E., "Aggadah: The Language of Jewish 'God-talk.'" *Judaism* 19 (1970): 158–73.

————, "Rooted in Reality: In Defense of Aggadah." *CCAR Journal* 22 (1975): 3–10.

Katz, Robert L., "Empathy in Modern Psychotherapy and in the Aggada." *HUC Annual* 30 (1959): 191–216.

Klenicki, L., "Notas sobre el midrash." *Revista Biblica* 34 (1972): 267–70.

Künstlinger, D., *Altjudäische Bibeldeutung*. Berlin, 1911.

Kuhn, Peter, *Gottes Trauer und Klage in der rabbinschen Überlieferung: (Talmud und Midrasch)*. Leiden, 1978.

Lachs, S. T., "Exempla of Yemenite Midrashim from MS Adler, 1702 J.T.S." *Gratz College Annual of Jewish Studies* 1 (1972): 37–43.

Lauterbach, Jacob Z., *Midrash and Mishnah*. New York, 1916.

————, "Midrash Halakah." *Jewish Encyclopedia*.

LeDéaut, R., "A propos d'une définition du midrash." *Biblica* 50 (1969): 395–413.

————, "Un phénomène spontane de l'herméneutique juive ancienne; le targumisme." *Biblica* 52 (1971): 505–25.

Lehrman, S. M., *The World of the Midrash*. New York, 1962.

Levine, Howard I., *Mḥqrym bmkylt' wbmsnh pshym wbb' qm'*. Tel Aviv, 1971.

Lieberman, Saul, *Mdrsy tymn*. Jerusalem, 1940.

————, *Sqy'yn*. Jerusalem, 1970.

Luzarraga, J., "Principios hermenéuticos de exégesis biblica en el rabinismo primitivo." *Estudios Biblicos* 30 (1971): 177–93.

Mach, Rudolf, *Der Zaddik in Talmud und Midrasch*. Leiden, 1957.

Mandelbaum, B., "Two Principles of Character Education in the Aggadah." *Judaism* 21 (1972): 84–92.

Mann, Jacob, *The Bible as Read and Preached in the Old Synagogue*. Vol. I. Cincinnati, 1940; vol. II, edited by Isaiah Sonne, 1966.

Maori, I., "Hsp't hmdrs 'l trgwm hpsytth ltwrh bbḥyrt hmlym." *Tarbiz* 46 (1977): 212–30.

Margulies, Reuben, "Ṣywny hpswqym btlmwd wbmdrs." In *Spr ywbl qwbṣ twrny yws' l'wr lṣywn hwp't krk h'rb'ym sl "syny"*, edited by Yehudah Leib Maimon. Jerusalem, 1957.

Marmorstein, Abraham and Kittell, Gerhard, *Tannaitische Midraschim: Übersetzung und Erklärung*. Stuttgart, 1937.

Marmorstein, Arthur, "The Background of the Haggadah." *HUC Annual* 6 (1929): 141–204.

————, "Mḥqrym b'gdh." In *Zkrwn yhwdh*, edited by Simon Hevesi et al. Budapest, 1938.

Marx, Gustaf Armin, *Aramäisch-neuhebräisches Handwörterbuch zu Targum, Talmud und Midrasch*. Hildesheim, 1967.

Maybaum, Siegmund, *Die ältesten Phasen in der Entwicklung der jüdischen Predigt*. Berlin, 1903.

Melamed, Ezra Zion, *Hyḥs sbyn mdrsy-hlkh lmsnh wltwspt'*. Tel Aviv, 1966.

————, "Mdrsy hlkh bmsnh wbtwspt'," In *Bar Ilan*, edited by Samuel Bialoblocki. Jerusalem, 1964.

Merchavia, C., "The Church Versus Talmudic and Midrashic Literature." In *Htlmwd br'y hnṣrwt*. Jerusalem, 1970.

Mirsky, Samuel Kalman, "The Schools of Hillel, R. Ishmael and R. Akiba in Pentateuchal Interpretation." In *Essays Presented to Chief Rabbi Israel Brodie on the Occasion of his Seventieth Birthday*, edited by Hirsch Jakob Zimmels. London, 1966.

————, "Trgwmym m'rmyt l'bryt bsprwt hmdrs whg'wnym." In *Peraqim* 4 (1966): 9–28.

Nádor, Georg, *Jüdische Rätsel aus Talmud und Midrasch*. Köln, 1967.

Nardoni, E., "Algunas consideraciones sobre el Midrás." *Revista Biblica* 33 (1971): 225–31.

Neusner, Jacob, "History and midrash." *Judaism* 9 (1960): 47–54.

Noy, Dov, *Hsypwr h'mmy btlmwd wbmdrs*. Jerusalem, 1968.

————, *Motif-Index of the Talmudic-Midrashic Literature*. Ann Arbor, 1954.

Osserstein, Abraham, "Mdrs yhwdy 'wrygnys." *Tarbiz* 46 (1977): 317–18.

Peretz, Yizhak, *Blsnwt drsnyt*. Tel Aviv, 1964.

Petuchowski, Jakob, "The Theological Significance of the Parable in Rabbinic Literature and the New Testament." *Christian News from Israel* 23 (1972): 76–86.

Porton, Gary, "Midrash: Palestinian Jews and the Hebrew Bible in the Greco-Roman period." In *Aufstieg und Niedergang der römischen Welt*. Berlin, 1972–79.

————, "Toward a Definition of Midrash." In *Approaches to Ancient Judaism*, edited by William Scott Green. Missoula, 1978.

Rabbiner, Zemach, *Beiträge zur hebräischen Synonymik in Talmud und Midrasch*. Berlin, 1899.

Rappaport, S., *Agada und Exegese bei Flavius Josephus*. Frankfurt a. M., 1930.

Rathaus, Ariel, "Reading the Bible in the Midrashic Tradition." *Service International de Documentation Judéo-Christienne* 9 (2) (1976): 12–18.

Renzer, J. S., *Die Hauptpersonen des Richterbuches in Talmud und Midrasch*. Berlin, 1902.

Robert, A., "L'exégèse des Psaumes selon les méthodes de la 'Formgeschichteschule.'" In *Miscellanea biblica B. Ubach*, edited by Romualdo Maria Diaz Carbonell. Monteserrat, 1954.

Safrai, S., "Tales of the Sages in the Palestinian Tradition and the Babylonian Talmud." *Scripta Hierosolymitana* 22 (1971): 209–32.

Saldarini, A. J., "Johanan ben Zakkai's Escape from Jerusalem: Origin and Development of a Rabbinic Story." *Journal for the Study of Judaism* 6 (1975): 189–204.

Schäfer, Peter, "Zur Geschichtsauffassung des rabbinischen Judenthums." *Journal for the Study of Judaism* 6 (1975): 167–88.

Scheiber, A., "Aggada und Antikes." *Acta Antiqua* 20 (1972): 421–28.

————, "Antike Motive in der Aggada." *Acta Antiqua* 17 (1969): 55–59.

————, "Antikes in der Aggada." *Acta Antiqua* 19 (1971): 393–402.

————, "Antikes und Aggada." *Acta Antiqua* 17 (1969): 449–57.

Schwarzbaum, H., "Talmudic Midrashic Affinities of Some Aesopic Fables." *Laographia* 22 (1965): 446–83.

Seeligmann, I. L., "Voraussetzungen der Midraschexegese." *Supplement to Vetus Testamentum, Congress Volume*. Leiden, 1953.

Shinan, Avigdor, "Midrashic Parallels to Targumic Traditions." *Journal for the Study of Judaism* 8 (1977): 185–91.

Slonimsky, Henry, "The Philosophy Implicit in the Midrash." *HUC Annual* 27 (1956): 235–90.

Sperber, D., "Varia Midrashica." *Revue des Etudes Juives* 129 (1970): 85–92.

———, "Varia Midrashica III." *Revue des Etudes Juives* 132 (1975): 125–32.

———, "Hlkh mn h'gdwt w'gdh sbhlkh." *Ha-Ṣofeh* 4 (1971).

Stein, Edmund, "Die homiletische Peroratio im Midrasch." *HUC Annual* 8–9 (1931–32): 353–71.

———, *Philo und der Midrasch.* Giessen, 1931.

Strack, Hermann L., *Introduction to the Talmud and Midrash.* New York, 1931.

———, *Kommentar zum Neun Testament aus Talmud und Midrasch.* Munich, 1922–56.

Theodor, Julius, "Midrash Haggadah." *Jewish Encyclopedia.*

———, "Zur Composition der agadischen Homilien." *Monatsschrift für Geschichte und Wissenschaft des Judenthums* 28 (1879): 97–113, 164–75, 271–78.

Thyen, Hartwig, *Der Stil der jüdisch-hellenistischen Homilie.* Göttingen, 1955.

Townsend, J. T., "Minor Midrashim." In *The Study of Judaism, Vol. II: Bibliographical Essays in Medieval Jewish Studies.*

Vermes, Geza, "Bible and Midrash: Early Old Testament Exegesis." In *Cambridge History of the Bible* I (1970).

———, *Scripture and Tradition in Judaism.* Leiden, 1961.

Wartski, I., "The Greek element in an enigmatical midrashic homily." *Tarbiz* 35 (1965): 132–36.

———, *Lswn hmdrsym.* Jerusalem, 1970.

Waxman, M., *A History of Jewish Literature from the Close of the Bible.* New York, 1960.

Weber, Ferdinand W., *System der altsynagogalen Palästinischen Theologie aus Targum, Midrasch und Talmud.* Leipzig, 1880.

Weingreen, J., "Exposition in the Old Testament and in Rabbinic Literature." In *Promise and Fulfillment; Essays Presented to S. H. Hooke in Celebration of his Ninetieth Birthday*, edited by F. F. Bruce. Edinburgh, 1963.

Weinreb, Friedrich, *Wie sie den Anfang träumten: Überlieferungen vom Ursprung des Menschen.* Bern, 1976.

Weinstein, N. I., *Zur Genesis der Agada.* Frankfurt, 1901.

Wertheimer, Solomon Aaron, *Bty mdrswt.* Jerusalem, 1893–97.

Wilken, Robert L., *Aspects of Wisdom in Judaism and Early Christianity.* Notre Dame, Ind., 1975.

Wolff, Mathieu, *Variétés homilétiques sur le Pentateuque tirées du Midrasch.* Paris, 1900.

Wright, Addison G., "The literary Genre Midrash." *Catholic Biblical Quarterly* 28 (1966): 105–38, 415–57.

Wuellner, Wilhelm, "Haggadic-Homily Genre in 1 Corinthians 1–3." *Journal of Biblical Literature* 89 (1970): 199–204.

Wynkoop, J. D., "A Peculiar Kind of Paronomasia in the Talmud and Midrash." *Jewish Quarterly Review* n.s. 2 (1911): 1–23.

Zeitlin, S., "Midrash: A Historical Study." *Jewish Quarterly Review* 44 (1953): 21–36.

Ziegler, Ignaz, *Die Königsgleichnisse des Midrasch beleuchtet durch die römische Kaiserzeit*. Breslau, 1903.

Zunz, Leopold, *Die gottesdienstlichen vorträge der Juden, historisch Entwickelt*. Berlin, 1832.

————, and Albeck, Chanoch, *Hddrswt bysr'l*, 2d ed. Jerusalem, 1954.

PART II MIDRASHIC BOOKS

Genesis Rabbah

Albeck, Chanoch, "Introduction." *Midrasch Bereschit Rabbah*, edited by J. Theodor and Chanoch Albeck. Berlin, 1936.

Barth, Lewis, *An Analysis of Vatican 30*. Cincinnati, 1973.

Buber, Salomon, *'gdt br' syt*. Cracow, 1902.

Freedman, H. and Simon, Maurice, *Midrash Rabbah* (English). London, 1939.

Glogau, Jehiel Michael, *Nzr hqds*. Jessnitz, 1719.

Goldman, Edward A., "Parallel Texts in the Palestinian Talmud to Genesis Rabba." Rabbinic thesis, Hebrew Union College, 1969.

Greenspan, Yehudah, "'ywnym bbr' syt rbh." In *Yavneh Me'asef I*, ed. by Samuel Klein. Jerusalem, 1939.

Gutmann, Joshua and Josef Schächter, *Mdrs br'syt rbh*. Tel Aviv, 1942.

Heinemann, Joseph, "Mbnhw whlwqtw sl mdrs br'syt rbh." *Bar Ilan Annual* 1972, 9:279–89.

Heller, Bernhard, "Der Abschluss von Theodor-Albecks Bereschit Rabba." *Monatsschrift für Geschichte und Wissenschaft des Judenthums* 78 (1934): 609–15.

————, "Theodor-Albecks Bereschit Rabba." *Monatsschrift für Geschichte und Wissenschaft des Judenthums* 71 (1927): 466–72.

Künstlinger, David, *Die Petichot des Midrasch rabba zu Genesis*. Krakau, 1914.

Leiner, Jerucham, "H'rwt lmdrs rbh." In *Spr ywbl*, edited by Yehudah Leib Maimon. Jerusalem, 1957.

Lerner, Mayer, *Anlage und Quellen des Bereschit Rabba*. Berlin, 1882.

Levine, Ephraim, "A Geniza Fragment of Genesis Rabba." *Jewish Quarterly Review* 20 (1908): 777–83.

Margel, Moses, *Der Segen Jakobs*. Berlin, 1900.

Marmorstein, Arthur, "The Introduction of R. Hoshaya to the First Chapter of Genesis Rabba." In *Louis Ginzberg Jubilee Volume on the Occasion of his Seventieth Birthday*. New York, 1945.

Odeberg, Hugo, *The Aramaic Portions of Bereshit Rabba*. (With a grammar of Galilean Aramaic). Lund, 1939.

Silberman, Hayyim, *Mdrs rbh*. St. Louis, 1919.

Sokolof, M., "H'bryt sl br'syt rbh lpy k"y w'tyqn 30." *Leshonenu* 33 (1968–69): 25–42, 135–49, 270–79.

Shapira, D. S., "Qwntrś h'rwt wh'rwt lbr' syt rbh." *HaDarom* 25 (1967): 141–55.

Theodor, Julius, "Der Midrasch Bereschit Rabba." *Monatsschrift für Geschichte und Wissenschaft des Judenthums* 37 (1893): 169–73, 206–13, 452–58; 38 (1894): 9–26, 436–40; 39 (1895): 106–10, 241–47, 289–95, 337–43, 385–90, 433–41, 481–91.

———, "Drei unbekannte Paraschas aus Bereschit Rabba." *Festschrift zum siebzigsten Geburtstag Jakob Guttmanns*. Leipzig, 1915.

Ungár, Simon, *Beresith Rabba Exegesise*. Budapest, 1890.

Wünsche, August, *Midrasch Bereshit Rabba*. Midrash: Bibliotheca Rabbinica, Bd. I. Leipzig, 1881.

Leviticus Rabbah

Albeck, Chanoch, "Midrash Wayiqra Rabba'." In *Louis Ginzberg Jubilee Volume*. New York, 1946.

Heinemann, Joseph, "'mnwt hqwmpzyṣyh bmdrs wyqra' rbh." In *Hasifrut* 1971, 2:808–34.

———, "Prswt bwyqr' rbh smqwrywtn mpwqpqt." *Tarbiz* 37 (1968): 339–54.

Künstlinger, D., *Die Petichot des Midrasch Rabba zu Leviticus*. Cracow, 1913.

Margulies, Mordechai, "Introduction." *Midrash Wyiqra Rabba*, edited by Mordechai Margulies. Jerusalem, 1953–60.

Weiszburg, Gyula, *A Midrás Leviticus Rabba*. Budapest, 1890.

Wünsche, August, *Der Midrasch Wajikra Rabba*. Midrash: Bibliotheca Rabbinica, Bd. 3. Leipzig, 1884.

Pesiqta de Rab Kahana

Buber, Solomon, "Introduction." In *Pesikta de-Rav Kahana*, edited by Solomon Buber. Lyck, 1868.

Goldberg, A., "Psyqt' drb khnh [mhdy] dwd mndlbwym 1962." *Kiryat Sefer* 43 (1968): 68–79.

Künstlinger, D., *Die Petichot der Pesikta de Rab Kahana*. Cracow, 1912.

Mandelbaum, B., "Introduction." In *Pesikta de-Rav Kahana*, edited by B. Mandelbaum. New York, 1962.

———, "Psq' dsqlym mpsyqt' drb khnh." In *Mordecai M. Kaplan Jubilee Volume on the Occasion of his Seventieth Birthday*, edited by Moshe Davis. New York, 1953.

Wünsche, A., *Pesikta des Rab Kahana*. Leipzig, 1885.

Zinger, Z., "The Bible Quotations in the Pesikta de Rav Kahana." *Textus* 5 (1966): 114–24.

Pesiqta Rabbati

Baumberger, Bernard J, "A Messianic Document of the Seventh Century." *HUC Annual* 15 (1940): 425–32.

Braude, William, *Pesikta Rabbati*. New Haven, 1968.

Friedmann, Meir, *Mdrs psyqt' rbty*. Sklav, 1806.

Grözinger, K. E. and Hahn, H., "Die Textzeugen der Pesiqta Rabbati." *Frankfurter Judaistische Beiträge* 1 (1973): 68–104.

Margolloth, Ephraim, *Zr' 'prym*. Lemberg, 1853.

———, *Psyqt' rbty drb khnh*. Warsaw, 1893.

Mekhilta de Rabbi Ishmael

Berlin, Naphtali Zebi Judah, *Mkylt' drby ysm"l*. Jerusalem, 1970.

Geiger, Abraham, *Urschrift und Übersetzungen der Bibel*. Breslau, 1857.

Ginzberg, Louis, "'l hyḥs sbyn hmsnh whmklt'." In Qwbṣ md'y lzkr msh swr, edited by Louis Ginzberg et al. New York, 1944.

Horovitz, H. S. and Rabin, I. A., Mechilta D'Rabbi Ismael, 2d ed. Jerusalem, 1960.

Kadushin, Max, A Conceptual Approach to the Mekilta. New York, 1969.

Lauterbach, Jacob Z., "The arrangement and division of the Mekilta." HUC Annual 1 (1924): 427–466.

———, Mekilta de-Rabbi Ishmael: A Critical Edition. Philadelphia, 1935–49.

Lieberman, S., "Pysq' ḥdsh bmkylt' wpyrwsh." Sinai 75 (1972): 1–3.

Schäfer, P., "Israel und die Völker der Welt, zur Auslegung von Mekhilta de Rabbi Yishma'el baḥodesh Yitro 5." Frankfurter Judaistische Beiträge 4 (1976): 32–62.

Towner, Wayne Sibley, The Rabbinic "Enumeration of Scriptural Examples." Leiden, 1973.

Treves, David Moses Abraham, Mrkbt hmsnh. Lemberg, 1894.

Wacholder, Ben Zion, "The Date of the Mekhilta de Rabbi Ishmael." HUC Annual 39 (1968): 117–44.

Mekhilta de Rabbi Simeon ben Jochai

Epstein, J. N. and Melamed, E. Z., Mekhilta D'Rabbi Sim'on b. Jochai. Jerusalem, 1955.

———, "Mekhilta de R. Simeon b. Jochai." In Mbw'wt lsprwt htn'ym, edited by Jacob N. Epstein. Jerusalem, 1957.

Ginzberg, L., "Mekhilta de R. Simeon b. Yohai." In Festschrift zu Israel Lewy's siebzigsten Geburtstag, edited by Marcus Brann. Breslau, 1911.

Hoffmann, David, Mechilta de-Rabbi Simeon be Jochai. Frankfurt a.M., 1905.

Horovitz, S., Beiträge zur Erklärung und Textkritik der Mechilta des R. Simeon. Breslau, 1919.

Lewy, Israel, Ein Wort über die Mechilta des R. Simeon. Breslau, 1889.

Sifra

Berlin, Naphtali Zebi Judah, Ḥydwsy hndy"b mwwl'zyn. Jerusalem, 1969.

Biderman, Jacob David, Spr' dby rb hw' spr twrt kwhnym kwll mdrsy htn'ym lspr wyqr'. Jerusalem, 1959.

Eliakim, Hillel ben, Spr' dby rb. Jerusalem, 1960/61.

Epstein, Jacob N., "Sifra." In Mbw'wt lsprwt htn'ym, edited by Jacob N. Epstein. Jerusalem, 1957.

Finkelstein, Louis, H'rwt wtqwny nwsḥ btwrt khnym. New York, 1946.

———, Twrt khnym 'l py ktv yd rwmy mnwqd. ('ssm'ny No. 66.) New York, 1956.

Friedmann, M., Sifra, der älteste Midrasch zu Leviticus. Breslau, 1915.

Ibn Chayyim, Aaron, Qrbn 'hrn. Dessau, 1742.

Joël, Manuel, Notizen zum Buche Daniel. Etwas über die Bücher Sifra und Sifre. Breslau, 1873.

Koleditzky, Schachne, Spr' dby rb. Jerusalem, 1960/61.

Malbim, Meir Loeb, Spr' dby rb. Bucharest, 1860.

Meir, Yisrael, Spr' hnkr' twrt khnym. Piotrkow, 1911.

Neusner, Jacob, A History of the Mishnaic Law of Purities. VI. Negaim Sifra. Leiden, 1975.

Porges, N., *Spr' dby rb*. Breslau, 1915.

Safrin, Isaac Judah Jehiel, *'śqyryt h' yph*. Lemberg, 1848.

Samson ben Abraham of Sens and Jacob David ben Israel Issar, *Spr' hw' twrt khnym*. Warsaw, 1866.

Weiss, Isaac Hirsch, *Spr' dby rb hw' spr twrt khnym*. Vienna, 1862.

Winter, Jakob, *Sifra*. Gesellschaft zur Förderung der Wissenschaft des Judentums, Schriften Nr. 42. Breslau, 1938.

Sifre

Berlin, Naphtal Zebi Judah, *Sifre*. Jerusalem, 1959.

Elijah ben Solomon, *Spry*. Vilna, 1866.

Epstein, Jacob N., *Mbw'wt lsyprwt htn'ym*. Jerusalem, 1957.

————, "Mkylt' wspry bspry hrmb"m." *Tarbiz* 6 (1936): 343–82.

Finkelstein, Louis, *Prolegomena to an Edition of the Sifre on Deuteronomy*. Philadelphia, 1932.

Friedmann, M., *Spry dby rb*. Vienna, 1864.

Horovitz, H. S., *Spry dby rb*. Leipzig, 1917.

Horwitz, Zebi Hirsch, *Zh spr spry*. Sulzbach, 1802.

Joël, Manuel, *Notizen zum Buche Daniel. Etwas über die Bücher Sifra und Sifre*. Breslau, 1873.

Karl, Zvi, *Mḥqrym bspry*. Tel Aviv, 1954.

Koleditzky, Schachne and Zolty, Jacob Bezalel, *Spry lhtn' h'lhy rby sm'wn bn ywh'y*. Jerusalem, 1947/48.

Levertoff, Paul P., *Midrash Sifre on Numbers*. London, 1926.

Lichtstein, Abraham, *Zh spr spry*. Dyhernfurth, 1811–20.

Lieberman, Saul, "l'tyqwny gyrs' wt bspry." *Tarbiz* 3 (1933): 466.

Nathansohn, Joseph Saul, *Zh spr spry*. Lemberg, 1865.

Pardo, David, *Spry dby rb*. Salonica, 1799.

Rabinowitz, Alexander S., *Mslwt ltwrt htn'ym*. Tel Aviv, 1928.

Sifre Zuta

Bruell, Nehemias, "Der kleine Sifre." In *Graetz Jubelschrift*. Breslau, 1887.

Epstein, Jacob N., "Bryyt' qtw'h bspry zwṭ' sbylqwṭ." *Tarbiz* 13 (1943): 69.

————, *Mbw'wt lsprwt htn'ym*. Jerusalem, 1957.

————, "Spry zwṭ' prsh prh." *Tarbiz* 1 (1931): 46–78.

Horovitz, H. S., *Siphre ad Numeros adjecto Siphre zutta*. Corpus Tannaiticum, Sectio 3, pars 3, 1917.

————, "Der Siphre sutta nach dem Jalkut und anderen Quellen." *Monatsschrift für Geschichte und Wissenschaft des Judenthums* 50 (1906): 68–86, 169–84, 406–25, 581–88; 51 (1907): 164–72, 334–42, 462–70, 609–16; 52 (1908): 217–25, 318–27, 578–90, 697–707; 53 (1909): 190–98, 328–43, 563–76, 657–73; 54 (1910): 28–43.

Joskowicz, Jacob Ze'ev, *Sifre Zuta*. Lodz, 1929.

Lieberman, Saul, *Spry zwṭ'*. New York, 1968.

Index of Passages

BIBLE

RABBINICAL LITERATURE

(Tractates alphabetically arranged)

Index of Subjects